An honest history of Shotokan Karate

Dedications

This book is dedicated to several people. All of them have influenced, assisted, pushed, cajoled and often beaten me into realizing very important things on this journey. First to my Sensei, who not only provided guidance but fed my need for information, assisted me in finding the physical way and encouraged me to research and review the mental way. Dingman Sensei was one of the best guides a student could have, a true Sensei! He was and still is one of my inspirations and the reason that I am a traditionalist despite myself.

To the other instructors that have helped me train and learn, like Terry Proctor, Jarvis Kohut, Saeki Sensei, Tanaka Sensei, Yaguchi Sensei and all the others who have come into my life and taught me new techniques, new ways to move, some valuable life lessons and how to be a great person (thinking of you Proctor Sensei specifically) I thank you for your time, your efforts and your dedication and I want to let you know that you have been great role models as I came up in Karate.

To my seniors, those that are still with us and those that are no longer with us, I want to thank you very much for encouraging, pushing and prodding the student that I was and the push you still give me as I look through my memories and remember your inspiration. Specifically, I want to thank two seniors that I have lost. Bruce Derraugh was one of those guys that you train with and he just shows you how to respect others. He was one of the people that taught me what being Sempai meant. He was lost to us in 2005 but when he lived…he lived. He also gave me a chance to make a living when I first opened my massage practice years ago. He supported me and never asked for anything in return, letting me work on him and his spouse and paying me double my asking price because I went to his home…he drove and fed me too! An amazing guy!

Also, to Scot Robertson who was one of the men that taught me to think first, act only after thinking second as well…something I have yet to master but will remember to work on. One of the most even tempered and thoughtful people I ever met, and a someone that shared my love of Bruce Lee. He was a gentle giant on the Dojo floor who could have taken you apart if he wanted to and used his Karate and Judo to make people feel totally out of place in a club, but instead he used his voice and his demeanor to make you feel welcome and as if you were his best friend right from the get go. Scot saw me through hard times and then left when he had pointed the way for me. He was a true inspiration and someone that I call a brother in Karate!

To the vast ocean of seniors who I trained with and who scared the hell out of me, forced me to move, made me work hard and more importantly made me a better person and gave me knowledge that was both physical and mental, I bow to you! Ous! I cannot repay everyone or even mention all of you from the JKA of Manitoba Headquarters days, from the 80's, 90's and 00's who inspired me, who showed up and bled with me and made the hardwoods cry with our perspiration. To those that helped me build stories and to those that helped me improve and study myself as much as the art of Karate I thank you!

To my students, and my juniors, who remind me every time I am at the Dojo why I do what I do. I am in awe of you every time you step into the Dojo and give your all. I promise to strive to provide the best teaching I can, to respect your efforts and to encourage you the way I was pushed, encouraged and to know when to use the stick and when to reward you with the carrot!

To my family…I thank you for being there to support me, give me the push to be the person I am and the freedom to find out who that was. The encouragement to review things for myself and not take things at face value, the different points of view on life and the hope that what I am doing has value. I lost my brother Al when he was in his mid-30's so that gave me 30 plus years of knowing one of the best people to walk this planet, he showed me what heart, guts, determination, a great sense of humor and love meant and how to share it!

To my wife, who is forced by law to put up with me and to love me and to understand me (the last part I am sure I test from day to day). Without you I would not have the time to do what I love and without you I would not enjoy my passions. You march with me on this crazy journey as a partner and wife and you support me and force me to keep it real by calling me on my craziness and by grounding me reminding me that I am now old and should not do what a young man does, then forgives me when I don't listen and can't walk the next day!

And lastly to my Emma, My **"*bestest*"** friend, my everything. Daddy has no words as to how you inspire me. Dingman Sensei once called you a Samurai and said you had many battles to fight but you would overcome great odds, he had no idea how right he was, and how you do so with grace and joy. You are the true master and I am the student. You teach me how to love, laugh and given me true purpose! To my little Samurai warrior Daddy says I will hold your hand going forwards and be the person and the Daddy you deserve, and the best-*est* friend I can be to the best of my ability!

Introduction

    1983 I walked into the **JKA of Manitoba** on Albert Street. 10 years old and having had trained previously at a different Karate club, I was excited, scared and ready to train. Little did I know that would start a lifelong passion for training and find me learning from men I think of as mentors and one that I see as a father and the definition of the title "Sensei"!

    Over the years however I was exposed to a great deal of rhetoric and Dogma that proved to be false. It often led to slight embarrassment when I would retell a story only to be told that the story could not possibly be true! And then the person correcting me would point out some simple but unquestionable reason why it was not possibly true. I also met a great deal of people, and idols that ended up disappointing me by retelling the same false swill I had so harshly found out were not true and honestly a few of them just turned out not to be worthy of my admiration for various character flaws that came out over time. I also have met people that invigorated my thirst for knowledge and have made my training more than just fun, but exciting and life changing.

    This book will serve as an honest history of Shotokan Karate and came out about in a unique way. I went through a long period of "Karate depression" as things in my province began to change. My instructor got older, his heir left the group and I found myself running things a lot more. A position I never wanted and to be honest one I was not ready for. I had started a Blog to learn more and force me to research Karate from a more legitimate stance as far as research went, and a way to share my ideas with others in a way that gave me some freedom to express myself.

    I honestly did not want to be retelling stories and re-teaching old classes that I had been taught. I wanted some authenticity to what I was doing and the blog forced me to question myself all the time, keep me honest and help me organize my thoughts. In 2010 the blog became something I would turn to when I wanted to work out a class or look into something and post it to ward off the Dogma clowns and help me inform others. A few hundred blogs later someone came to me with the idea of creating books out of the blogs. I thought about it and decided that my first book would be to clear up the hyperbole that we get when we asked our seniors about the history and past of the JKA or how Karate was made.

This book is a result of that only and shows my point of view or opinions after doing hours and hours of research after looking into the false narratives that were presented to me. I am not writing this book to upset anyone, to pick on anyone or bully anyone. The stories that I am telling are clear, open and transparencies that we often lack as students. We miss details and we often retell stories that are false and meant to be used to "Market" our organizations. This book is looking to offer up the history and events that made the JKA the great organization that it is today as well as stating that the other groups are also great! Note that…that is important, I have met so many people who are not JKA who are great people, and of a matter or point of fact…I have met people on both sides of the coin who just so happen to be not so great.

If you read each chapter in succession you will see a lot of the information is repeated, treat each chapter like an individual post and take breaks in between. My goal is to introduce some truth, some facts and some fun with this book. It's also important to note that the book also used to be 3 books. However, upon review I figured it may be easier to digest this whole subject as a single book and just go from there. It is my hope that it helps you to learn a bit, enjoy a lot and learn some of the true and honest history of Shotokan Karate. The book presents things as honestly as I possibly can, it is not just my ideas but also presents my views, I have a hard time splitting the two and I hope that you realize that when reading this book…which used to be the little blog I used to just make things clear for me.

An honest history of Shotokan Karate

I am going to be honest here and say that in "An Honest History of Shotokan Karate" I am not going to apologize for what I am saying, it's a blog-based book with some really cool history upgrades to trace Karate form the ancient Okinawan roots to the modern groups that teach Karate. I also don't apologize for being pro-JKA. I am a JKA member and always will try and be a JKA member. I know it's not a perfect group, but honestly, I don't see any alternative that comes close. I like their Karate and while I am accused of being ridged and inflexible in my approach to Karate, I won't change. I recently had to add WKF rules to our club and we are learning them, but honestly, we are doing all this through JKA eyes and our WKF…. Looks like JKA guys doing WKF rules.

What I am trying to say is that if you think my point of view is too ridged or my stance on some things is skewed or bias, well yes...I am and it is. The Honest History part however is going to be about as honest as it comes. Brutal facts will get tossed out that may actually upset people, and I am warning you up front, I don't care! The point of this book is to look at things from a clear point of view, to call people and groups out for telling lies, inaccuracies or using Dogma to sell memberships, including my own instructors and seniors, and then to move past it and enjoy the truth. It's not to be mean, or point out that others have taken advantage of the lack of education by the general public, or even to say some should not teach...heck if the Karate is good teach! It's to just set some ground rules and to bring a few things to light that may be more interesting than the fraudulent Dogma.

Karate to me has been a life passion, to the point that I recall most things in my life based on what I was doing in the dojo at that time or around major events like tournaments or seminars. I love Karate to the point that I warned my now wife before we got married that I was already married to Karate, she would be my mistress. Only my little girl takes president over Karate honestly and my wife knows this and accepts it. She makes a great deal of fun of me...but she accepts it.....I think.

This book is going to dip into the history and try to blow some common false stories out of the water! It will challenge you to look things up and research beyond this book and it will only be a guiding hand not a sign post. I am not going to really post where I found things, because I think you need to do the foot work to appreciate the knowledge, much like Karate itself, you will be offered different ideas but you have to do the work to progress! After the history is done, I will have some fun with some common stories and Dogma that don't play out true and some are totally false and made up. And if you think I am wrong you can get ahold of me and tell me....with some notes and proof, I like to learn too you know!

Again, the point of this collection of Blogs, mish mash of historical fact is to cut through the marketing dogma that has been rolled out to us over the years to sell Karate to us, which I found sad. The truth in most cases is far more interesting than the catchy stories that were told that could never be true, it's also nicer than the harsh stories some groups have told about other groups and its way more educational than the story book lies we were fed growing up in Karate.

Please don't read any of this as an insult to other groups or individuals. I am the first to admit that I am JKA through and through and never want to leave the JKA, but I have great respect for men like Nishiyama, Kanazawa, Yahara, Asai, Okizaki and others who left the JKA.

I enjoy learning from the few Shotokai people that I have encountered and while I have seen a great deal of seniors behaving poorly, I still respect the sweat and tears they put into Karate training. I will never take that from anyone!

For this book to be a success in my eyes it must do two specific things, and well. First it has to provide a source for Karate or historical education, even one factoid learned is a home run for me. And second, it should get you researching, looking things up to confirm or argue against it. That will make this book worthwhile for me and the hours of research and writing the blog and this book will then be worth it as well.

So, let's get into it shall we!

1372 King Satto of Chuzan

To truly understand the relationship that Karate has to its Chinese roots one has to go back several hundred years to the rule of King Sato of Chuzan, whom also was known as Chadu of Chuzan. Chuzan was one of the three original kingdoms that formed the island of Okinawa. Chuzan was the middle kingdom between Hokuzan to the north and Nanzan to the south. The island was ruled by warlords and chieftains before Satto amalgamated the island into one nation.

Satto was the son of Seii of Chuzan, a Governor of the Urasoe district. Seii was a young monarch when he was put on the throne and his rule was infested with issues because his mother was corrupt and used his young age to damage the reputation of the Chuzan thrown by using her position to conduct less than legit business and damaged support for the monarchy at that time. Satto took power when his father died in 1349.

When Satto seized the thrown when his father diet, he took advantage of a unique situation that had come up to help cement his position and give him more authority in building his power to rule over Okinawa and a solid claim to the whole island. In 1372 a Chinese envoy arrived in Okinawa and came to the court of Satto straight away. This Envoy requested admission of Chinese cultural supremacy and that Okinawa send representatives to then capital of Nanjing with tribute to the Hongwu Emperor. Satto jumped at the chance to pay tribute to China as it affixed his position as the King of Okinawa with the approval of the Qing Empire behind it.

While this did not last long the fact that he took this opportunity was a major event in the formation of one single Okinawan ruler.

In 1374 he sent his brother Taiki with a large tribute to the emperor. The Chinese ruler took the tribute and every year expected the same. For this price Satto Chadu of Chuzan became the first king of Okinawa and also received presents back from China and the Royal seal to again show his true rule over all of Okinawa. In the eyes of the largest power in the whole of Asia he was the ruler of his small island nation, for the court of China had befriended him and he felt protected by their opinion of him.

The custom of investments being sent to China continued for 500 years, each year the investments would go to China and it allowed Okinawa to trade openly with the largest single country in the world at the time. Satto also opened up trade with Korea, Thailand and also Japan after this and Okinawa became a trade hub for Asia. He did this by using smaller islands in his kingdom to trade with the other countries so as to not upset any one partner. One country would take in goods from Korea and then trade them to Thailand or silk from China would land on the main island, were purchased then sold to Japanese merchants off of a smaller island. The trade program made Okinawa not only important in Asia pacific trade but very wealthy.

Satto did one other thing that was perhaps even more important to the true development of Karate, he established the Chinese Immigrant community of Kumemura in 1392, a short distance from his new capital of Shuri. This community served as diplomats, interpreters and other related roles in the trade industry, but more importantly to the development of Karate ….they passed on Chinese culture and Martial training to locals. This exchange of fighting arts meshed with the local wrestling styles and became what we now see as Karate today.

Despite his great efforts, the kingdom was still split into three distinct kingdoms. Satto's son Bunei was next to take the thrown and he focused a great deal of his time and effort on growing the commerce and trade with different countries and empires, such as Korea and Siam. Satto had succeeded in being recognized as the king of Okinawa but it was not actually a single nation, it was still three nations that worked independently of each other. In reality the chieftains of the other two regions of Okinawa had died around the time that Satto had passed away but Brunei was so transfixed with the wealth that he was accumulating with Naha being the busiest port in the area and him benefiting financially from trade that he did not make moves to unify the islands three major kingdoms. The island would not be unified until his son was overthrown by a rebel named Hashi in 1406 that the island nations were truly united under one king, Sho Shisho, Hashi's father.

This political coup d'etat lead to the longest dynasty of kings in Okinawan history, however it was the hard work of Satto that lead to the relationship with the Chinese that began the fertile development of Chinese boxing into local fighting styles and from that generation of fighting came Karate's earliest roots. It was only because Brunei was so transfixed with the wealth that the was being brought in that the Satto dynasty fell, after 5 years of doing nothing about the rebel attacks mind you.

This new dynasty maintained and promoted the relationship with the Chinese and grew the trade route that would eventually change from a Chinese business endeavor to a reason that the Japanese would take this island nation and make it a province of the Japanese Empire.

The Importance of the Kumemura area for Karate.

During the rule of King Satto a small village or community of scholars and diplomats was established to house the many businessmen, envoys and scholars that came to the islands to do business and establish a relationship between China and Chuzan. The importance of this community, established in the port city of Naha, cannot be underemphasized. The Chinese Empire would not openly trade with other countries like the Empire of Korea and Japan, but as an intermediary the Okinawan Kingdom was a perfect middle man! Chuzan used small island ports to transfer Japanese, Korean or other countries goods to their own boats and then traded with the Chinese or the other nations they had a trade relationship with.

The Chinese government sent reams of envoys, bureaucrats, diplomats and scholars to this small island nation and started to conduct trade through the business men at this foreign port. More importantly with the envoys and important businessmen came many body guards, military escorts and other men sent to protect and influence the trade specialists. These martial artists were of Fujian origin and many learned Fujian white Crane style of boxing along with a few other fighting arts in their home towns. They brought their fighting skills with them and on occasion taught it to the local Okinawans that they lived beside and did business with.

The community itself lasted from 1392 to 1879 when it was dissolved upon Okinawa's formal annexation by Japan, and the city of Kumemura was absorbed into the prefectural capital of Naha, and is now known simply as Kume area in the city of Naha. However while it existed the town was a central hub for Chinese society in Okinawa and a point of exchange between the two cultures. You would walk down the street and see rich Okinawan business people hurrying along to meetings with Chinese trade envoys or merchants wearing rich Chinese clothing having tea in Okinawan tea houses. All the time the Fujian warriors were acting as body guards to the wealthy.

A different reason to take the very nature of Kumemura into consideration is the continued belief that Okinawans were farmers and fishermen and thus Karate was created from the poor farmers of Okinawa. This is not a true picture at all of the roots of Karate and further the Okinawan people did not form the art to defend against Samurai, it was formed a generation or two before Samurai would visit Okinawa.

The area known as Kumemura and Shuri, as well as most of the areas around Shuri such as Naha another Island towns and cities were very filled with the wealthy, educated and cultured people who ran the island with more scholars and businesses to help collaborate with the Chinese and create a solid trade industry. It had more wealthy businessmen than rice farmers and many more bureaucrats and businessmen than fishermen or labors. The towns around Kumemura were vast and sophisticated cities of that period and the cultural exchanges went both ways, the Okinawans had a long history of culture that they could bring to the table but they also were very open to absorb the Chinese aristocratic way of life and to adopt the impressive Chinese culture along with its writing, culinary habits and of course the martial arts that they brought with them.

The island of Okinawa was a cultural melting pot. Along with trade and education came religion. The Chinese brought Confucianism with them to the areas around Shuri/Naha and many of the youth that studied the traditional Chinese classics were exposed to this "new" religion or philosophy and ingrained it in their own culture. The previous prevailing religion was one of Animistic ritual and seen as backwards by the Chinese and Japanese, this religion was chased out by the new foreign and exciting theologies.

As the island became more and more populated with Chinese government officials the Animistic religion began to fade as the ruling Okinawan officials, Kind Sho Soken and Sai On, began to replace the existing religion with a more "modern" Confucian/ Chinese influenced practice. They also took on Shinto and other religions from abroad as well. They absorbed and altered religion and culture from multiple countries including Japan, Siam, Korea and of course China and then turned out slightly altered religious practices and cultural ideals and passed them onto the countries they traded with.

The replacement of many standard and accepted Okinawan cultural pillars meant several things for Okinawa at the time. They were able to tighten bonds with both China and Japan by changing the view that they were backwards and naïve natives that could be dominated by more modern and forward thinking countries and they were taken a bit more seriously as partners and not seen as a nation used for their position in the Asian island chains off China, And this also lead to many gifts and expensive patronages from Chinese Emperor at the time. The Okinawan people became cultural Chameleons with their ability to view and then absorb and implement many of the changes that the new relationships brought with them, a skill they would call upon to save the nation several times.

The Chinese Emperor gave many gifts to Okinawa and helped convert the island nation from an agricultural based society to a more commerce focused society with gifts of Confucian temples and sending many scholars to help educate the upper class of Okinawa, and with the education came Martial arts as well! They pushed trade and taught the Okinawans how to use the trade route to create a new source of wealth for the Ryukyu Kingdom. This help created a new focus and made the Okinawan people much more reliant on the trade routes, while they maintained their traditional fishing and agriculture, the wealthy did not rely on those industries to cultivate power and wealth.

The Kumemura area was very important to all parties directly involved in trade in the area (China, Japan and Korea specifically), and not just the Okinawans. The Chinese were not creating settlements on Okinawa to simply enlighten the Ryukyuan people, they sold a lot of their Silks and textiles through Okinawan businesses to Japan, and Japan needed the Okinawans as the Emperor of Japan and his government had "Closed the doors" to outside trade, but saw the Okinawans as a "Japanese" adjacent province conveniently. The Japanese used the Okinawans to trade discreetly with China, Korea, Siam and anyone that they could reach out to through this convenient intermediary.

Okinawa became very wealthy as a trade hub between Java , China, Japan, Siam, Korea and many others. Korea playing a major role in purchasing in the North needed Okinawa as much as the Chinese and Japanese did. At any time in history the Koreans were at war with Japan and or China and Okinawa was the only place they could use to be a go between for business. War was war but business must go on was the mentality of the time. The war was that of the state not the business world.

The Okinawan people were at a strange point in their history. They were trading partners with China and depended on the Chinese to recognize their monarchy so they could exist as a kingdom, however they traded with all the countries in the area, often clandestinely.

They were also living as a subservient nation to Japan. Japan felt that Okinawa was a "protectorate" of sorts and they were part of the Japanese Empire in a way. This worked for the Ryukyuan people as they could then deal with the Japanese and trade with them, something not open to everyone. But that meant that they must be Chinese and Japanese in appearance culturally while trying to maintain their own cultural ethnicity and identity. A balancing act that would prove very difficult for them and one that required a flexibility and mastery of cultural pliability on their part. For the most part they felt this was the cost of doing business in the region, and business…was good!

    This relationship with Japan led to an interesting twist in their culture. Even though the Okinawans were seen as servants to the Japanese court, they were forbidden from taking on several of the Japanese cultural idioms but expected to be as Japanese as possible. They were forbidden to speak Japanese, wear specific Japanese clothing, or partake in Japanese culture. This was not only acceptable by the Okinawan people but also served two purposes that assisted them in their business dealings in the area. First it kept the Chinese in the dark about how close a relationship the Okinawans had with Japan allowing them to trade with all those countries in the area and not show their political hand, and gave the Okinawans the "in" they needed to gather information and send it back to Japan or China to gain favor with the different monarchs in both countries.

    The insistence on a cultural divide also kept the Okinawan culture separate from the Japanese culture, this made it much easier to justify the poor treatment that the Okinawans received at the hands of the Japanese and also restricted the "rights" that the Okinawans would have if they had any grievances with the Japanese government or their treatment by the Japanese in business deals or in general. The Japanese created this invisible cultural division and did not realize that the little bit of latitude it created for them also worked against them at times, and for the Okinawans whom they felt they were oppressing and subjugating.

    The process of ensuring that Okinawa maintained a degree of freedom and fluidity in its cultural links to each trading partner was over seen by a magistrate or a minister of Cultural education in the Kumemura area. His job was to make sure the Okinawans had a unique cultural character to show the Chinese and even select to adopt enough Chinese culture to make the Kumemura area seem Chinese enough to put the Chinese at ease and make information gathering easier for the people selected to watch over the Chinese emissaries to Okinawa. This also allowed the Okinawans to take on some of the culture that was being brought to Okinawa as a cultural exchange with the Chinese and not get in trouble from the Japanese overlords. The Ryukyu nation also did the same going the other way by ensuring they were adopting appropriate levels of Japanese culture and displaying this to the Japanese while ensuring that the Chinese did not view this exercise and see that the Okinawans were perhaps close to the Japanese that was necessary for them to maintain ties to China. This exercise was a huge undertaking and would have been a very delicate balancing act that the whole nation undertook to prosper in a very unique situation.

All this hard work and sculpting of the Okinawan culture, especially in Naha and around Kumemura was greatly effected at the end of the Ming dynasty; The Manchu/Qing dynasty took China and Chinese culture by storm in 1644 and they made changes to every aspect of Chinese culture and with that put demands on the people, including those living in Okinawa's Kumemura area to change along with them. However before this the Chinese empire of the Ming was established after rebelling against the Mongol Juan empire, they were completely opposite from the Mongols, they were organized, culturally distinct and ran a very efficient country focused on property for all, including making peasants lives much easier after the harsh rule of the Mongols had oppressed the people.

The Ming Dynasty was an "invasion" of Manchu people that had overtaken the Mongol culture more than it had overthrown just a ruler. The new Dynasty was founded in Northern China and took the rest of China city by city till they held all of China. The new rulers looked to change the very fabric of Chinese culture and this carried over to all their international affairs as well. They looked to influence the Okinawan people and spread the culture they had implemented in China. They also looked to culturally subjugate the Okinawans more and create a small outpost of Chinese influence so they could not only trade with Japan but also spread their influence further than the Chinese shores.

This cultural influx brought to China made life very interesting for the local Ryukyuan people for several reasons. As the Ming Dynasty started to put more pressure on the Okinawan government to become more "Chinese" the Japanese were also starting to make a foot print on the Okinawan people. This radically different culture was not easily meshed with the Chinese culture however. The Satsuma clan, having taking over officially running the Island nation behind the scenes for the Japanese Emperor, took the steps forcing the Okinawa to make changes that effected the way they dealt with the Kumemura area and the Chinese living there.

First they stopped the economic support of the area creating a vacuum with the wealthy business class and also the political bureaucrats that had become accustomed to doing business in this area. And just as the aristocrats in Shuri, or the Anji, grew more influential and powerful, the Japanese began to change their minds about the political use of Okinawa a go between for them. The Anji were previously used by the Japanese to perform minor information gathering on the Chinese but now the Japanese felt they could not be trusted and changed their use of the Okinawan people to just commerce and trade.

The changed that the Japanese had placed on the Okinawans created an opportunity for the Ryukyuan people to expand their own influence in the area. The changes created an opportunity to experience different freedoms as well as creating a new focus for the people.

The locals changed their approach and began to reestablish the traditional Okinawan culture as well as taking the funds that were going to Kumemura and changed the payments to support the Shuri people. The young men of Shuri, now much more wealthy began to travel abroad to Fuzhou and Beijing to learn more about the Chinese culture and with it they also began to learn more about Chinese martial arts, but very little was brought back to Okinawa in that regard for some time as those that traveled selected to stay in China. For nearly four generations the Kumemura community had a monopoly on Chinese cultural exchanges and served a very important place in Okinawan society, now that the monopoly that was established was dissolved and new inroads to learning Chinese culture and customs were release, Shuri became a much more influential center and Kumemura began to decline.

During the height of influence that the Kumemura area had in Okinawa, the *Yukatchu* or Scholar officials were created as part of the Okinawan caste system to study with the Chinese. It was these bureaucratic that traveled to China, Japan and abroad and also served to run the government in Okinawa. These scholars were also the cast that studied martial arts in China and from the Chinese in Kumemura. The influence of Fujian martial arts is obvious when you look at the Kata and systems that have been passed down to modern Karate systems. Goju ryu for example has Kata that are still practiced in both White Crane and Goju ryu. The masters we have seen as corner stones of modern Karate, like Chatn Yara and others served as Yukatchu to serve the Okinawan Emperor and it is highly suggested that this class of scholar Bureaucrats continued to exist in one way or another until the more modern masters like Azato and Itosu served the Ryukyuan King.

Much later the area known as Kumemura became a hot bed of anti-Japanese sentiment and many of the community fled to China after the Kingdom was dissolved and the Japanese military moved on the island. The brutal assimilation of the Okinawans by the Japanese meant that the culture was being molded into that of a Japanese island, the cultural influences by other nations was scrubbed from the island violently. By the time that Japan Annexed the island much of the ties to China had been severed and as the Meiji restoration set in the complete transformation to a Japanese rural province was completed.

The old rule of not looking or sounding "to Japanese" so as to allow China to do business and feel comfortable on the islands was replaced with a staunch new approach by the invading Japanese mainland. The locals were now expected to speak Japanese perfectly and they were to dress and act as though they were Japanese. The radical change happened very quickly but was presented at the end of a sword; the locals had no choice but to totally reform their cultural identity to be not only a bit more Japanese but to be Japanese.

The Kumemura area was enveloped and taken over by Naha and now is not much more than a local neighborhood that uses the name to identify itself. During the Meijin restoration Japan went through radical reformation and changes, but Okinawa took up the changes with difficulty and it took a while to complete which showed how far they had come from the cultural chameleon they previously were. Okinawa lagged behind in taking up the Meijin restorations perhaps a bit slower because of the radical changes that were needed compared to other areas in Japan. The heavy influence of China over most of the islands was set deep in the culture and change does not come easy in Japan, it takes generations, and the Meijin reforms were to take less than a few years to set in.

Yoga's hyperbolic connection to Karate

One quick story or sales Pitch I want to debunk right now is the notion that Karate somehow "Comes from Yoga Asana". A few points that need to be made up front is that SOME of what we call Karate comes from Chinese martial arts, this is true and provable with the brief history I am laying out here, however there is a lot of influence from indigenous arts and Japanese arts to, so its not so much a straight line as it is part of a greater tree.

The Kumemura area brought Chinese martial arts to Okinawa and they merged into what we now call Okinawan Karate, again provable, but when you start saying Yoga influenced Karate you are not only reaching...you are wrong.

Sometime in the 17th century Budhidharma, or several Indian Monks who became collectively known as this singular person, traveled to China to teach Buddhism in China. According to the story the Monks in China were in such bad health that this Budhdharma had to teach them a healthy way of living and introduce Yoga to them so they could physically withstand the vigor's of meditation. When you look at the written history of this however it falls apart fast.

First off the one book that is pointed to as proof of his teaching Qi Gong style kung fu to the monks or something that changed into this is the Yi Jin Jing, which most sources I have red suggest is full of errors, stories that are far to amazing to be true and claims that are so fantastic they can only be questioned and considered hyperbole or just outright falsehoods.

Also Qi Gong appears to existed long before Budhidarma crossed the boarders into China over the Himalayas, as did Indian fighting arts…and Chinese Fighting arts. To really answer the question of the link between Karate and Yoga…by way of Kung fu (Chinese fighting arts) you have to first see if you believe that Budhidarma was a single person, or if scholars are now suggesting that he is not a single man but made up of several men who's stories merged over time. Also, you have to realize that the human body can only do so many things, it's not unlimited in its ability to move….we have two arms and two legs and a large number of combined postures, but not infinite. By this is suggest that the Zenkutsu Dachi Oi Zuki position one takes to accomplish the front stance straight punch….only looks like The warrior pose a bit….Because we only have two arms and two legs.

While it IS true that some of the origin story of Karate DOES come from Chinese arts like Fujian white crane, to suggest that we have roots in the Indian arts of Yoga and Ayurvedic arts is buying into history and stories that are a little more than questionable in their origin!

1429 and the unification of the Ryukyu kingdom

Back tracking slightly, we see the rule of King Sho Hashi of Okinawa, the great unifier of Okinawa as being a pivotal character in the development of Okinawa and finally as a province unified under Japan. In 1429, King Sho Hashi completed his exhaustive quest to bring together the kingdoms of Chuzan (Central Mountain), Hokuzan (Northern Mountain) and Nanzan (southern mountain) under one Ryukyu kingdom. Known in Japanese as Sho Hashi and Chinese as Shang Bazhi, King Sho Hashi was an Aiji of Shoshiki Mairi. He was an administrator in the beginning but he gained power when he led a rebellion against King Bunei in 1404 and he elected to put his father Sho Shisho in power. When his father passed he took the thrown after a long battle to unify the war lords and recreate Ryukyuan society with the new caste system.

Hashi undertook the cultural changes that made solid political and business ties to China possible. He sent envoys to Nanking to ensure that China knew his Father was the leader of the island nation and that he was to be the focus of any political talks that China undertook on the island. Hashi was sure to let the Chinese know he had put his father in the place of the king showing himself as the king maker! He also put Okinawa in place as a tributary of the Chinese government and friendly to their causes in the area. He undertook a venture to "civilize" the people of Chuzan and thus adopted many elements of Chinese Culture. All of this showed not only his military prowess and skills but his understanding of politics and bureaucratic strategy.

After establishing his "Civilized" nation centered on Shuri castle and posting King Sho Shisho as the monarch, Hashi began to expand his new kingdom. When he saw Hokuzan, a northern neighbor as being a military threat to his father's rule, Hashi planned the military attack and overthrow of that region to bring it under his father's kingdom. In 1419 Hashi took his father's army and began a military campane against the warlords who ran this region. After three Hokuzan Aiji (local lords) turned to his side in the battles Hashi stormed the Hokuzan castle in Nakijin gusuku and after a pitched battle the warlord and all his closest retainers committed Suicide and left Hashi with the whole northern neighbor nation of Hokuzan under his father's rule.

A year after this Hashi's father passed away, and one year after establishing his rule in the unified nation, Hashi sent a request to be recognized as the ruler of this area by the Chinese Imperial Court and received it quickly. In 1422, King Sho Hashi succeeded his father officially as the king of Chuzan and appointed his brother warden of Hokuzan and in 1429 moved to overthrow Lord Taromai at the capital of Nanzan, thus unifying the island nation and truly starting the Sho (Shang)Dynasty in Okinawa and allowing him to start a closer relationship with China.

King Sho Hashi did not affect major changes on the existing system to make changes that would help him not only rule but also build a system that would allow for progress and easier interactions with other cultures. He left the system of farmers paying Aiji (lords) taxes in the form of goods and laborers paying taxes as well in place. The local Aiji backed the maintenance of the current system knowing they would benefit and develop their riches as long as they were loyal to the new king.

Sho Hashi then ensured that Aiji were made to owe their allegiance to his royal government in Shuri, and thus kept the lords in place for a time, but as servants to the government not independent warlords who would challenge Sho Hashi or the rule of the Ryukyuan kings after him. They effectively became land owners and fewer rulers of sub states under Sho Hashis rule.

Sho Hashi turned his attention to expanding trade with China and other Asian nations as well. Many documents exist chronically the Okinawan trade missions to Siam, as well as many relics and rare architectural items that chronically his emphatic expansions into trade.

All of the efforts to transition from a the previous warring states to a unified state made it possible for the island nation to become a trade-centric nation, which helped unify the people, bring in outside wealth and influences the Okinawan culture. This change also help develop the unique caste system that the Ryukyuan people adopted by merging Chinese and Japanese ideas on society. The fusion of cultures made for a uniquely Okinawan culture, one that saw the Chinese ceremonial robes worn by kings and other high officials when meeting Chinese officials and the wearing of Japanese swords by aristocratic members of society when meeting with the Japanese envoys. These cultural examples were but a few elements that were adopted into Okinawan society under Sho Hashi.

Sho Hashi died at the age of sixty eight, in 1439, and the royal court appointed his second son Sho Chu as his successor. The court sent out emissaries to the court of China and the Shogun of Japan in Kyoto and many other kingdoms in the area to ask for investiture from them to recognize Sho Chu as the new Emperor or ruler of Okinawa.

The First Sho Dynasty lasted till 1470 with seven successful kings. Each of the rulers showed proficiency at being culturally flexible and working with the system that Sho Hashi had put in place. They each adopted both Japanese and Chinese clothing, culture and mannerisms to help them work with the two opposing juggernaut nations they traded with. Each progressive ruler in the dynasty created inroads, made cultural changes and politically significant policy changes to help them smooth the trade with the ever changing landscape they faced, and for the most part they were very successful at this.

Sho Chu was appointed "Warden of Hokuzan" by his father Sho Hashi and after Sho Hashi died he became the ruler of Okinawa. Under his reign the Ryukyuan people began trading with Java. His son was installed as the new Sho king when his father died in 1444. Sho

Shitatsu was the eldest son of Sho Chu but only ruled for 5 years and his Uncle Sho Kinpuku took the thrown when he died in 1449. Under Sho Kinpaku many different building projects took place, such as a damn and cosway that connected many of the smaller islands. When Sho Kinpuku died a succession dispute took place between his younger brother and his son, In this dispute the Shuri castle burned down and killed both of the potential successors. Another younger brother, Sho Taikyu, took the throne at this time.

Sho Taiyku was one of the younger sons of Sho Hashi (6th child) and served after his brother died trying to take the throne after Sho Kinpuku died. He was a devote Buddhist and constructed a great number of Buddhist temples in Okinawa. Under Sho Taikyu the use of Maritime trade increased and was refined as a business. The island nation saw a big influx of trade with other nations and many Luxury goods found their way to Naha and Shuri. Naha, a port city once known for being a fishing village and harbor with lower caste Ryukyuans only, became a prosperous looking port town with estates and fancy homes owned by local lords. However Taikyus support of Buddhism was not something that the locals did not support Sho Taikyu's support of Buddhism and this focus also put a strain on the royal treasury.

When Sho Taikyu died in 1460 he was succeeded by his son Sho Toku who would be the last in the first Sho dynasty. Coming to power as a young man he inherited a nation that thrived but he had an empty royal treasury. Portrayed as cruel and violent by history he under took many military campaigns to expand Ryukyuan rule to smaller islands in the Archipelago that make up Okinawa now. Most of his military campaigns were failures or cost far more than they brought in. His rule was seen as a complete failure and he was generally portrayed not only as cruel but greedy as well with no true leadership skills. He died in 1469 as a young man, possibly at the hands of his own military.

Sho Toku was replaced with his chief vassal Kanamaru who took the name Sho En, thus maintaining the respect for the Sho line, but establishing a second dynasty. Sho En was born into a peasant family and worked his way up after becoming a servent to Prince Sho Taikyu. After Taikyu became the King Kanamaru was made the royal treasurer and after this he was put in a position to oversee foreign relations and trade. As Sho Taku was depleting the royal treasury he became very unpopular with the bureaucrats and it has been suggested that Sho En was put into power after they had Sho Toku killed.

The second dynasty lasted over 19 generations till the Satsuma clan forced King Sho Tai to abdicate and move to Japan as a way of absorbing the kingdom as a whole. The kingdom had already been invaded and was basically being run by the Satsuma clan under the Tokugawa Shogunate. This ended the rule of the Ryukyu kingdom, which had been established, unifying the nation and reigning for more than 400 years. With the fall of the Sho dynasty in Okinawa came the period of absorption for the Ryukyu kingdom into the Japanese nation.

1609 Shimazu clan invades

Taking a slight step back, The Shimazu clan was the ruling *Daimyo* (lords) of the Satsuma Shogunate and spread their power over the provinces of Satsuma, Osumi and Hyuga in the *Saikaido* (West sea circuit) area of Japan. They were actually an ruling clan and hereditary vassals or allies of the Tokugawa Clan, who unified the Japanese feudal *Daimyo* under the Tokugawa Shogun, but they were seen as outsiders to the royal court.

The clan was one of the best established and wealthy clans in Japan and with the loyalty of the Shogun and their loyalty to that post they were very powerful and influential. The founder of the clan, Shimazu Tadahisa was the son of the Shogun Minamoto No Yoritomo and received his domain of Shioda in Shinano province in 1186. They helped establish the Tokugawa Shogunate and also were sent to invade the island nation of the Ryukyu Kingdome in 1609 by the Shogun to bring the Island nation under Japanese control.

The invasion of the Ryukyu kingdom was more than just a land grab however, it was a battle over plans for the islands to be used as a jump off spot for an invasion of Korea. The Japanese Feudal leader Toyotomi Hideyoshi ordered the kingdom to support the invasion of Korea, but the Ryukyus were tributaries of China at the time and as such could not contribute to the invasion because it was well known that had the Japanese taken Korea that China would be the next target. If the Ryukyu kingdom had supported Japan, not only would they lose a status as tributary and thus their ability to trade with China, but they would have lost a lot of the wealth that came with being associated with and doing business with the great dynasty as a go between with Japan and Korea itself.

As the Japanese were also using the Ryukyus as a trade route this is clearly a case of cutting off your nose to spite your face. The Okinawan people were not going to endanger their trade wealthy by supporting the Japanese and they were not going to anger the Japanese and fall to them completely. Again, this took a great deal of social savvy and political chameleonship on their behalf.

The Japanese armies invaded Korea without the aid of the Ryukyu kingdom and then, despite knowing they could lose a great trade option, turned their attention to the Ryukyu kingdom itself. When Hideyoshi passed away the Shimazu clan of Satsuma took the islands nation under the new Clan leader and Daimyo Toyotomi Hidetsugu. This was made possible because the Ryukyu rulers had previously aligned themselves with China and not paid respect to Edo (ancient seat of rule in Japan) as was expected. The Satsuma clan was given full permission to invade and take the island Nation as a prize.

April 1609, three thousand men and more than one hundred war junks sailed from Kogahima and took the island without any resistance. The Okinawans were told not to fight by the king and simply bowed down to the Japanese invaders. The island was sacked and many cultural treasures were looted and taken to Kogoshima and the island became a tributary of both China and the Satsuma clan, with the Japanese taking ultimate control and using the island as a political agent against China. The Okinawans had been trained to be good at working both sides of the situation and were culturally flexible. A great deal of information exists that suggests that the Okinawans took the invasion in stride and continued working on building up their wealth as a trade port while working both China and Japan as intermediaries feeding both nations information that was favorable towards Okinawa first and foremost.

Because the island nation was a tributary to both countries, and Japan had closed its doors to both Europe and all other outside nations, Okinawan was one of only two ports that offered a connection to the outside world. The ownership of Okinawa was very valuable and the Shogunate knew that the small island chain meant more power and access to textiles and supplies that they did not have in Japan. This arrangement worked for them as long as the invading forces did not show their hand to the Chinese and openly show that they now were the true rulers of Okinawa, which in fact worked better for the Ryukyuan people than it did for the Japanese.

The Shimazu rules introduced several laws that would ban commoners from wearing the double swords or even owning them. The Shimazu saw everyone not a true Japanese Samurai as being a commoner. This lead to an interest in Okinawan gentry and military in studying the martial arts to offset the disadvantage they had against armed Samurai in civil self-defense situations. Again making Chinese martial arts study more attractive to the Ryukyuan people than before.

The Shimazu also made other changes and laws that influenced the development of Karate and also the society of Okinawa in general. Firstly they set about moving all the Aiji or ruling class to Shuri. This move started out the development of Shuri as a real Royal, cultural and political capital. With this the mobilization of craftsmen and goods jump started an ideology of a nation. Previous to this the provinces were localized and travel and goods did not move very freely as it was not required for commerce. This new ideology started the nation feeling more like a nation and not a set of wards. The island soon became more economically integrated and territories more specialized.

It's important to note again that the Satsuma invasion was relatively bloodless and they also insisted that the kings not take on a Japanese character and culture so the many temples, monuments and structures that were erected at this time were more Chinese in appearance. King Sho Shin built a new palace, and interestingly the large Dragon pillars erected at the entrance to the palace were neither Chinese nor Japanese in style. The pillars were those of Thailand and Cambodia, reflecting far reaching nature of the Okinawan relationships for trading along the Asian cost. This showing that Okinawa was not just involved in cultural exchanges, forced as they may have been, with Japan and China.

By invading Okinawa and taking it as a tributary and then an oppressed nation under their rule the Satsuma clan set in motion a series of changes in Okinawan culture that lead both directly and indirectly to the formation of the martial art we know as Karate. By requesting that the local gentry and members of the court essentially spy on the Chinese and yet offering a great physical threat to the new spy network, the Japanese encouraged the Okinawans to become proficient and study Chinese martial arts. Couple this with the total emersions in Chinese culture by the Okinawan ruling class, and anti-Japanese sentiment all created an atmosphere for growth in martial training on the islands. As a practitioner of Japanese Karate the irony that the very Japanese art I study was actually created to defend against the Japanese is not lost on me.

1872 Japan Annexes the Ryukyu Islands

The Japanese influenced and administered the direction that Okinawa and its people went from 1609 to 1872 and the dictatorship essentially ended the autonomy of the Kingdom. The Ryukyu kingdom was stuck for a period in duel subordination to both Japan and China.

However in 1872 the Satsuma clan and the Japanese government began to formally make moves to annex the islands as a province of Japan. Up to this point the Japanese were happy to rule the island but use the kingdom as a go between and spy network to watch over the Chinese and alert them to any political plans by other nations to move on Japanese interests.

In 1872 the Kingdom of Okinawa was "reconfigured" to be the Ryukyu province of Japan. Several years later, in 1879, the Ryukyu kingdom was completely dismantled and the islands became known as the Okinawan Prefecture. Then King Sho Tai was "requested" to move to Tokyo at that time to ensure that the envelopment of his nation went smoothly. Prior to his being moved to the Japanese mainland Sho Tai was actually left in charge of daily business on Okinawa. He was given the title of Marquis Sho Tai and given a compensation for his family and servants to live on in Japan. Most Japanese history books tend to gloss over this change and show instead that Okinawa was "always a state under Japan".

For a short time after the Ryukyu Kingdom was dismantled the Chinese emissaries continued to visit Okinawa in hopes of maintaining a peace and a natural trade route with the people of the Ryukyu Islands, the Chinese had come to use and see the value of the unique relationship they had with the Ryukyu kingdom and felt the value of the trade route with their enemy. Most of the emissaries faked ignorance of the Japanese take over out of convenience and hoping to maintain the relationship and trade route. In 1866 the last official mission from the Qing Empire visited Okinawa and established that China recognized King Sho Tai as the ruling emperor of Okinawa. This was followed by a1874 Tributary envoy to China from Naha and just five short years later the government of Japan officially reformed the kingdom into the Okinawan Prefecture.

The Reality of the move the Japanese made is that they felt that they no longer had to put on a show for the Chinese, the Japanese military was more modern, stronger and they felt that they were a force in the region that the Chinese would have to respect. The doors had been thrown open to the world by Admiral Perry's visit to Japan and the truth was that they felt that China was not as big a threat as they had been in the past. Also, the removal of the Okinawan king to Tokyo signaled that he was done as ruler of anything, his title and stipend was to maintain some semblance of friendly relations with Okinawan, but the hard facts were that they had taken the island and the Ryukyu Kingdome was conquered and over.

The king was moved to Japan, but many of his officials were left in Okinawan to run the country, some acquiring permission to return after first going to Japan with the king. They were left to administer a new country/province that was formed in the image of many western countries. They set up government posts and set about creating a new political entity that would run the province. Some of these men had been assistance and body guards to the king before the ruling family was removed and some were Karate exponents that learned the art to defend their king.

All of this past history had formed Karate by forcing the Okinawan people, especially those in command of the nation, to learn the martial arts to protect themselves from armed occupation forces and with the cultural exchanges they had been given the opportunities to learn and adapt the fighting arts of China, Thailand, Korea and Japan and to build and personalize systems of fighting under the pressures of occupation.

Was there a ban on Karate?

The romantic in me wants to say yes, but the truth is that Karate was never banned for practice in public or for any one person officially. Yet it remains a common misconception that Karate was banned in Japan/Okinawa by the Japanese at some point. Some say that Karate was banned when the Satsuma Clan invaded and took control of Okinawa, but this is simply a largely convenient misconception and a large extrapolation on a true banning.

When the Satsuma Shimazu Daimyo took control of Okinawa he stopped a common social trait that Okinawans had practiced for years, the wearing of the two swords that samurai used, or *Daisho*. The *Daisho* was worn by Samurai in Japan to represent social power and personal honor, it showed they were of the warrior class and often the upper cast members would wear them to show their status. However the Okinawans wore them as mostly a "costume" adopted to show the ties Okinawa felt they had with Japan, and as a way of showing the Japanese that the person wearing the *Daisho* in Okinawa were of higher rank socially than others. While the Japanese wore the *Daisho* with Kimono and battle Armor in a silk Obi, the Okinawan upper class wore them with Chinese robes and normally through a rope style belt. However they still came to symbolize that the wearer was a higher social cast than others, thus they served their purpose for a time.

The Shimazu rulers had the Okinawan gentry stop the practice of wearing the *Daisho* by giving an edict to the King stating that only true Japanese Samurai could wear the *Daisho*, however the delicate relationship and the fact that Japan did not want the Chinese to know the true relationship to Okinawa made a straight *Daisho* banning impossible, it would have revealed the Japanese as the true rulers of Okinawa. The royal edict was instead made as a "Social suggestion" to the Okinawan King and his gentry and it was still equally expected to be followed despite the means in which it was given. A heavy suggestion by a powerful nation is still often seen as an order regardless of how nicely it is given.

Shortly after the Japanese invasion forces settled in to rule the Okinawan country in secret, the Satsuma clan generals requested that the King Sho Nei, as a new Satsuma vassal ordered that all Okinawans give up the wearing of *Daisho* and could not replace them with other weapons. The need for a weapon was not really the reason that the *Daisho* was adopted in the first place, so giving them up was not seen as a big deal. However, the ruling army also stated that they could not carry other weapons, however this was a rule for commoners only. Court guards, police and other security persons could carry weapons in the line of duty, such as when protecting the King…but not the *Daisho*. They often used more common weapons like clubs and staffs to do the policing.

Karate as it were was never banned because the Samurai of Satsuma were never really aware of its existence, and those that were felt the Katana was more than enough to make this empty hand fighting useless anyways. The Ego of the Samurai would never allow them to ban an unarmed fighting art when they saw their Katana as being superior in every way to a man who only had his hands and feet to fight with. The Japanese also may have seen Karate as an off shoot or version of their own Jujitsu, however this has never been verified and honestly Karate was so scarce at that point that they may not have made much notice of it at all.

So, Karate was not banned, and at the time the Shimazu Samurai occupied Okinawa only a hand full of people were practicing the art anyways. It was limited to court guards and other wealthy and influential government representatives along with a hand full of others. The likely hood of a samurai feeling that they needed to ban a Self-protection art that they probably were not really aware of is slim and unlikely; the fact that we only have reference of a ban on weapons and nothing saying an unnamed fighting art was banned says something itself. It is far more probably that this fable was created with a bit of truth, but more as a marketing tool to show how "Deadly" Karate was….I mean if the mean and skilled Samurai feared it enough to ban it then it had to be dangerous and worth training in for self-defense right?

If we fast forward to World War II and note that Karate itself was only suspended briefly till the Karate masters took on American service men and convinced the occupying allied forces that Karate was simply a form of exercise shows that Karate was itself was never banned even during the complete destruction and demoralization of a nation after they lost a world war. The Japanese Karate masters thought quickly and avoided getting their art banned even in the face of a complete breakdown of their society.

Karate was never banned in its history. Not when the Shimazu clan invaded, nor when the Americans and allied nations took the island from the imperial government and over took Okinawa during and after World War II. As I said, this was more than likely a very good attempt at marketing the martial art to the masses by pointing out how deadly it was, but it was made with little fact or truth to the suggestion of it being banned. Perhaps the age old masters felt it was best to coop the weapons ban and use it to bring in new members, however in more modern times, a banned art may not be seen as very favorable.

Karate Growth and development post Annexation

Between 1872 and the 1900's many young students who had been training under masters during that time began forming their own styles of Karate based on what they had been taught and what they developed on their own, but as of this time the names of the styles were still loosely affixed to the locations they trained in. For instance you would get a wide variety of practices that were associated with Naha and Shuri areas even if the actual instruction and training was in different styles and systems completely. As an illustration you can see that Funakoshi Sensei would visit Itosu and Azato sensei (and many others) and train with them, but the Shuri style of Karate he learned from each master may have had some similarities, but vastly different in others. Also, some masters lived in the same town, taught different versions (or even completely different systems) but they were still called by their regional location and not a separate style.

Each master would specialize in different Kata, different training and have specialties that followed this specialization. They would build up their own personal training and keep the core similar but focuses would vary greatly, or they would train in completely different systems, but still all were known by the same name based on the town or area they trained in. Some would be kicking experts while others had hands like stone from Makiwara conditioning. The systems began to differentiate and develop separately in a vacuum as the old system of government changed and the need for royal body guards was lost. The ruling class now wealthy land owners and business people were no longer training often together, this lead to the variations of early systems that we see as the true starting point of what we know as Karate now.

The expansion of Karate over the next generation included new students such as Miyagi Chojun studying and refining the Hard Soft style of his master, which soon became known as *Goju ryu* Karate under Miyagi, Kenwa Mabuni who created the *Shito ryu* system and many others who focused their training on different aspects of Karate or different branches as they formed. Many other masters began forming their own styles and teaching them, often with their name affixed to it, like *Motou ryu Shorin ryu* and others. The styles began to cement themselves as well. Itosu Sensei was experimenting with different ideas and creating Kata for new students that would introduce them to his style of Karate. It was a period of growth, research and development by many talented instructors and their clubs.

Itosu was not the only one experimenting at the time with different ideas. However, his experiments had far reaching implications. He began with a dissemination of the major Katas he taught. He broke them down and took key elements to create a single beginner Kata he called *Channan*. This Kata embodied the very fundamentals of his Karate but over time he felt that it was way too long and while rudimentary and basic, it offered no advantage for his teaching. He took that Kata and further broke it down into the *Pinan* Katas. Actually he first created one single *Pinan* Kata and further split it down from that point to what we know of as the *Pinan* Katas now (which were then translated and changed slightly by Funakoshi to become the *Heian* Katas we now know). More importantly he began thinking about the future of Karate and who should be training. A big shift in training was on the horizon and people who were making these changes were thinking of the longevity of the art, no longer thinking of it as a tool to protect a royal family the systems began to take on a much different approach and a fundamental shift in thinking about its importance in development of the practitioner.

Karate began to be something that all members of society could train in, not just the military and body guards or noble families, which presents a vastly different history than we are often told by unwitting instructors duped by early marketing attempts. The systems began as a rich persons fighting art, as the art taught to the wealthy and upper class protectors of the royal family and became an art that would be taught to the middle class in Okinawa, a class that had not really existed prior to this shift.

The invasion of Okinawa, the annexation and then modernization of Japan created a new audience for Karate. A new focus for training and started the true evolution of Karate as we know it. The formalization and stylization of training began and as the key players in the creation of Karate were no longer training as a group the systems began to expand, new Katas were created by the founders of the systems and expansion, exploration and research went crazy. All of this created an environment for growth and diversification of the systems. And it also created and environment for some of the founders of more modern systems to step into them and begin to learn, develop, research and diversify their views and philosophy on training in Okinawa Te or Okinawan hand.

Funakoshi Gichin, early years

This is where our hero comes in! Funakoshi Sensei was born on November 10th, 1868 In Shuri Okinawa to a once wealthy, prestigious and reputable family. The original name of the family was *Tominakoshi*, and the family was known as well off scholars and vassals to the royal family who taught the village governor and his family classical Chinese writing and handled other educational matters of well off families who governed the area. The family had been provided a large stipend and land to live off of; however Funakoshi's father, Gizu, was a very heavy drinker and gambler and squandered the money. Because of this Funakoshi and his family worked the land next to their hired help and made ends meet by selling what they grew on their land while trying to maintain an sense of belonging to the upper class in society. As such Funakoshi was raised with the attitude of an aristocrat but the work ethic of the working class.

Young Funakoshi was born at the end of the Ryukyu Kingdoms life span and just before Okinawa became a prefecture after Annexation during the *Meiji* period. The *Meijin* means "enlightenment rule" and the period was one of great social and economic cast system changes in Japan. The social changes were brought on by wealthy business people overturning the old social norms to take power from the ruling class and throw the cast system out the window! A great deal of the social norms were upended and society was in turmoil as change after change came about and the Emperor of Japan took back a lot of the control over the country from the Daimyo's and Shogun, this was the start of the modern era in Japan. So Funakoshi lived during a time when the Island nation was just getting used to a shift towards being Japanese and not Ryukyuian and a period in which what it meant to be Japanese was also changing drastically.

Some of the major changes in the cast system were actually physical in nature. For instance it was now illegal to carry the traditional double swords of the Samurai or the *Daisho*! Not only was it illegal but the clothing people wore were now more western and they probably stuck out more. Those that continued to wear the traditional Japanese style clothing could not wear the swords regardless. Also the hair styles were changing and the traditional top knot or *Chonmage*, a symbolic hair cut with a shaved top and front of the head and the hair at the back folded and oiled to hold the Samurais helmets in place during battle was illegal.

The *Chonmage* was a status symbol during the pre *Meijin* era and played a big part in identity for the early Japanese cast system. Many of the families of upper class status at the time were opposed to the changes and the new laws, including Funakoshi's family. The Funakoshi family was actually very vocal about the new laws and against the changes. As the Funakoshi family was seen as very influential and an educated family their opposition to this law was seen as dissent by the local government bodies who were tasked with enforcing the new laws. The government did not take kindly to the opposition and punished many of the families by any means they could find.

Funakoshi's family was viewed as dissidents and trouble makers by the local political body and this affected the status of Funakoshi himself. Funakoshi Sensei originally wanted to be a medical doctor and even took the board exams to become a doctor and passed the stringent examination with perfect marks. He was well read and educated in both Chinese classics and modern Japanese writing, however his families notorious status had kept him from joining the royal medical academy and helped set in motion the very important events that would help create Karate as we know it. As Funakoshi was well educated and a very intelligent person who was essentially barred from entering into medicine, he made the fortunate choice to move into the "Family business" and become an educator. A change in direction that would have huge implications in the way Karate was transferred to the mainland later.

It is important to note that a lot of the fairy tales about how Karate was banned came out of the actual laws that the *Meijin* restoration created, such as the banning of "Samurai swords" or the other weapons of the warrior class in Japan. The stories and explanations were much more interesting if they were applied to Karate and everyone at the time and specifically that Karate was illegal, however and to be clear, Karate was not on the radar of the ruling class at that time. Okinawa and its fighting arts were seen as rather rural and of little importance at the time. The *Meijin* restoration was the force of will that the new ruling class or merchant class was bringing to force against the warrior class to seize power from them. The rural province of Okinawa played little role in the changes that were being made on the big islands at the time.

Karate was not really illegal, however if anyone carried weapons or showed the traditional Samurai fashion at the time it would have been illegal, this would have carried over to Kobudo weapons. No record of any imperial law actually exists that outlines a distinct legal restriction for practicing Karate. It is however more likely that the story grew out of the stories of the restoration and not from some mysterious edict that suddenly appeared about a relatively unknown fighting art from a rural province during the *Meijin* period.

Funakoshi Sensei actually grew up in a fairly normal home, many facts that are presented state that his class level was fairly high in the cast system and he was very educated and raised, as most Japanese children, mostly by his grandparents. He lived with them in their home while his father, in sharp contrast to the political position his family had in the cast system, worked odd jobs and worked to make ends meet after he had spent the stipend his grandfather had provided for the family. By all accounts young Gichin Funakoshi was an exceptional student and while he suffered from many ailments that made him a weaker child he was not any different from most kids. He had childhood Asthma but again it was a time when medical attention was different for children than it is today, most of those young men that took up Karate would have been seen as frail by today's standards.

The biggest influence on Funakoshi Sensei's life was born early on when he began school. He was frail, as stated, and yet a great student. His future was perhaps set because of his social status and the family financial issues, but his early years formed the path for him. It was in this school that a young and "sickly" Funakoshi met and befriended the son of famous Karate master Anko Azato (Yasutsune Azato). Azato was a well-known Karate instructor in Okinawa, but he was unique in that he was also a *Kenjutsu* instructor and as this art was a key Japanese martial art and held in high regard by the new Japanese government, Azato had managed to maintain the status and stature he previously held with the cast system as a guard and government official in royal service. As luck would have it Azato's son and Funakoshi soon became good friends and Funakoshi was taken in as a student by a very picky Azato Sensei.

Azato was a military chief and a body guard of the king of the Ryukyu kingdom, he was also one of the finest Karate masters on Okinawa, And he was also very picky about who he taught Karate. He only had a small group that he trained and was notorious for turning away students. A student of Sokon Matsumura and friend of many other instructors of the time, he had a great number of fairy tales and stories attributed to him that made him sound like a superman himself. Azato himself was a *Tunchi* (Village chief) in the cast system and as such held authority over Asato Village, a small hamlet halfway between Shuri and Naha. He was provided the best options for training and was uniquely trained in horseback riding, Sword fighting and wrestling as well as the local fighting arts he learned from Sokon Matsumura, which all colored his system and makes his students style look slightly different from other instructors systems.

As I pointed out Azato was a good friend to many of the well-known instructors of the time. He was especially close to Anko Itosu, a fellow upper class fellow who worked for the Ryukyu Royal family. Itosu was a *Pechin* or lower ranking Ryukyuan upper cast member. He was raised in a very strict home and was educated in the Chinese classics and Calligraphy that mostly upper level cast families would have the chance to study. Unlike Azato Sensei however, Itosu was trained under Chikudun Pechin, a much less respected and known instructor of Tode. While Itosu had originally started training under Matsumura he changed instructors when Matsumura told him he was mediocre and lacked skill. Itosu only moved his training back to Matsumura when Chikudun passed away. Funakoshi also had the opportunity to train under masters like Kentsu Yabu, Chotoku Kyan, Higashionna Kanryo, Matsumura Sokon himself and other instructors of the time. This was the custom in Okinawa at the time, senior students or personal students would be sent for periods of time to train under other masters and round out their training.

Young Funakoshi trained most of his Karate life with Azato, studying a hybrid art that formed his movement patterns that we see in Shotokan today. The system was a merger of the *Kenjutsu (Jigen ryu)* that Azato had studied and the *Tode* (Okinawan fighting system, one of the original names for Karate on Okinawa along with simply *TE* or hand) of which he mastered under Matsumura. Funakoshi only had a handful of students to train with and as such the majority of his training was apparently *Kata* as was traditionally the norm at the time. He would do drill work with the few students that Azato trained but mostly his training was in a deep study of the Kata that he learned from Azato and other masters. It is commonly said that Funakoshi Sensei mastered only 15 Kata prior to leaving for Japan, this is not true at all. In his book Karate do Kyohan he lists off Kata that he studied under other masters and the list is very extensive and even has Kata that are not practiced today.

Through Azato Funakoshi met and studied with Itosu. This was said to have been after Matsumura passed away in 1901 and Azato passed away in 1906. Funakoshi had already been training for roughly 28 years under his master and only trained with Itosu for about 8-9 years, most of which he was a full time teacher in the school system. Funakoshi however shared his passion for the Chinese classics with Itosu and it was said that they were very close friends more than instructor and student. A lot of information about the duration of time, when he actually trained with and to what extent Funakoshi trained under Itosu is set in a lot of confusing fable, rhetoric, guess work and marketing stories, making it hard to be very accurate in this regard.

While Funakoshi is said to have called his friend "Master Itosu" he reserved "Sensei" for his teacher Azato, yet another example of internet "mind porn" that I have found while researching the relationship that Funakoshi had with Itosu. Itosu had a large group of people who trained with him and Funakoshi would have been seen as senior to all of them as he was much older than most of the young men training under Itosu at the time and he had been working as a school teacher longer than most had been training in Karate. Also, the use of the term "Sensei" is and was more akin to the term "Teacher" than most of us think today. It was not a term restricted to special occasion, it was more of a title used for school teachers and some suggest one that was not used in Karate until it came to Japan.

It is commonly said that Funakoshi studied very hard under both Itosu and his direct instructor Azato and learned the more popular styles of Karate of the time; being *Shorei* style and *Shorin* style. However the truth is that this is a distinction that was put forward by Funakoshi to explain the different characteristics or performances of the different Kata. The truth is that some of the Kata were *Suri-te* system Kata and others were from the *Naha-te* system, which went on to be known as both *Goju ryu* and *To'on ryu* systems of Karate. In his book Karate Do Kyohan Funakoshi uses the *Shorin* and *Shorei* to make a distinction between Kata that are lighter and dynamic and those that are "heavy" and tenser body movements. He is not the first or the last to make this distinction and it is of interest that he uses the *Shorin* name to denote the "Shaolin" influence that Karate most definitely has, it's not by any means an accurate separation as *Seisan/Hangetsu* is a Kata that comes from Shaolin white Crane training by way of whooping Crane system Chun fa (kung fu) and listed as *Shorei* by Funakoshi. In other words Funakoshi used a very easy to understand, if not inaccurate, tag system to denote types of Kata he was teaching to clarify why some of the Kata he taught seemed to teach often opposing principles.

Funakoshi graduated and became a school teacher while training with Azato, most accounts show that he continued to train religiously with Azato and often traveled to Azatos home in the village of Asato many times a week at night after work. Between his graduation at the age of 18 and his 21st birthday in 1888 he worked odd jobs to support his family. When he was 21 he was hired by the Okinawan School division as an assistant school teacher. It was then that he was married and started his family. His wife Gosei was also a Karate adept and many stories of her wrestling skills and Karate skills have been shared to illustrate her prowess at fighting, however many have been used to confuse Gosei with the wives of both Itosu and Azato, both of which may or may not have trained in Karate. Funakoshi Sensei still was not taking on students, he supported his family, his parents and grandparents on his salary for teaching, three dollars a month as an assistant school teacher all while making the nightly trips to train with Azato.

Funakoshi's wife is said to have taken day jobs working in the rice field and weaving fabric at night to help support the family. She encouraged his training in Karate and often trained herself. While this much is known about her there are not a lot of stories about Gosei Funakoshi other than this. Once Funakoshi moved to Japan there are a few mentions of her, such as her joining him in Japan during the war with the children, however she apparently passed away a short time after moving to Japan. Most of the early writings of Funakoshi obviously involve his teaching or training in Karate. His biography is one of training and teaching and a great read, but not a lot of stories about his family life are printed.

Funakoshi Sensei: the Karate instructor

Funakoshi was a school teacher in 1888 and worked his way up to being a full teacher and worked in the school system for some time before he retired and moved to Japan in 1922. He became a senior student of Itosu after Azato died in 1906 and he had been working with Itosu on a very important project. No real written account exists as to who had the idea first or who did what, but Funakoshi and Itosu Sensei both worked on making Karate part of the Okinawan Middle School curriculum. Coincidentally Funakoshi was a middle school teacher at the time that this occurred in 1901 which suggests correctly that he was highly involved in the move to put Karate into the daily curriculum of the schools. He worked with other Itosu students to create a workable syllabus and approach the school system to include Karate training as part of the daily fitness focus for students.

Most accounts of Funakoshi paint him as a reluctant instructor early in his teaching career, he would appear to have been much more comfortable in the role of student or administrator of Karate rather than leader or instructor. At that time Itosu, a very influential and ambitious man had been looking for ways to make Karate much more relevant, beyond its original role in Okinawa and seeing the young school children as a perfect audience for Karate Itosu worked with his junior Funakoshi in finding ways to implement a program in the school system. Funakoshi was not the only instructor that was working on this goal however, Itosu had a number of students whom went into the teaching profession.

Itosu had many students who began teaching in the school system around this time; men like Kentsu Yabu, Shinpan Goshukuma, Hanashiro Chomo and his junior Funakoshi, who was by now a full instructor and who was approaching the end of his career as a school teacher at the time. Itosu formulated a way to bring the teachings to the school children by making his system much easier to study and breaking down the principles of Karate, creating new Kata for the students and making Karate much more easy to train in. This was a big move for Karate in general and despite some push back from more traditional instructors the idea grew and what was once an elite training regimen that was focused on defense and often the ability to end life, and an art restricted to the higher cast families became more common place and much more accessible to anyone wanting to train in the art. The old Okinawa of strict cast and structure came crashing down with the Meijin restoration and a more western social structure became the norm in Okinawa, and in Karate.

Lots of people point to the post Meijin attitudes about Okinawa or other "Foreign" countries by the Japanese as being proof of racism, intolerance, prejudice and sectarianism; however it is more an extension of the cast system that formed entire identity of early Japan. The Okinawans had a similar cast system and it was very difficult for them to give this up at the time. However being on the lower end of the post Meijin restoration adjustments to society the Okinawans were much more open to accepting the merger of cast levels and open up Karate and other formerly restricted practices to everyone, I am not saying that sectarianism did not exist in Okinawa, it was however overshadowed by the realization that even though they were now "Japanese" the Okinawan people were going to be seen as a uniquely "Different" part of Japanese society.

In 1901, the commissioner of Public schools, Shintaor Ogawa was sold on the idea of introducing Karate to the school system by Funakoshi and Itosu and officially recommended it to the Japanese ministry of Education. For their part the Japanese ministry of Education allowed this "Back water" idea to be introduced to the Okinawan school system, but they stopped short of total acceptance of the system into "Japanese" Schools. The minister of Education for Okinawa felt so strongly about the idea that he suggested all normal school and first public high schools in Okinawa have Karate as part of the daily training for students. This recommendation was accepted as a pilot plan in 1902, Karate joined other more traditionally Japanese arts like *Kendo* in the school system.

Itosu Sensei had little idea of what the school system was like, he was not practiced at the policies and general navigation of the school system, but he had Funakoshi as a guide. Itosu had Funakoshi appointed the head of his endeavor, apparently, because of his career as an educator and his experience with the school system. Funakoshi also had the personality of a politician and had shown that he was a great mediator and negotiator. Funakoshi was to act not only as the chief instructor for the new school project but also as the diplomat that dealt with, trained and indoctrinated the other instructors who felt slighted for not being included in the program. This gave the new venture the added push of outside instructors suggesting and promoting participation in the school program. Previous to this a instructor who was not part of the endeavor may have tried to undercut the programs and forbid their own students from participation, and put the whole project in jeopardy. But now with the push from many of the respected instructors on Okinawa the program was set to be a huge success.

At the age of 33, in 1896, Funakoshi had started teaching his own interpretation of Karate, merging the systems that he had been taught by Azato Sensei, his primary instructor, and systems and ideas he had learned from training with other instructors over the years. Azato Sensei was by now an older man who was still teaching Funakoshi but not as often. When Funakoshi announced he would be teaching what Azato had taught him it brought students from all over Okinawa and more money for his family. Funakoshi was teaching small groups of dedicated students the system that he was building prior to the school systems program taking off. Funakoshis Karate was very different than the system he was introducing to the school system. The school program was built around Itosu's softer, more Chinese looking system with shorter stances, higher postures and Funakoshi was teaching a linear system that was based more on Azato Karate. The process continued in the schools with Funakoshi leading the charge, but privately he was teaching a very different system.

By 1910 Funakoshi had developed several students in Okinawa who would carry on his teachings in Okinawa and help him look for new ways to spread his Karate to the mainland independent of Itosu and his group of Karate students. Funakoshi's system was linear and explosive but also leaned heavily on his personal philosophy that Karate should be used for health, self-defense only if necessary and to improve the character of the practitioners. He also believed he was passing on the traditions of his masters. Funakoshi was more focused on avoiding fights and felt that avoiding confrontation had much more honor in it than winning or engaging in a fight. He believed it took more courage to walk away from a fight than to defeat an opponent. This is significant because Funakoshi was born and reached adulthood during a very important yet violent time in Okinawan history.

With the changes of the *Meijin* restoration, the total destruction of the native cast system and the revolutions in industry the whole country was changing and this created shock waves in its society, which lead to a great increase in violence on the island nation. Ironically Funakoshi saw the changes directly as he was recruited to assist in many of the *Meiji* restoration changes as a school teacher during much of the changes. Despite his families opposition to the changes it was his job to assist with many of the changes, often holding down the youth who were having their "top knots" removed and disarming youth who insisted on wearing the double swords that their previous cast allowed them to wear. This all affected his personal philosophy and his creation of his system of Karate.

Funakoshi also began giving public demonstrations to different groups. He used this as a way to spread his Karate and also as advertising for the school system program he was essentially put in charge of. The demonstrations started to become popular and larger and larger groups would come to watch them. Funakoshi would perform his Kata, do some Kobudo demonstrations and eventually take questions from those that had come to watch the demonstration. The groups got bigger and bigger and were a significant part of raising interest in Karate on the mainland. In 1911 Captain Yashiro of the Imperial Navy visited Okinawa and saw Funakoshi doing one of his demonstrations. For the first time a military man from Japan watched a Karate demonstration and was so impressed with Funakoshi's brand of Karate that he issued orders for his whole crew to visit and witness this new art, many of them decided to learn Karate in the short stays they had in Okinawa.

Prior to the military interest in Funakoshi's Karate he had not shown much interest in going to Japan, but fueled by the first visit of steady military and now government groups training with him as they stopped over and did short stints in his training, Funakoshi was showing growing interest in going to Japan. One of the most prestigious visits that Funakoshi had was when Admiral Dewa of the imperial Navy first fleet visited Okinawa and a dozen of his commanders and offices stayed a full week to train with Funakoshi. They then brought back stories of the Okinawan fighting system and showed some of the training they had received to others. This started a very big interest in the new exotic art that they had seen with their mainland friends and colleges. The Imperial Navy specifically brought back favorable words of the Okinawan style of fighting to others and this started a movement to get instructors of the art back to Japan. Funakoshi was mentioned specifically as a great master of the Okinawan art and this created a great deal of issues for him at the time. However Funakoshi followed the ideals of his instructor

Azato and promoted others names when he was talking about Karate, this seemed to stymie the issues for him and placated others jealousy for a short time at least.

1902 Karate moves to the schools and beyond

Going back a bit, to 1900, Karate broke away from being taught to the local upper cast members for the purpose of protection of the King of the Ryukyu nation, the old guard had long since retired, the king was swept away to Tokyo to live out his day as a willing political prisoner and had his title changed so his royalty was changed to be lesser and more manageable by the Japanese government. The former military attaches and council were now left with little to do, some had gone into political and government office to assist in running the province but most retired to their lands and were not just land owners renting out to farmers who worked the lands. During this short instability after the kingdom fell to the Japanese those that were Karate exponents had little time to teach as they were remaking governments to run the island, but after this most that had retired moved into teaching the arts and took on new students.

By 1902 Karate was no longer a specialized training program for the body guards of the king; it was more of an open practice and used to supplement the finances of most of the old retired masters. Karate was beginning to be introduced to the Okinawan school system as previously discussed and public demonstrations held by Funakoshi Sensei were giving the programs a great deal of momentum. Itosu and his students were running a great deal of the Okinawan school systems Karate program with Funakoshi as the head instructor but most of the direction being given by Itosu directly to his students. The Karate being taught was now almost completely Itosus system as Funakoshi was moving away from running the program and focusing on his own Karate and giving demonstrations publicly. He would soon give a very important demonstration to the Crown Prince in Tokyo and the move begins plans to move to Tokyo. However, back in 1902 Itosu was busy changing the Karate that was taught to the palace body guards and royal court members. The Kata was changed to remove techniques so that the Kata was easier to learn and teach to younger students and most importantly the Karate that was developing continued to grow and change and progress into something similar to what we see in many styles practiced in clubs today.

The systems where refined and a great deal of the "Effective" techniques were removed. A lot is said about this in some clubs, but the most devastating moves that were removed were taken out to make them more acceptable for practice in modern society. Things like eye pokes, throat strikes and other "less than" clean techniques were removed so that it was more practical for teaching children and other members of society, not that the Katas were less effective, they were just more cleaned up. For instance *Wanshu* (*Empi*) apparently used to house a lot of groin strikes, these were removed and converted to other techniques to make them more acceptable to the general public. With the changes the expansion ideals were starting to shift as well. The focus of moving to the schools only started to shift into making Karate open to the public in general and clubs began to open that specialized in teaching Karate to the public. Many of Funakoshi's peers in the school systems Karate program were part time instructors of Karate and held down day jobs, only a few were school teachers. The transition from small groups of students training in school was an enormous step for Karate. It is important to note that while Itosu and his group headed by Funakoshi opened the door for Karate to be in the school, other instructors like Chojun Miyagi also worked in the school system after the door was opened and did so independently of Itosu and his changes to Karate. This meant that early *Goju ryu* was taught in schools like Itosus *Shorin* system was.

Moving Karate to the schools created a central point for practice for many instructors however. It also opened the door for cross training for all students, not just the select few as it had been. Prior to the movement to the schools many of the styles had been scattered and or disorganized in their practice. Most were family styles and not codified or organized.

Each system had a "Style" of Karate based on the influences of the instructor in that area. The formation of the school curriculum forced many of the traditional family groups to organize and systemize their training programs and create formal training criteria for them out of the chaos of the unmodified systems. With this came a need to name the different systems and show the influences that were being used to create the system. For instance, if you lived near Naha your system was influence by the systems in this area and was categorized as *Naha-te*.

Itosu worked hard to make the School Karate style very easy to learn and broke down concepts and training into workable chunks for children. He created Kata that were just 20-ish movements long for them to learn and worked with his seniors to implement a curriculum that would attract the interest of kids. He was brilliant and created the student friendly system that progressed from an easier to follow system to a more difficult senior end training. Itosu also created the *Pinan/Heian* kata series to help beginners develop the physical skills and understanding that they needed to move up and then stylized them into a curriculum so that there was a set bath for students to follow in learning. And this was all before the classic Kyu/Dan ranking existed. While *Naha Te* and *Shuri Te* moved into the school system and changed, the *Tomari Te* system seemed to stagnate and shrink. Members of the *Tomari te* style were having issues incorporating the changes that would be required to move into the school system and most importantly they did not accept much of the changes. Chotoku Kyan, who was born in *Shuri* and had studied under Kykan Oyadomari and Kosaku, both *Tomari Te* masters, was said to have been very difficult himself but stated that Oyadomari and Kosaku were even more bull headed and against change. Kyan represented the old *Tomari* guard and was set in his ways and focused on small groups of adult students only while keeping traditional training and focus exclusively. Granted Kyan is also known to have been a bit "rough" around the edges and have some "unique" training methods. He encouraged his students to visit brothels and drink heavily so as to get into fights and test their skills. Kyan also was a heavy drinker and had a nasty temper.

  Not surprisingly *Tomari te* never made it as a separate style and did not make it into the school system, again not surprising. *Shuri Te* was the dominant style in the schools and influenced all other styles that continued to exist, even into teaching and working with adults. The only problem was the growth rate was out of control, many of those visiting Okinawa would train for a while with a junior instructor used to teaching kids and then after a short time they would go home and say they mastered the art, but really they only learned a bit of the watered down art taught to kids, they did not understand nor were they often exposed to advanced ideas, they learned school kid Karate and it became the norm!

  I want to be clear and say that not only did *Shuri* styles like Shotokan and *Shito ryu* leave the island for the mainland but also at the time styles like *Goju ryu* began to develop separately from the *Shuri* and *Naha* styles and gained a great deal of popularity, then also joined the *Shuri* cousins in Japan. All of this progress was only made possible because of the ground work that Itosu, Funakoshi and the students had done for decades before the move to the schools and after they moved to the schools. The expansion into the school system directly led to the public demonstrations which Funakoshi and others performed and this led to the introduction of Karat to the mainland and for once....something invaded Japan from Okinawa, and not the other way around. It is also important to note that while Itosu and his students moved into the schools, they were not the only ones. *Goju* also had school clubs and made good use of this innovation to create a wave of popularity for the *Naha* based system.

Funakoshi Sensei: The demonstrations that changed everything.

Shortly after Funakoshi helped Itosu set up his school program he began giving public demonstrations of his Karate. Some think that this is to offset what he saw as a big shift in the system to push Karate into changing into a kid friendly system from what he believed in. In 1906 Funakoshi put together a demonstration of his Karate, the first big demonstration that would focus on his system of Karate and the biggest in Okinawan history. Prior to this Funakoshi had also been known as the head student of Itosu's and a leader of the school program. He had given plenty of demonstrations, but all of them pretty much had been to market Itosu and his school program to others, his main demonstrations had been used to market his second instructors program, but after a few years he began giving demonstrations for his system of training. While his original demonstration in 1902 to Shintaro Ogawa had gotten the ball rolling he was now pushing his own system and trying to promote his own training. The demonstration was so popular that an "Elite" team was developed made up of masters like Gosuku, Mabuni, Motobu, Kyan, Ogushuku, Ishikawa, Tokumura and Yahiku. The team performed demonstrations for two years and were busy highlighting the different styles of Karate in demonstrations across Okinawa.

By 1917, the use of Karate in the school system was very deeply ingrained, the classes were huge and a major success. The Minister of Education requested that Funakoshi travel to Japanese to demonstrate to his peers on the big island. The demonstration was organized but raised little fanfare initially. Demonstrating to adults a program that was geared towards kids was not exactly a world changer. However his visit to Japan had created enough of a stir because of his teaching military members to attract the attention of the crown prince of Japan. Over the years Funakoshi continued to train with many masters and was recommended by Itosu and Azato to many of their peers for training and continued improvement. He was uniquely skilled and knowledgeable in many of the smaller styles of Karate on the island and seen as a expert in many of the Okinawan styles others had never seen. He was named the Chairman of the Okinawan martial arts society and also the head instructor of the Okinawan teacher's school. He was a much respected instructor on Okinawa and seen as senior to most of the current masters on the island that are now seen as his peers.

The crown Prince Hirohito actually visited Okinawa in 1921 en route to Europe; he was presented with a demonstration by Funakoshi that was put together by Captain Kanna, the commander of the destroyer that the prince was traveling on. As an Okinawan by birth Kanna made sure that the demonstration had Karate in it. The demonstration was a big part of the Gala that was being held at the Shuri Castle as a part of a major cultural event. Funakoshi and his Okinawan students were invited to appear as part of the cultural event and were to demonstrate the Karate system that was in the schools at the time as the Gala was sponsored partially by the Okinawan Educational Society who were a big part of getting Karate into the schools , but this time he made the demonstration about his style of Karate and only mentioned the school program in passing. The crown prince was so impressed that he invited Funakoshi to do several demonstrations in Japan.

A while later, in April of 1922 Funakoshi demonstrated Karate at the Women's higher normal school in Tokyo and at the first national Athletic exhibition as a key demonstration. These demonstrations were such a success that Funakoshi decided to stay in Japan and never did return to his home in Okinawa. Funakoshi was a newly retired 54 year old school teacher that has traveled to the mainland to make a second career of out of teaching Karate. Funakoshi was the son of a broke *Shizoku* (Okinawan upper class) and a retired school teacher with a small pension, which was barely paying his expenses. The trip to japan was an opportunity to make enough money to continue to support his family.

When he first got to Japan and after the initial fanfare, he had to take odd jobs to pay for his living expenses. However as his demonstrations began to attract students and they became a staple of any fairs or athletic events he started to be very well known in Tokyo and his art was being well received, he started to attract more and more students. His innovations and his ideas began to influence others who were teaching Karate in Japan at the time and Karate began to spread across Japan.

Eventually Funakoshi found a room in the *Shidobata* in Tokyo (a dorm for Okinawan students and travelers). To pay his way he became the custodian of the dorms, sweeping and cleaning up during the days and then teaching at night. He also did some gardening and ran errands for people during the day. At that time his son Yoshitaka traveled from Okinawa after Funakoshi's first student and assistant, Shimoda Takeshi, had passed away in 1934, and acted as his assistant and demonstration partner. Shimoda had been an expert in *Kendo* and *Nen Ryu* as well as other arts, but he had fallen ill after a long trip and passed away suddenly. Yoshitaka was a bright young man who had trained with Itosu and several others and was forward thinking and ready to help his father out growing the new family business.

Funakoshi began teaching individuals in private classes while he continued to give demonstrations, but an idea after a demonstration at a university led him to open a club in the college. Soon many colleges had Karate clubs and Funakoshi and his son were teaching at the clubs. They also opened clubs and had other seniors teaching at them that had trained under Funakoshi personally and were passing on his system. The seniors and Funakoshi taught and collected funds and soon as they had earned enough money to rent a facility in *Meishijuku* district of Tokyo and then moved to the Meijiro district to open the first real stand-alone club which was called "the Shotokan". The club opened in 1939 and a plaque was mounted so students could see it when they entered the club. The plaque welcomed them to the training hall of 'Shoto', the pen name of Funakoshi. The Shotokan was the first hall that was reserved for teaching Funakoshi's fusion art of Karate and it began the art form we all know now as Shotokan, the largest style of Karate practiced in the world.

While Funakoshi and his son focused on traveling and teaching while doing demonstrations he sent his seniors to teach at Takudai, Keio, Wasada, Chuo and other colleges, these programs in turn sent students back to the main club to learn at the headquarters. Funakoshi had taken Itosu's idea of teaching in schools and created a Karate empire out of the idea. Regardless of what opened the door for Funakoshi and his system, Funakoshi and his students provided the hard work that catapulted him and his system and made it the success we see today. Funakoshi also began using his knowledge of writing to start writing his books and create a new way for people to learn karate and assisted with the growth of Karate in Japan.

__Karate's name change "Chinese Hand" to "Empty hand"__

Most students have been told the story of how Gichin Funakoshi changed the name of Karate from "Chinese hand" to "empty hand". It's often toted as a major change in the direction of Karate and a mile stone in the acceptance of Karate by the Japanese people, this puts Funakoshi in the position of both savior and innovator in Karate…..This is both a simplification and exaggeration of what actually happened and a fabrication of who was responsible for the change to the name. While it is true that Funakoshi had change the name of many of the original Okinawan names used for the Kata make them more likely to be accepted by the

Japanese students he hoped to attract when he moved to Japan, there is also little truth to the assertion that he was part of the change of the arts actual name.

The assertion that Funakoshi, at this time, started making the change to "Karate-Empty hand" would be flawed for several reasons. To start with "Karate" was the term used by most people in Okinawa when referring to the art, it was much more likely to be called Toude/Tode or Te by the practitioners of this time, and while it was much more popular with a greater number of people in Okinawa it was still not a "common practice" with the masses. You also have to realize that Okinawan people did not have the same hang ups that the Japanese did about China and things foreign to them.

They would probably think nothing of calling a art for "Tang (Chinese) hand" while the Japanese would be aghast at the use of the "Chinese hand" title. While it may have been a great idea to use a different name for the system in Japan, the Okinawan people were more than happy to call it Te or whatever they wanted to. And that's just talking about those that practiced the art. The fact is that Karate was not and still is not much more than a fringe practice in Okinawa to this day as it was back when it was just a local art. Its not like the style had even a dozen brick and mortar buildings that would allow for club practice. Back when Funakoshi was learning and living in Okinawa it was more of a private style of self-protection passed down to a limited number of people.

Prior to the change over the use of the "Kanji" or Japanese pictographically writing used to write Karate meant "Tang hand" or "Chinese hand. Again, it was not a commonly practiced art and still very much tied to the Chinese systems that it came from.

So, when did the swap out of *Kanji* happen?....the earliest known use of the new writing for Karate, and the use of "Empty hand" over "Tang hand" was by Chomo Hanashiro in his book "Karate Kumite", and it was published in 1905. Wait....Another interesting point...."Karate *KUMITE*", many of my Shotokan peers and instructors insist that early JKA members "Created" Kumite. Before this the practice was only Kata , Kihon, Kobudo, Drills and conditioning exercises. Guess that's not true as well. Actually the book outlines basic Yakusoku kumite or pre-arranged sparring and showed that Kumite existed prior to World War II. Chomo Hanashiro was a peer of Funakoshi Sensei and a student of both Matsumura Sokon and Itosu Anko. He was also one of the Okinawan school system teachers that were tasked by Itosu to help spread Karate into the school system. He took over much of Funakoshi Sensei's duties when Funakoshi left for Japan and was seen as a highly educated person who was also a Karate master in his own rights. Also Itosu's "10 precepts of Karate", written in 1908, used the Kanji for "Empty hand" as well. Itosu was seen by many Karate instructors as the Authority on Karate in

Okinawa at the time and upon his death many of his students were seen as the new masters, Hanashiro Chomo being at the head of that list.

For 28 years the written name of the art bounced between "Chinese hand", "Empty hand" and the spoken name between Karate, Tode and Te. It created a great deal of confusion for new students and may have contributed to the separation between Japanese Karate and Okinawan practices. Many of the innovations that came out of Japan were seen as "Empty hand" changes and the traditional Okinawan style remained "pure" and unchanged from the alterations that Itosu had made. However many of the Okinawan members who were returning from Japanese schooling were practicing the same art in Japan but came home to confusion when the name was different. In 1933, 11 years after Funakoshi started teaching in Japan, a semiofficial head of the Butokukai visited Okinawa and suggested that the name be changed to allow Karate to be more readily accepted and not viewed as exotic (read Chinese) in Japan. The official pointed out that the name change had already been completed for all clubs in Japan as the "Chinese nature" of the styles had also been altered to make it more palatable in Japan. The Chinese monitor had also not gone over well with the Japanese, but once it had changed the fighting art had caught on very well in Japan.

In 1936 a big meeting was held by the Okinawan masters to discuss the current affairs of Karate in Okinawa. The meeting was held and masters like Chomo, Kyan, Choki Motobu, Juhatsu, Chibana, Chotei Motobu, Genwa and Shiroma all met in Shuri to find ways to promote the art. It is said that at this meeting Chomo brought up the name change to the group, and it was also said that the change was not meet with a warm reception by everyone. The meeting itself was said to be an interesting one with several attendees dead set against the change from "Chinese" to "Empty" Kanji and some were not only opposed to this change but chastised Chomo noting he had used this change for nearly 3 decades prior to the meeting and he was now trying to force his views on them. In the end the masters all felt that the change would be acceptable as it allowed for expansion into Japan and an easier transition for students coming back from Japan. They relented due to economics and logic, but many of them privately stopped using Karate all together and began using style names like Shorin Ryu over Karate.

As further proof that Funakoshi was not the spear head in this movement as a great deal of the propaganda suggests, in 1922 Funakoshi had his first book on his art published as he was trying to market the system in Japan and draw in more students. To find a title for his system he turned to a more descriptive name than simply "Chinese hand" or even "Empty hand", he used **Ryukyu Kenpo Tode**. It is important to note that the use of "Kenpo Tode" is a different way of writing "Chinese hand". However by including the "Ryukyu" in the title he was ensuring that others knew that the system was of Okinawan origin and not simply Chinese. He also referred to the art as Tode when he gave his first Black Belt certificate a few years later in 1924. Funakoshi eventually converted and began using "Empty hand" in the name of his art, and while he was not the first to use this term he was more than likely the most influential person to use the changed name at that time. The change to the name made sense in the end and was a huge move for the Karate masters of their time to have made. In the early 1930's Japan, and therefore Okinawa, had invaded China and a forced nationalistic ideology was being pushed in Japanese society; it made teaching an art with "China" in the name a hard sell, then you add that the Okinawan masters were still seen as lower cast or foreign and you can see that they wanted to limit any friction and opposition to them teaching, a simple name change was needed. Like many, Funakoshi took the change and ran with it. The name change helped Karate get a foot hold and then grow and set up a solid foundation in Japan for Karate and allowed for a focused expansion into what is now what we know as Karate today.

Karate in Japan: Judo's influence over Karate

So, Funakoshi is in Okinawa, The name of the art has changed to "Empty hand" and he is working odd jobs, living in an Okinawan Hostel and has students in the Universities and its growing to the level of a movement for him and his students. But what was the launch point of all of this? What influence made his system so different from others that his system was the biggest in Japan at the time? The answer is actually a set of situations and lucky happenings that made up a formula of success that I am sure was mostly made up of pure luck.
After the Japanese crown Prince left Okinawa he extended an invitation to Funakoshi and gave a formal recommendation that Funakoshi demonstrate the art on the mainland. You can hypothesize as to why this was, but the honest truth is that he saw a cultural system that impressed him. He more than likely saw the system as a cohesive practice that he could bring to Mainland Japan to illustrate a positive cultural component of Okinawa, not a fantastic fighting art that would be such a big influence on the Japanese, after all they had a strong history of fighting arts that they saw as far superior to the Okinawan Chinese influenced system. However Funakoshi was smart enough to see the opening and opportunity to bring the fighting arts forwards, and more than likely a second career as his teaching career was now at an end.

In 1922, after letting Itosu know he would be leaving the teaching program in the schools Funakoshi left for Japan. Upon arrival in Japan Funakoshi began going on a tour and doing demonstrations at many different events, including the 1922 National Athletic Exhibition of Ochinomizu in Tokyo. It was at this event that his first sponsor approached him and asked him to stay in Japan. The Sho family funded his stay and helped with any paper work he would need to fill out to stay on the mainland. The Sho family was a direct decedent of King Shotai, the last king of Okinawan. The Family saw value in brining Okinawan influenced culture to Japan, they too were looking for a second shot at their original family business, meaning they would use Karate and any other Okinawan art to show that their culture was not the inferior social structure that the Japanese had put forward in taking their kingdom from them.

The actual arrival of Funakoshi was much less exciting than one would think. As the "most noted" man of Karate from Okinawa he was met with no real fan fair, no one really thought much of his visit once he came to Japan. He was after all a 51 year old mild mannered retired school teacher from Naha and was not only smaller than most people but well past his physical prime by this point in his life. He was by all accounts quiet, conservative and the farthest thing from a showman, not exactly the kind of man you would expect to lead a movement that would see Karate become what it did. He held events and partook in existing events to show off his Karate, but pictures of the time sow a small man and his students doing Karate to big groups of people, most of which were not really paying attention to the event. He did not present fantastic *Embu* like we see today and a few writers of the time portray the man as quaint and small, not a good portrayal of a man that would create a movement. The fact that he was approached by a Kendo instructor to stay on in Japan was seen as a lucky turn of events for him. After a while however other patrons stepped up to pay for his teaching, including an art group and finally other well-known Japanese martial arts masters.

After staying in Japan and giving multiple demonstrations, Funakoshi was approached by the founder of Judo, Jigaro Kano, with a personal request to demonstrate his art at the famed Judo Headquarters the Kodokan Judo hall. It was suggested that at that point Judo saved Funakoshi and Karate, he had been working so hard and with little money to live off of and was close to throwing in the towel and moving home. Funakoshi was living in student dorms doing menial jobs and only the Okinawan people were interested in his art, and some suggested it was more to talk to a fellow Okinawan who had been of some status from their homeland, not because he was a great instructor or he taught a famous style of Karate, at that time his style was new to everyone…including him.

Judo had never invited an outside martial art to demonstrate for them in their home Dojo, actually they fought for pure judo training and had turned away several Jujitsu instructors who had wanted to teach, demonstrate or work in the Kodokan….or worse, they would let them teach then turn master Judoka instructors on them and beat them up, showing Judos superiority. At the time Karate was also seen as a provincial or back water style of fighting and seeing as it was not even a grappling art it was may have been viewed as a less than worthy art by some, or as not a threat to the superiority of Judo in the field of fighting. Regardless, it was invited by Kano none the less. Judo came from the Samurai arts and still held tight too much of its attitude and grandeur. But Kano was a forward thinking person and saw something in Karate and requested a semi private demonstration for him and his senior instructors and students.

Kano had a lot in common with Funakoshi from the start, both were educators, with Kano being a university professor and Funakoshi a school teacher with classical education. Both men were seen as well-educated and Kano felt a great deal of respect for Funakoshi. The reason for this may have been mostly because the respect was mutual, Funakoshi apparently treated Kano with the kind of respect that one over the Judo master while other Karate instructors who had visited the mainland had treated Kano with contempt and as an advisory. Kano had very poor interactions with other Karate instructors and some described the meetings as insulting and aggressive meetings where Kano was treated as an adversary and not an emissary. Kano and Funakoshi were also closer in age than some of the other instructors, Kano being 8 years Funakoshi's senior and someone Funakoshi would honor as a senior in age for sure. Knowing Funakoshi's conservative up brining he would have acted appropriately and humbly with the Judo king, this is what created the bond and the first big opportunity for Funakoshi in Japan to really cement his place in Japan.

Funakoshi brought is student Makoto Gima to perform at the Kodokan (at this time it was still in the Tomisaka area of Tokyo), both of them performed in front of 100 black belts. Gima had studied for years under Yabu Kentsu in Okinawa, and now that he was in school in Japan he had transferred his studies to Funakoshi Sensei and had been a key advisor in the early formation of Funakoshi's system of Karate. Gima's early studies were based in the Shorin system that Yabu taut and had learned from Itosu Anko, Yabu being a school teacher himself and one of Itosu's school program teachers, the system he learned at the time was the basic Shorin system that childeren were learning in Okainwa at the time. The change to Funakoshi's Azato based Shorin system brought his teaching in line with Funakoshi's training and gave Funakoshi an advisor that was trained in the more used system Itosu was teaching, this gave him a good mix of the hard Kenjitsu influenced system and the softer inclusion based system of Itosu.

Gima and Funakoshi demonstrated Naihanshi Shodan (Tekki Shodan) and Funakoshi performed Koshokun (Kanku Dai). The demonstration went into application and movements performed to show both attacks and counter strikes, grappling movements and Bunkai in general. This fed right into the Kodokan's wheel house and apparently caught the attention of the black belts leading many of the seniors to ask questions and get involved in the demonstrations. Apparently the demonstration was very animated and Kano and his black belts not only asked questions but were shown and involved in dynamic applications of the Kata.

After hours of demonstrations which saw Kano and his students get very involved int eh demonstration and performances, the group asked Funakoshi and Gima questions about the art and began to see the commonalities and applicable differences between the two systems. One must remember that while Funakoshi took Itosu Shorin ryu and Azato Shorin ryu to create his Shotokan (name used later) system, Kano had merged several systems of Jujutsu into his art of Judo. He had taken studies with instructors from Tenjin Shin'yo Ryu and merged other systems with this base to create his hybrid, so he had a great deal of respect for the approach of his younger Okinawan counterparts Karate system.

Kano and his students were very impressed and a system of Cross style exchanged began to occur as a friendship was formed between the two men. Kano had a great deal to offer Funakoshi as he was well established and well known in Japan and could bring many supporters to Funakoshi and his system. Kano worked very hard to make Funakoshi and his assistants feel invited and comfortable, going to the lengths of serving dinners that were traditionally Okinawan and not exactly common to the pallet of the Japanese. These efforts solidified the bonds of friendship and respect that they shared and helped Funakoshi in harder times when he first came to Japan.

During the demonstrations and exchanges Kano took note of several of the throws that Karate had, the names had to be changed but the throws were solid and he took them into his system as well. Funakoshi demonstrated many of the grappling applications in the Katas and throw a great number of willing participants at the events. Kano shared ideas with Funaksohi as well and the friendship between the two grew considerably. Funakoshi used a few of the Japanese Martial artists ideas to create some changes in his Okinawan based style that makes it look a bit different and unique from other systems as well.

Outside of the technical changes that were made, most were minor adjustments some major changes were also made that created a unique opportunity for the systems developments. During the events Gima and Funakoshi borrowed Dogi's from the Judo group (uniforms) and wore them to do the demonstrations. While Gima appears to have borrowed a black belt, Funakoshi used a traditional sash to close his Dogi top. The use of belts in Karate had not yet been common place and belts were not used yet as well. The reason that Gima was given a Black belt and Funakoshi opted to use a black sash was said to be an idea that Kano came up with. In order for the smaller Okinawan's to be taken seriously they must at least show that they are the same ranking as the senior Judoka's that were in attendance.

Funakoshi enjoyed the use of the Dogi so much and shortly after the exchange demonstrations Funakoshi had the original Karate Keikogi (practice uniform) made up of much lighter material, but used the same design. Funakoshi noted that the use of the uniform allowed for much more freedom of movement and also something to hold onto when grabbing an attacker to throw or sweep them. However the Karate uniform was of much lighter material because the Judo Dogi was much warmer than he liked and the use of grabbing and throwing in Karate is limited. He did adapt a Obi or belt in place of the sash as he felt that the Sash was to Chinese and would not go over well with new Japanese students.

While Funakoshi came away with a new uniform and the structure for ranking his students, as the Dan/Kyu system had not been firmly established until this point, Kano did not come away from the meetings empty handed. Kano developed the Shoulder Throw (Ippon Seio Nage) from the movements in Heian Sandan as demonstrated by Funakoshi and he also developed a specific foot sweep that was inspired by the Naihanchi kata. Kano was constantly developing and researching, adapting and changing movements to create a much more fluid and effective art. While Judo change slightly from the meetings it has essentially been the same, with the same movements taught in the exchanges between Funakoshi and Kano, since the 1920's. You can still see the influence that Funakoshi had on the already established Judo juggernaut today.

Once established in Japan as a serious martial artist, Funakoshi found his circle of students beginning to expand and grow. With the help of Kano's interest in his style of fighting and as the word about this spread as to his skills, Funakoshi became more and more famous and felt it was necessary to stay in Japan and spread his style and build even further interest in Karate on the mainland. Some people feel that it was at this time that he went to his masters in Okinawa and asked to stay on in Japan to teach. Several people write that it was only after he dipped his toes in the Japanese student pool that he saw value in staying and went back to Itosu for permission to stay, however Itosu had already passed away in 1915 and his original instructor, and most influential person in his Karate life, Azato had passed away 10 years prior to his leaving for Japan. It is far more conceivable that Funakoshi simply felt that he had to stay in Japan to keep his style growing and provide a base for Karate in the larger population that Japan offered over Okinawa. Also, funds were limited and the economy of Okainwa did not offer a retired school teacher the same options that Japan did. In Japan he was provided students with a lot more free funds to spend on leisure than he would in Okinawa. He stayed in Japan to create a second career post retirement, and after his meeting and exchanges with Kano and the Kodokan students he was now famous enough to make this work.

First Generations students

In 1922 Funakoshi performed his last of three trips to do demonstrations in Japan, having been asked back three times and having traveled home two times. On his third visit he gave an improved demonstration that inspired groups to seek his instruction in this strange system of Okinawan fighting. He was showing that he was growing as an instructor, a showman and using skills he had picked up to excite people about what he was teaching. One of those men was **Jigaro Kano**, soon becoming a close friend. Kano was the founder of Judo and held in high regard in Japan. When Kano asked Funakoshi to teach in the Kodokan it sealed the fate and lead directly to the prosperity of Karate on the mainland. Funakoshi and Kano Sensei shared a lot of ideas on how to organize the systems that they were teaching, they also shared some technical aspects of training but mostly they worked with each other on how to organize the systems they were teaching to make them easier to grasp, more organized in syllabus that could be easily passed no and more importantly they shared ideas on how to market their systems and how to create growth in the martial arts at that time.

Kano respected Funakoshi and became fast friends with him, Kano had taken the unusual steps in letting Funakoshi teach in the Kodokan, Something that he had not done prior to this. He also incorporated some unique Karate throws that Funakoshi taught him into his Judo system, something that he was known for. Kano had studied several styles of Japanese Jujitsu and was known to have incorporated many aspects from different arts and systems to create his system that he began calling Judo. He also was known to research and develop different throws with his students and "play" with ideas on how to improve the current throws or bring new ones on board, the fact that he took a few from Karate is not a shock at all.

Both men also shared a similar back ground, being educated and from well off families. Kano convinced others to train with Funakoshi as well and thus allowed Funakoshi to live in Japan earning a decent living and allowing Funakoshi to send money back home to his wife and children. This was all exceptional and had not been done by Kano before demonstrating the close ties and bonds that he had formed with Funakoshi and the deep respect he had for the Okinawan retired school teacher.

Funakoshi decided to make Japan his home and began teaching for an artist's guild to help pay for his living expenses and thus established one of the first true Karate clubs in Japan at the Meisi Juku, a dormitory for newly arrived Okinawan students. Funakoshi also began writing about his style in 1922 and had his first book published called Ryukyu Kempo: Karate. His system was starting to form roots and students were taking up the style and Funakoshi was formulating his system, students were studying and helping to develop the system and the first generation of dedicated students were becoming entrenched in the Shotokan systems history.

Many of his students were transient and had studied in Okinawa previously. Funakoshi knew that if Karate was to take off he would need to move into a more mainstream base for his style to find stability and students that would not train for a time then leave. Looking at what Itosu had been trying to do in Okinawa with the school system, Funakoshi established the first Collegiate Karate club in 1924 in the gym of the Keio University. The group took off and soon other schools began opening Karate programs and Funakoshi was kept busy sending students to teach as well as teaching on his own. This offered great stability as well as some of the great first generation instructors.

In 1936, several of Funakoshi's students started raising funds to construct a free standing Dojo. The Dojo was named the "Shoto-Kan" after the pen name that Funakoshi used when writing poetry. From his original college/school based programs and his Dojo he developed his first generation of students. These students included Takagi, Yoshida, Obata, Noguchi, Egami and Hironishi.

One of his more famous and most devote students was **Takeshi Shimoda**. Shimoda was a student of Kendo and also studied Ninjitsu. In his 30's when he began Karate he would be Funakoshi's demonstration student and one of the most influential people in the budding new system as it began to develop. Funakoshi brought Shimoda with him everywhere as he traveled around the country performing Karate demonstrations for crowds, with the demonstrations often taking on a carnival like atmosphere, the two would show their new system to the crowds trying to build Karate's population in Japan. Unfortunately while he was an extremely skilled student, he passed away while he was very young. He became ill with an unknown illness while traveling with Funakoshi and passed away suddenly.

Before Shimoda passed away Funakoshi took on several students that would travel with him giving the demonstrations. Shimoda would still be the most senior and run most of the demonstrations but along with Shimoda was **Shigeru Egami**, a student of Funakoshi's that had been studing at Wasada University and upon graduation took up training and traveling with Funakoshi, Shimoda and eventually Funakoshi's son Geigo. Egami was also a student of Judo, Kendo and Aikido before joining Karate and as such his Karate was seen as slightly different from his peers. Egami focused much of his training and administrative duties on the formation and running of the College league that was in charge of all the different university groups. Soon after Funakoshi passed away they united and formed the Shotokai and continued to grow and develop parallel to the JKA.

Isao Obata was also an early student of Funakoshi's, but he tended to walk the line between the two groups of Shotokan/Shotokai students, the future JKA and the Shotokai group. Not only was he an active member of the Shotokai, he helped form the JKA with the help of his juniors. Like most of his peers at the time he had trained in other arts in school; like Judo, Kendo and Kyodo, and his ventures into Karate came only after reading Funakoshi's first book. Obata had even transferred his schooling to Keio University to find training with Funakoshi, who it had been rumored was going to teach at the club. Obata became so involved with the growth and expansion of Karate that he dedicated the rest of his life to training and administering Karate, he also arraigned and participated in post-world war two activities to build Karate back up, becoming the driving force in forming the JKA and rebuilding it after the war. He also put a great deal of his personal wealth into the growth and development of Karate.

Jotaro Takagi was also one of the early student of the Chuo university clubs and became a strong force and administrator of the Shotokai. In 1995 he became president and principle of the organization. Takagi became the president of Mitsubishi Jishu Co and used his place as a President and then Chairman to help build up the Shotokai. Under Takagi the Shotokai has stuck to the path that was set out by the former presidents and heads of the organization. However, he moved the headquarters of the Shotokai to a newer facility as well as doing a lot of legal work to ensure the emblems and properties of the organization remain protected for generations to come. Takagi ensured that the organization was following the vision that Egami had for the organization and maintained the proper spirit in training. He passed away in 2016 after a life time dedicated to Karate and maintaining the focus of Shotokai.

Hiroshi Noguchi was a student at Wasada University and was a senior teaching at that club for the rest of his life. He was one of the seniors that came together initially to form the JKA and help Funakoshi Sensei out financially. Like many martial arts masters of his time, Funakoshi Sensei was not financially well off and teaching Karate cost him much of the money he had saved from his family funds just to travel around the country demonstrating. Noguchi was also the first Wasada Karate Captain and represented the team. While Noguchi never sought the lime light he helped develop many great masters that presented Karate to the world. **Mitsusuke Harada** and **Tsutomu Oshima** all count Noguchi as a big influence in their Karate lives. Noguchi was seen as senior to Egami and many others in the Shotokai.

Genshin Hironishi started his training at Wasada University and went on to teach at Chuo and Senshu universities as the head instructor of that clubs. Hironishi was a close friend of Gigo Funakoshi and a staunch traditionalist. He was one of the group that came together to form the Shotokai and along with his close friend Egami he ran the organization. Hironishi was well known for his ill temper and being hard on students as well as his super traditional stance on training. Hironishi was seen as the keeper not of Funakoshi Gichin's Karate, but the Karate of his son Geigo. When Egami passed away Hironishi took over running the Shotokai as the president and held office until his death in 1999. His super traditional stance was tempered slightly as he was also responsible for founding the Shotokai's stance and practice of sport Karate. The system that was created was seen as super traditional sport. His main focus was on traditional Karate however. This may sound strange as I will show that the Shotokai was against tournaments and sport Karate when the JKA was forming, and this was seen as one fo the major rifts between Shotokan and the Shotokai, however the advent of sport involvement for the Shotokai came a long time later when sport Karate had already become very popular and the Shotokai recognized that they needed to participate in this style of training to remain relevant.

Tamaro Yoshida was an early student of Funakoshi's that left for the United States and settled in San Francisco's China town. Yoshida was known to be a favorable person and enjoyed teaching. Moving to the States for business and to raise his family he melted away into his teaching and became somewhat anonymous compared to his peers. Known as a staunch supporter of traditional Karate and a student of both Funakoshi Senior and junior as well as a junior and student to Obata Isao, Yoshida was a quiet and unassuming man but one that focused his training and teaching on the lessons he learned under the Funakoshi's and his other seniors. Yoshida was also perhaps one of the first instructors in North America from the

Shotokai group. With Yoshida teaching in the states, many of his early students opened clubs and preceded the JKA invasion of clubs by more than 2-5 years.

Hironori Ohtsuka was an early student of Funakoshi and amongst the seven men that Funakoshi first gave the rank of Shodan, or first level, too. He received his Shodan in 1924 along with Tokuda, Akiba, Shimizu, Hirose, Gima Makoto, and Kasuya Shinyo. Ohtsuka began his martial arts training learning Japanese Jujutsu under his uncle, Chojiro Ebashi and then moved to learning Shindo Yoshin Ryu Jujutsu from Shinzaburo Nakayama. In 1921 Ohtsuka received his teaching license in Jujutsu (his Menkyo Kaiden) and became the fourth master of that school. However in 1922 Ohtsuka began training with Gichin Funakoshi and studied medicine. He established a medical practice and specialized in treating martial arts injuries. By 1928 Ohtsuka was an assistant instructor with Funakoshi Sensei's School and also traveled to train with Mabuni and Motobu in Kobudo and other aspects of Karate. When Shimoda passed away, Gigo Funakoshi stepped in to take his place and began teaching his way. The new training was harder and much more rigorous. Ohtsuka began complaining that the new way was far too difficult and he soon left the Shotokan to form his own training group that came to be known as the Wado Ryu school. This school combined his Shotokan Karate knowledge with his Jujutsu training.

Makoto Gima began his training in 1912 and was one of the students that performed the demonstration at the Kodokan doing Tekki shodan and some basic drills. Gima Makoto was born in 1896 in Okinawa and after graduation from the Okinawan Shihan Gakko (higher normal school), Gima left for Tokyo to study at the Shoka Daigaku (present Hitotsubashi University.) Gima began training with Master Itosu and his senior student K.Yabe. He came to Japan after Funakoshi sensei and settled in the Meisei-Juku (Okinawan student dormitory) and began training with Funakoshi Sensei. After Graduation from Hitotsubachi university in 1923, Gima entered the teaching profession and taught at a commercial school and worked for the Kajima Corporation Company. Gima never joined the JKA or Shotokai, instead he began training with Kanken Toyama and eventually started teaching his own brand of Shotokan that was influenced by his training in Shudokan under Toyama. His style of Karate is referred to as Gima-ha Shoto-ryu and very popular in Canada's west as well as small pockets in Japan and Europe.

Shinyo Kasuya was a professor of German Language and literature at Keio University in 1924 and asked Funakoshi sensei to teach a group of students and university staff at Keio. Kasuya was a German Language and literature professor and became an advisor to the group. The group became known as the Karate Research group of Keio University. The group was organized and sanctioned by the university, making it the first collegiate karate club in Japan, and it is still active to this day. Shinyo Kasuya is credited as being the person that gave Karate its "in" with Universities and because of his hard work university clubs began opening with Funakoshi and his students running the majority of the clubs. Clubs opened at Takushoku, Chuo, Shoda (now Hitotsubashi), Gakushu-in, Hosei, Nihon, Meiji and many others.

Many of the first generation students, especially those that received Shodan under Funakoshi, went on to open their own clubs and run their own styles of Karate. Some stayed to teach, but the entrepreneurial spirit was strong before World War Two and the attitude was that Japan was taking the world by storm. They spread out and began training with other younger instructors and many began working towards the imperial dream of expansion. Some are lost in the mysteries of time and others may have died during the war. The timing was right for expansion, but the timing for Karate's expansion would also be somewhat halted by the governmental expansionist mentality and the want to go to war itself. The war would have a great impact on Karate…for good…and bad!

These were the first generation instructors, known now as the golden age of Shotokan before it became a system that it is now known as and before it became as popular and well-rounded as it is now. The systems early seniors helped establish a foot hold in Japan for Funakoshi and his art as well as began building the now popular art. Several never received the recognition of a Shotokan Shodan, others were the first Shodans given by Funakoshi but all of them created opportunity for the system to take hold.

One cute story I have been told is about the first demonstration that Funakoshi Sensei and his students held at the Kodokan. The story goes that Funakoshi Sensei showed up with a few of his students and were requested to give a demonstration of the Karate applications. They were getting ready to do the demonstration when asked by Kano if they wanted to change out of their street clothing into "Proper training attire" . The Karate men had no idea what Kano was asking as they trained in everyday clothing most days.

Kano proceeded to offer Funakoshi and his students the Dogi that they used in Judo to work out in. The story says that Kano provided a personal Dogi to Funakoshi as they were about the same size and Funakoshi Sensei took the offer but tied his Dogi shut with a sash he had that he normally used to close his traditional Japanese top. Thus was born the use of the Dogi or Keiokogi in Karate.

I know that Judo provided us with the "Karate Gi", however I cannot find any source for this story other than the instructor who told me this cute story.

Early Karate in Japan and the creation of the Shotokai's roots

Funakoshi had been staying at the prefectural student dormitory at the Shidobata, Tokyo and had a small room alongside the entrance. His daily duties he were assigned to pay for is room included cleaning the dormitory grounds during the day while students were all in school, which left the evenings for teaching. Other than the public demonstrations, for which he set up many, Karate was still not very well known and was generally restricted to the Okinawan nationals that lived in the dormitories and came to train with Funakoshi from outside. His funds were slight and he had left a great deal of his pension at home to take care of his wife and children, and he also sent home what he could to help support his family.

After deciding to stay on in Japan, Funakoshi Sensei began teaching Karate full time, first at an art guilds studios and then moving his classes to the school at Meisho Juku Dormitories and moving his residence to this new location as well. The new full time teaching brought in little money, but private classes he taught earned him a living wage and brought even more notoriety to his teaching and his new fancy Okinawan fighting art. He also began doing something that would influence his systems growth a fair amount more than teaching in small Dojo's and doing private teaching, he began writing books about his Karate system. This helped not only promote his Karate further, it also helped attract more students of note and helped him codify his system.

The books attracted several noted students, including famous Sumo fighters and rich benefactors, which all helped bring in more students and brought up his income, making his stay in Japan much more comfortable for him. Prior to this he had lived a rather poor life, existing on meals at the dormitories and living on a very restricted income, with the books being published and more students coming in he could push forwards his vision of what Karate would be by purchasing better uniforms to train and demonstrate in and promote his club with better marketing.

Another idea that he used for growing his system was a familiar approach that had been used for spreading Karate to the masses in Okinawa. Having seen how the educational system in Okinawa had helped spread his instructors system and he was after all living and teaching in a university dormitory at the time, he felt that pushing to have Karate as part of the curriculum or at least as an extra-curricular activity would benefit him and the students. Funakoshi approached the school and began teaching in the University gym and offering classes, which were very popular with young Japanese students.

Funakoshi moved his focus to the university system themselves; he set up clubs in Keio University, followed by Chuo, Tokyo and Wasada University. All of these clubs were very popular and he had junior instructors teaching for him when he was unable to attend, he used the term "Captains" and presented them with ranks to reflect their seniority and authority over the classes. The university clubs began to grow and the most famous club of the university clubs was Takushuko University club, which was not only a focus for Funakoshi but the largest and most respected club in the group.

With the new clubs established in the university system, Funakoshi had created the very first Japanese Collegiate Karate programs and his style was spreading and growing rapidly. His success also bread success for other Karate instructors as well. Taking a page from Judo, Funakoshi began giving out ranks to members. Leaving the old Menkyo system behind he provided "Dan" ranking certificates to people he felt could help spread his system of Karate. He gave Shodan rankings to Jikken Tokuda, Hironori Otsuka, Eiyu Akiba, Toshinyuki Shinizu, Hirose,Makoto Gima and Shinyo Kasuya on April 10, 1924. While Gima and his cousin Tokuda had trained extensively in Okainawa only Otsuka had previous Martial arts training. The ceremony was long and very formal, seeing Funakoshi call up each recipient, giving them both a certificate of rank and a black belt to wear. Each of the members were collegiate students and instructors who helped Funakoshi Sensei transform Karate from a mysterious, foreign, mystically based art to the more modern and scientific martial art and sport that it was to become.

After a short period of time, and some very tough times, Funakoshi had opened his first school in Meishojuku Tokyo and then moved it to Meijiro after finding a much more suitable location. The school attracted more students, many of which were wealthy and working men. Men like Takagi Nakayama, Yoshida, Obata and Noguchi. All these men would go on to influence Karate a great deal, as well as helping to spread Karate through Japan. The "Shotokan" was formed and a large contingent of the students was not in the university anymore, they were working or started Karate after University. They had different ideas, larger ideas that saw Karate spreading and becoming a industry with for profit Dojos popping up all over Japan. A professional division would be set up to help create instructor and the spread would be business like. However a growing number of University students were against this approach.

In 1930, Funakoshi's senior students at the university clubs saw a need to band together to help promote the style in general and to build an organization to propel the system even farther into the mainstream, but the way they felt it should be. It was also in this year that the Dai-Nippon Karate do Kenkyukai was formed. The organization was essentially a group used to standardize practice and create a way for clubs to exchange information, train together and formalize a governing body for the university group. While Funakoshi was the leader of this group, much of the organization was led by senior university instructors. The name change in 1939 to the Dai-Nippon Karate Do Shoto-Kai as the Shotokan Dojo was built in Zoshigaya, Toshima-Ku district. Gichin Funakoshi served as the first Chairman of the group from 1936 till 1957, but again most people will admit that the actual decisions were being made by a small group of University based instructors and Funaksoshi, while only 62 and showing no signs of slowing down, was much busier than one would think growing his system.

At the age of 62 Funakoshi was still doing demonstrations with his direct assistants all over Japan at any event that would have him. He also taught a great deal at different clubs. The organization was set up with him as the president and chair person, but by all accounts he had little to do with the actual day to day organization of the university groups by this time. After Funakoshi passed away Egami Shigiru took over as president and the chair fell to Motonobu Hironishi, after Giei Funakoshi had been honorary chair for many years.

The Dai Nippon Shoto-kai is simply known as the Shotokai today. They did change their focus from a University based group to grow into other ventures and stand-alone clubs and many of the members earn a living as professional instructors today. One other tenant of the group that has fallen by the way side is the participation in Kumite and tournaments. One of the reasons for this was a notion that Funakoshi did not approve or or teach Kumite at all so the Shotokai originally did not teach this as one of the pillars of training as the Shotokan based groups, and even the Shotokai, do today. It is very hard to imagine Karate without the Kumite for sure!

It was a common misconception made about Funakoshi that he had never actually seen a Kumite class or taught Kumite in his life time. However he did not accept that Karate should include Jiyu Kumite, and he was dead set against this type of training. The truth is that far more complex than this however. As part of the growth and acceptance plan for Karate, Funakoshi gave the task of formulating Shiai Kumite rules and development of the types of acceptable Jiyu Kumite to his son Gigo Funakoshi and several of his students. While Funakoshi

Gichin himself never partook of Jiyu Kumite his students and his son most certainly did...and with his blessing and directive to do so.

The Shotokai was formed out of a group of likeminded University men that followed the teachings of early Shotokan. The changes that were going on in the professionals division made up of the JKA roots were ignored and often seen as "not Shotokan" or "Not the teachings of Funakoshi". The group seemed to gravitate towards the early teachings of Funakoshi, his son and those that were passed on by Egami Sensei which were developed after both Gigo and Funakoshi Sensei had passed away. They were slow to change and maintained the ideals of being "not about professional Karate". The roots were set with the University groups and they would be hard and slow to change. A great deal of the teachings that were passed on were less than scientific and more about spiritualism and the mental side of Karate.

1922 Otsuka and Funakoshi Karate

In the 1920's Funakoshi was doing a lot of traveling between clubs in universities and traveling all over Tokyo and outside Tokyo to teach and give demonstrations. To do this he used a group of first generation students to help with the teaching and to help give demonstrations. He had several junior instructors that traveled with him regularly, many passed away in World War II or gave up Karate after they graduated school. However one instructor traveled a great deal with Funakoshi and his senior student Shimoda and helped give a great number of demonstrations with them. His name was Hironori Otsuka and he was very influential in the development of Shotokan and later became the head instructor in his own system of Karate, Wado Ryu.

Otsuka was born in Shimodate City Ibaraki Japan and was the fourth son of Tokujio Otsuka, a doctor and wealthy benefactor to many Martial artists of the time. At the age of 5 Otsuka began training in Japanese Jujustu under his great uncle Chojiro Ebashi, a famous martial artist with a lineage in a Samurai clan. After years of training in the family arts Otsuka went to study at Waseda university in Tokyo an began training in various schools of Jujitsu in Tokyo. In 1921 he received his teaching license or Menkyo Kaiden in Shindo Yoshin ryu Jujutsu and became the fourth master of the school. It was expected that Otsuka would follow into the family business and become a doctor, but as his father had passed away prior to him finishing his schooling and he needed money to finish his degree, he took the opportunity to take a job as a clerk in a bank and continue to study and teach Jujutsu.

With his earnings from the bank Otsuka also went back to university and continued working towards his own medical degree. In 1922 he met and started training with Funakoshi Gichin at the university. Funakoshi had just finished publishing his book "Ryukyu Kempo Karate" and had exposed Japan to the art of Karate, which was often called Karate Jutsu. Because the art was growing rapidly Funakoshi saw a need for instructors to help him with demonstrations and with teaching at new university clubs. Funakoshi would often leave junior instructors to teach at new or smaller clubs, as there was no ranking system it was very common for relatively new members to be teaching even newer members. This practice often led to issues of continuity in the training. Often Kata was "interpreted" by new instructors or different training put in place that was counter to the general training regimen of the time.

By 1926 Karate had been implanted into the Japanese culture and Funakoshi had made many changes and adaptations to Katas, starting with their names, and created a new system and style of Karate which had allowed him to bring it to a new level of popularity and kept it growing at a staggering rate. The university groups were Huge and training in the gyms was often packed with students. The university clubs were roughly organized by Matsuda Katsuichi, Himotsu Kazumi and Nakachi K. Funakoshi would come out and teach classes and preside over them as well, watching as the seniors took terms leading the class. Otsuka attended Shichi Tokudo, a barracks situated in a corner of the Palace grounds in Tokyo. Funakoshi visited the club and assisted in teaching the classes Otsuka would accompany Funakoshi and take classes from him and his seniors. Otsuka was a brilliant young Karate student that loved Naihanchi Kata and was called on to perform it with Funakoshi at demonstrations, including a demonstration for royalty of Japan, Oshima Sensei did Heian Shodan at that demonstration.

Otsuka would participate in drills and "mock" fighting demonstrations for Funakoshi when he was teaching or demonstrating. At the time Kata and basics were pretty much all that were practiced in Karate, Kumite had not been introduced as of yet and the idea was seen as "low brow". Funakoshi had wanted to make Karate a gentleman's activity and fighting was seen as something that rough people partook in. Otsuka once faced a live blade of a Kendo master who had trained at Keio university as part of the demonstration. The sword was seen as a status symbol and linked the training to the upper class. At the right moment Otsuka swept the attacker off his feet and countered with a strike to the face. The demonstration was a huge success and the altercation was used as an example of why Kumite was not needed, just good hard training and the understanding of movement. Otsuka had been integral to the early development of the Shotokan Style and introduced Funakoshi to many of the aspects of Jujutsu that we see in our system today.

In 1927 Otsuka was traveling with Funakoshi and getting ready to graduate, open his own medical practice and settle down. As part of his duties he would ensure that the students who were left in charge of the clubs were teaching and maintaining the standards and system that Funakoshi sensei had laid out to them. Otsuka was traveling to a class being held at Shichi-Tokudo, the seniors at this club were named Miki, Bo and Hirakama. The three members taught at this Dojo and had adapted, on their own, a set of rules and practice for Jiyu Kumite (Free fighting) without permission from Funakoshi, and actually this was a practice that was in direct conflict with his wishes. The students would don Kendo gear and use the face shield and protective gloves to allow for full force strikes. This shows that the actual practice of free fighting was not a total unknown idea at the time. Otsuka observed and brought the information back to his instruct. Funakoshi was not pleased at all!

When Funakoshi was told about the free fighting by his junior students and the Shichi-Tokudo club he stated that the practice belittled the art of Karate, he banned the practice, however by all accounts the practice continued despite his banning free fighting. Funakoshi never returned to Shichi Tokudo and banned all top students from attending this club, assisting them or ranking any members. Otsuka, like his peers never went to the club again, but this event is said to have had a great impact on Otsuka and other instructors and actually may have been the moment that free fighting in Shotokan was created as an idea to develop over years. The description of the training however does sound more like a kick boxing event with safety gear, when the JKA began research into the art of Kumite they brought many seniors into the research and Kanazawa sensei tells a story about how he was told to punch a Kendo chest protector worn by a peer, his hand broke the wooden chest piece and he almost killed his peer. Because of this Control in Kumite was put forward as the most important part of training in Kumite.

Funakoshi taught a Kata based system that only had 16 Kata practiced at the time. The remaining were not added till later. His students were said to have the most precise and exact techniques taught anywhere. He would teach four hour long classes on one movement in a Kata and then push his students to the breaking point with one Kihon waza that he would have them repeat and repeat after working special exercises to push their body to be strong, quick and flexible. The only time that he suspended his training was for a short period after an earthquake in 1928 and the clubs in the university had been severely damaged. Most of the clubs in Japan had been damaged so bad that they suspended training. Funakoshi and his students however got heavily involved in the massive clean-up as part of their training, while other martial arts clubs took time off, his students and Funakoshi himself went to work cleaning up the debris and getting ready for classes again.

While Funakoshi's expansion of the style was taking place, and growing in leaps and bounds, other parts of his organization were beginning to unravel. Otsuka wanted to study with other instructors and go back to training in his family style as well. He began taking classes from Mabuni Kenwa and Motobu Choki. It was his relationship with Motobu that caused the most friction with Funakoshi however. Motobu and Funakoshi had a rough history and Motobu was also teaching a "rougher" form of Karate that Funakoshi did not much care for. The system that Motobu was working on included a set of two man "Sparring" Drills that was basically free fighting inspired, his views were very different than the system that Gigo and Gichin Funakoshi were teaching and Motobu actually suggested that his system was much more effective and any art that did not include it was weak. Otsuka began experimenting with the system and had been training in free fighting and looking for ways to apply it to his Karate since leaving Shichi Tokudo several years before. He introduced a great deal of his Jujitsu back into his training in Karate as well, which did not sit well with Gigo Funakoshi or his father.

By 1935 Otsuka had implemented a great deal of the changes that he wanted into his training and this had caused a major rift between Funakoshi and himself. All communication was stopped and Otsuka was no longer recognized as a Black belt in Shotokan Karate. Most people view the changes in the system that he taught as the only reason for the ill will and lack of communication between the two sides; however they conveniently leave out one very important detail. It is very polite to see his new system and his differing ideas as the reason for the split and the truth is it probably did not help, and served as a convenient answer when asked why Otsuka was no longer Shotokan, but the honest truth is much more embarrassing for the Funakoshi family.

The final straw for Otsuka was likely due to a personal issue that he had with the organization running the University clubs, or the Shotokai. The early group was made up of seniors who trained with Funakoshi, but the administration was actually run by Funakoshi's oldest son Giego. As tradition dictates the head instructor did not deal with the financial end of things, this fell to his son Giego and others in charge of the administration and finances for the Shotokai. The story goes that Giego Funakoshi, as Sensei Funakoshi's eldest son, was not only in charge of the bank account for the Shotkai, but he had a very bad gambling issue and ran up a great deal of debts with his bookies. Otsuka had been saving money from his practice and from his teaching to open a new Dojo for his instructor with the help from a few others. Otsuka was approached by Giei for assistance in the financial matter, which he suggested affected the organization. Reluctantly but out of loyalty to Funakoshi, Otsuka approached the seniors and acquired a "loan" for Giei to pay off the "organization" short falls.

Funds were taken from the bank and used to pay off Giei's gambling debt. What happened next, according to both Hironoshi Genshin and Harada Mitsusaka put a permanent rift between the Funakoshi family and Otsuka. Giei accused Otsuka of keeping all the money himself and not giving him the loan. Otsuka felt that his honor was taken advantage of and made a very big scene in defending his honor and stated that he had paid the debts. for Giei with the funds collected from the seniors and had put 200 yen of his own money in for this as well. Funakoshi's younger son, and a very tallented instructors in his own rights, Gigo stepped in and tried to quash this fight. However, the bad blood between Gigo and Otsuka had already gone too far. Otsuka felt that his reputation had been attacked and Funakoshi Gichin felt hat Otsuka had insulted his family in airing the dirty laundry. Giei made a big deal about Otsuka correcting him in public, even if he had misused the funds and misrepresented the situation in the first place. Otsuka had suggested that they were equals by defending himself against Giei very publicly and this was not how Giei saw the structure of the organization at that time.

Gigo raised the necessary funds and saw that the bank was repaid and that his brothers debt was covered with the banks. However, there was already bad blood between Gigo and Otsuka. While Gigo was seen as much more talented and often embarrassed Otsuka by correcting him in public and in class, Otsuka was supposed to be his equal…or even senior. By correcting him in public he was essentially putting Otsuka in his place as he saw it. Otsuka would hold his anger but it was obvious to those observing the situation that this type of dressing down did not sit well with Otsuka.

Gigo took care of the debt and ensured that the organization did not have a public black eye for not paying back loans, however Otsuka would speak openly about the situation and bring it up often, while ensuring that he commented that he had not been repaid. Because of his new interest in free sparring, Gigo and the senior Funakoshi made the decision to expel Otsuka and recall his Dan ranking. This was seen as a much more personal attack on Otsuka than the minor dressing down Gigo would give to him in public, however it came with the addition of a statement suggesting that Otsuka had learned nothing about Karate and stuck to his Jujitsu all this time. Essentially calling into question his knowledge and ability to teach their art.

Otsuka was immediately replaced by Gigo as the lead instructor of Wasada and most of Otsuka's senior students stayed with Gigo, whom they saw as a much better instructor and more qualified to teach them the Okinawan art in the first place. This was a major insult to Otsuka by his own students, essentially they showed no loyalty to him and when he left several suggested that the "upgrade" was much needed and welcomed by all.

Otsuka took this time to travel and study under other instructors. He also traveled and met with other martial arts instructors from different arts, like Aikido's Ueshiba Morihei. He then went on to create his own style of Karate using the influence from all the instructors he had trained with and those who influenced him. He used drills from Mabuni and used ideas that he had learned from Motobu. Ironically, his influence over Shotokan was actually putting a seed of change into the training. He left an idea about Free style sparring or Jiyu Kumite that would at first cause issues and have the seniors call it barbaric and low brow, and eventually see them implement the very thing that cause the rift between Otsuka and Funakoshi Gichin, and yet his Wado style did not start to use free fighting till well after the JKA started using this form of training. While Otsuka was vilified for his behavior over the loans that were given to Funakoshi's eldest son he may have made more of an impact that many would like to admit.

No! Mabuni is not the founder of Shotokan.

In 1927 Mabuni Kenwa moved from Okinawa to Japan to try his hand at teaching Karate on the mainland. A retired police officer he felt that the prospect of more stable finances was more appealing than teaching his instructors arts in a private family Dojo, after seeing the success of those like Funakoshi Gichin and his Shotokan Ryu he felt that the move would serve him well. Funakoshi and Mabuni knew each other from their time in the Karate Kenkyukai on Okinawa. The two had kept in contact after Funakoshi retired from teaching and left for Japan, Funakoshi had written Mabuni about Japan and the fact that it was a land of possibilities now that Karate had broken through to the Japanese and become part of a cultural revolution of sorts.

Back in Okinawa both Funakoshi and Mabuni trained with Itosu, however Funakoshi was not a full student. Funakoshi would always clarify that his Sensei as being Asato Anko and Itosu was only his second instructor because Asato had passed away. By the time that Funakoshi moved to training with Itosu he was already well versed in Asato's system of Karate and was not changing his approach. He assisted Itosu moving the system into the schools but he was seen as a senior from a different group. While Asato was Funakoshi's instructor and he was not going to change his training Funakoshi had acknowledged that Itosu had shown him the Heian Katas and the two additional Tekki Katas that were formed by Itosu. Much of what Funakoshi was teaching however was not "Itosu Karate" at all. Mabuni trained only with Itosu for the Shuri te side of his Karate training. Unlike Funakoshi, Mabuni also branched out and studied Naha style with Higaonna Kenryo, the instructor of Goju founder Miyagi Chojun. Some records show that Funakoshi had trained with Higoanna as well but only to learn or refine some of the Kata that Azato wished him to work on and not as a full time instructor as Mabuni had.

While Itosu may have introduced Funakoshi to the Pinan (later changed to Heian by Funakoshi) Kata, there is more than a little evidence that he did not adopt them at first and actually forgot them, thinking that they were for school children only. The evidence shows that Funakoshi approached Mabuni after his junior had come to Japan to teach and asked him to teach several of his students the Pinan Katas so he could incorporate them into his system of Karate as an entry level Kata. Back in Okinawa it was very popular to not only create an introduction Kata and have the new students train in them but many of the governing bodies were having instructors like Miyagi and others create introduction Katas for systems that did not have them already such as the Geikisai Katas from Goju Ryu. Itosu had developed the Pinan forms by himself, having taken parts of the Katas Passai, Koshokun, Ueshi, Chinto and Chinte to create the system of Katas that he used to introduce Karate to the new students at the junior schools his members were teaching at. The Katas were formalized by Itosu in 1904, this was some time after Funakoshi had trained with him and during a period that Funakoshi was working and teaching his students in Okinawa. Gima Makoto, a direct student of Itosu, Yabu Kentsu and Funakoshi stated that Funakoshi had just learned the Pinan katas right before departing for Japan in 1922, and he had not really trained in them for long.

While Funakoshi had used the Kata briefly while teaching in Okainwa Dr. Fujiwara Ryozo, a renowned Japanese historian and Karate student has shown that Funakoshi did have Mabuni reteach him the Katas in 1919 prior to his leaving for Japan. This suggests that while Itosu had instructed his students to use this series of Kata for the new students, Funakoshi did not actually use the Kata to teach with at first and had to relearn them a few years before leaving for Japan. Funakoshi apparently took up the Katas and changed them to "Shotokan-ize" them or make them more along the lines of the system his instructor had taught him. In fact the Heian Katas that we practice today represent the mechanical differences between the Itosu system and the Asato system. Not only can you see the changes that Funakoshi made in which

Kata was taught first, but the mechanics were changed to make the system of Kata practical for teaching Funakoshi's system of Karate. A fact backed up by a statement made by Mabuni that he had made corrections to Otsuka's Pinan Katas that he learned from Funakoshi in 1928 as they had been altered drastically and did not look like the Kata he was teaching.

When Funakoshi relocated to Japan he only taught 15 Kata in total. He felt that the 15 represented his style of Karate and explained that the 15 were the sum total of his training. He posted this in his book 'Ryukyu kenpo karate' in 1922. And again in 'Rentan Goshin Karate Jitsu' in 1925. Funakoshi explained later in his Karate do Kyohan that he knew many more Kata but he felt that the 15 were representative of what he wanted his system to be. He felt that many of the other Kata he had trained in were "Not representative of his system of Shuri Te style Karate". In his later book Karate do Nyumon or introduction to the Empty had (written in 1943) he states that he knew other forms like Ten no Kata, Chi no Kata, Hito no Kata, Rohai, Hakko, Hatsun, Shoto, Shoin, Hotaku, Jiin, as well as many others, but felt that others were not necessary for study to learn his system of Karate.

Shotokan Karate was "officially founded" as Funakoshi Sensei opened his own club and it changed to the Shotokan Dojo. At that time the Dojo taught a great deal of Kihon, the 15 Kata and lots of drills. There was no Kumite really and more senior Kata was not introduced at this time. The concept was that the Shotokan system held in it only the 15 Kata to study, and an in-depth study of the forms were used so that the students knew the kata inside and out. Funakoshi set up the system with the 15 Kata only, but after the JKA was formed by Nakyama, Nishyama, Obata and other seniors they felt that the 15 Kata was limiting and they began looking for sources to bring more Kata into the fold. Funakoshi send them to study with the Shito ryu Kata dictionary Mabuni Kenwa. The group of men gathered with other seniors and went to Mabuni and learned Passai Sho, Koshokun Sho, Gojushiho, Niseishi and Hito. These were later followed by Rohai, Unsu, Chinte, Jiin and a few others. All of these Kata were taught by Mabuni in Shito ryu at the time, however the JKA does not mention that they learned the Kata from Mabuni.

Mabuni was becoming a very big deal in Japan! Having mastered the art of self-promotion this somewhat quiet ex-police officer was creating a reputation as a Karate man in his new home. Many exchanges occurred between Funakoshi's established Shotokan School and his new Shito ryu system. Mabuni's son Kenei reported that Funakoshi himself would send his son Gigo to Mabuni to learn Kata. After Mabuni arrived in Japan he taught many of Funakoshis top students and Funakoshi himself would join the students to train in sessions with Mabuni. After training with Mabuni the seniors would take the Katas and study them, break them down and instead of teaching them as is, they would alter them and "Shotokan-ize" them to have them follow the Shotokan's style of movement. Nakayama Sensei has been quoted as saying that Master Funakoshi never stopped learning Karate "When he visited Mabuni, he told me to learn Gojushio and Nijushiho Kata so that we could address them more intensively later on". The senior students would then change the Katas and make alterations to make them more sensible and linear.

While Mabuni had a big impact into the translation of several forgotten old Kata into the Shotokan syllabus it should not be confused with Mabuni being a founder of the system, and it cannot be stressed enough that much of his teachings were altered drastically to get the outcome that Funakoshi wanted regarding the new Kata. No doubt Mabuni was an excellent Kata person and his memory of Kata was incredible, but you cannot now equate that to him being a founder of Shotokan, nor can you overstate his influence in the system. Mabuni was an important resource in adding to the number of Kata that Shotokan has, but an honest review of what occurred would show you that any other Okinawan that had a half decent knowledge of the Kata that were introduced would have had the same impact as a source for Kata to be changed later.

It is also important to note that Funakoshi's style of Karate went on to become much more popular due to the mechanics of its system and the linear dynamics that they held, the use of Kata Dachi (Stances) that were more natural to the Japanese and the importance that both Funakoshi and Asato put on introducing the mechanics that they use to create the style that later became Shotokan. Mabuni's Shito ryu system was much more Chinese and relied on mechanics that were unfamiliar to the Japanese. This led to a stalling out of the system and when Mabuni passed away he left a system that had, for the most part, remained much more rooted in the Okinawan/Chinese heritage than other systems and a system destined to not gain the popularity that other Japanese systems enjoyed.

Funakoshi Gichin, a classical man!

Funakoshi Sensei was a unique man! He was a highly educated person and his interests in the mind and how it works was often more prevalent than his peers. He used Karate to try and reach people and make them physically and mentally stronger, where many of his peers stopped at making Karate a fighting art designed to be used as a weapon only! He was also one of the educated class that helped bring Okinawa and Japan into the modern era in a way that was acceptable to the elders and the young alike. At the time of the Meijin Restoration many of the young were looking at the changes as necessary, while others held onto the past and the cast system were revered by the traditionalists. Funakoshi was tasked, as were others, with finding a palatable way to enforce the changes.

Funakoshi was both a humble man and a man that cherished respect and had a strong sense of honor. He preached humility and to strive to show good character. He preached this to his students and emphasized that they needed to seek to be honorable and use Karate only for improvement of life and health and not to gain fame or to feed their Ego. He was also a simple man that felt that things should be kept as simple as possible.

One of his favorite stories that illustrate how a person in Karate should behave was this; *"when a man of little character receives his first Dan he will run home and shout at the top of his voice to everyone that he is a first Dan. Upon getting his second Dan he will climb to the roof tops and shout and upon receiving his third he will jump in his car and parade through town blowing his horn and announcing his new rank!", "however when a man of good character gets his first Dan he will bow his head in gratitude, upon getting his second he will bow his head and shoulders, when he gets his third he will bow at the waist and walk quietly to the wall so no one notices him"*. One of my seniors told me that this was attributed to Funakoshi Sensei; I have never read anything directly saying he had ever said this. However, it is how I see Funakoshi Sensei, a traditional, humble man.

Funakoshi did not like competitions and felt Karate was for self-perfection and at worst to defend yourself. He studied Buddhism with Abbot Furukawa Gyodo of Enkakuji Temple in Kamakura and began practicing Zen meditation. His studies of emptiness and Zen can be seen in his Karate teaching and his use of "empty" in his rebranding Karate.

While Funakoshi Sensei was a very forward thinking person, he also had his roots firmly in the traditional Japanese way. He never spoke of simple matters and often would not succumb to modern ideals. For instance, the norm for the time was to wear western clothing, mostly of higher dress quality. Suits, dress shirts and sweaters and other dress wear was becoming the norm, Funakoshi however preferred traditional Kimono's and foot wear and wore this as a rule even when his peers had adopted the western clothing. I have seen pictures of him in western clothing but it is very rare and apparently he frowned on this and felt uncomfortable.

Funakoshi Sensei may have dabbled in modern clothing (I have seen only a few pictures of him wearing a white modern suit) especially around the time of the war. Most of the pictures of Sensei Funakoshi however show him in traditional Japanese clothing. And as a child he wore the traditional school child uniform when attending school in Okinawa. Other than the few modern suit pictures and the school uniform, almost all pictures of Funakoshi Sensei are of him in Japanese attire.

He also would not refer to common items by name as it was tradition to never do so. One story that Genshin Hironishi Sensei brought up was when he was helping him to pack when Funakoshi Sensei spotted a pair of socks on the floor and asked his grandson Ichiro to pick them up for him. His grandson wanted to play with him a bit and said "what?" to which Funakoshi Sensei waived his hands and said "those". Ichiro continued to play with his Grandfather and said "those what"! Funakoshi continued to ask for the "articles" without saying them and Ichiro continued to fain ignorance until the elderly master began to get upset with him and he had to give up his quest to get his grandfather to say "Socks".

Funakoshi Sensei was also a big advocate of the health benefits of Karate. While most of the masters grew up in a time and place were nutrition was not at its best and some were born with a genetic weakness or some kind of systemic issue such as child hood asthma, a recent study shows that Asthma and other childhood allergic diseases are more prevalent in Okinawa and Japan that other nations of similar economy and class structure. One of the best ways to deal with Asthma is to exercise to strengthen the lungs and the body.

Funakoshi was a forward thinking man and knew that a "fighting" art would not "sell" as well to the local Japanese as an art that was good for your health and followed the long standing code of Budo. Budo is the warrior way and he instilled both ideas into his Karate early on as well as a Okinawan twist on character development that he was taught by Azato and Itosu independently of his studies in Buddhism that also supports this. . *"If they taught me nothing else, I would have profited by the example they set of humility and modesty in all dealings with their fellow human beings."*

Humility seemed to have been a corner stone of his teachings, while he was both a venerated teacher and of higher cast, he also swept the floor and cleaned his Dojo, as well as acting as a gardener and handy man when he first came to Japan. This is not to say that his brand of humility is common in Shotokan training nor is it extended to all his students. Funakoshi was also known as a great political and social mediator. He was called in several times to mediate issues and his wife was also known as a great mediator in their Okinawan neighborhood. His skills were picked up, no doubt, from his training with Azato and Itosu whom were both members of the royal court. Because of the characteristics that he had and his knowledge of the different styles of Karate that he learned and merged into his own style, Funakoshi was the perfect person to help spread Karate in a country that was eager to learn this new fighting art.

His mix of philosophy and physical skills made his style very popular and also helped him build his group to be one of the strongest systems to date. Many masters followed him and tried to build on what he had brought to the table and failed, went home and their styles either dwindled and failed or stayed part of the Okinawan culture to come back to the main land years later. Funakoshi proved perfect for the expansion of Karate in Japan and his masters knew this even before he left.

Yoshitaka (Geigo) Funakoshi and an era of change

In the 1920's Funakoshi continued to travel around and teach all over Japan. His main assistant at the Meisujuku Dojo and for demonstrations was also **Takeshi Shimoda**, a student that had previous martial arts experience in the sword arts and some say Ninjitsu. Shimoda was a very talented student and by Egami Sensei's account very close to Funakoshi. He was fast and dynamic and with perfect form. He could hit you looking totally relaxed and destroy the target without looking like he even tried. His influence over Egami and even Gigo (Yoshitaka) Funakoshi was eminence.

How much Shimoda influenced Shotokan is questionable however and he was not to be a big influence in the end as his stay was short, but important. Shimoda took the designs that Funakoshi laid out for his Karate and taught and practiced the same as Funakoshi. Some pointed out that he was a perfect mimic and every movement was the same as the masters. He did not try and influence the nature or fundamentals of Shotokan by introducing his other training to the style.

Shimoda passed away in 1934 from unknown causes after a demonstration, some say heart issues, other an acute illness that took over after an intense trip that included a great deal of demonstrations, Funakoshi then turned to his son Gigo to step in and become his assistant and also demonstrate and teach in his absence.

Gigo (Yoshitaka) Funakoshi was born in 1906 which made him 28 when he took over as an assistant for his father. He had traveled from Okinawa to Japan when he was 17 however and got a job as a radiographer at a local ministry of education in the physical and medical consultation department. Gigo was the third son of Funakoshi and by far the most talented and most interested in Karate practice. He was born at home in Okinawa and diagnosed at an early age with Tuberculosis. He was a sickly child and frail growing up. His father recognized the same issues he had dealt with growing up and put him into Karate training at a young age. In fact his father sent him to train with his own instructors Azato and Itosu.

As Gigo had undergone the same training that Funakoshi himself had gone through he felt confident putting his son in charge of the duties of being an assistant to the chief instructor. Gigo soon took over running the universities and also took the full position as second in charge in the new Shotokan organization. While Funakoshi Gichin had taken a system that was purely a self-defense-based art and made it one that held much more philosophy and cultural dynamics to it and formed what is called Gendai budo, or A martial art based on the philosophy of "DO", Gigo began concentrating on separating the new Japanese Karate from the original Okinawan arts.

Gigo Funakoshi took up studying different arts, such as Kendo under Hakudo Nakayama and other arts to give Shotokan distinctive Japanese flavor to its practice. He recruited Shigeru Egami and Genshin Hironishi to help him train and develop his ideas and bring them to the forefront of training and really make primary changes in the system and how the techniques were used. More linear and dynamic and with much less "clutter" in movements and a definitive leaning towards stream lined movements the system began to take form. In the early days of training it was said that Gigo would engage many different training partners for his work outs because few could stand up to training the way that he did and not many could maintain for the full work out, he would therefore change in and out of partners to keep fresh or rested partners at the ready.

Because of his understanding of Japanese martial arts and culture, Gigo became a big influence over the formation of modern Karate. Gigo also went to other arts and studied from other people to introduce new techniques and alter the appearance of Shotokan. For the first time someone other than Funakoshi Senior was making changes in the style. Before Gigo introduced the radical changes the style was based on old To-de and Shuri-te systems that emphasized the use of the upper body and down played kicking and other lower body techniques. Lots of open hand attacks and short distance striking, the grappling and joint locking was commonly focused on as well as antiquated things like pressure point striking and close in grappling.

Gigo Funakoshi introduced variations and also developed the style as a more dynamic and explosive style that emphasized long distance attacks and defense. He lowered the stances and from Kendo he brought in the angles of movement and other movement patterns. He also introduced new techniques that had never been used in Shotokan or other Okinawa style fighting arts before. He brought the Mawashi geri, Yoko geri kekomi, Fumikiri, Ura Mawashi geri (Some credit Kase as the person that brought this to Gigo however), Ushiro Ura mawashi geri and Ushiro geri Kekomi. Gigo developed new kicking to bring dynamic and explosive movements to the system and excite new members with this precise and dynamic kicking method. It's important to note that many of the changes that he brought about existed, in some cases, in other styles or were being employed at the time by others, he refined their use and created a way to introduce it to Shotokan in a way that made the movements more "Shotokan" in the approach. He may not have created his additions in most cases but his refinements were revolutionary in some ways. He introduced very high skill movements that would never have been seen as practical in most cases, but the addition gave the system the flair that it needed and also created a new feel for some of its practice.

Gigo was especially known for his introduction of low stances and bringing Fudo Dachi and his more exciting kicking to the style. All of these folded into the existing curriculum and began to affect the way that techniques were done in general. Gigo also made many changes in the standard Kihon practiced. Before his changes the most common stances were a short Zenkutsu Dachi and Niko Dachi, he introduced the practice of Kokutsu dachi as the go to second stance and lengthened the Zenkutsu in basic practice. Some say he invented the stances, but they did exist before him, he just introduced them as a main stance selection in Shotokan Kata. Classic Okinawan style Kats use Neiko Dachi and not Kokutsu, and while they have deep Shiko dachi, most do not use Kiba Dachi as often as Shotokan. These key changes really separated the Shotokan from the other Okinawan style Katas.

Gigo introduces all of these new techniques in the book Karate Do Nyumon, of which he wrote the technical part of the book and his father wrote the forwards and the history part of the system. Gigo also made some major changes in how the techniques were done. For the first time a higher knee lift was introduced along with a new way of using the hip!

Gigo also spear headed several other changes in fundamentals of the style, such as the Hanmi position that was virtually unseen on Okinawa. Using the rotation of the torso to add power to a movement was not really well used in Okinawan Karate where they preferred the power on power techniques over use of physics. This also allowed for a smaller target area for the punch and a more economical way of addressing strength over techniques. He also began using the stance for power as opposed to using just the upper body to apply force. The thrusting of the back leg introduced more power to the newly minted thrust based style and doubled the power capacity of a stepping punch over just using the arm to punch.

Gigo also did one thing that may have put him on the opposite side of the issue from his father. He supported free sparring as a way of testing the system and worked with others to implement his ideas using the free sparring platform to prove that a technique or idea had merit and was worth implementing into the Shotokan system. Gigo's style was fast, explosive and used a new lower stance to generate power with longer attacks and chained techniques together with better foot movement and introduced foot sweeps and off balancing techniques for fighting. It was different enough to establish the system as being completely new and a more "Japanese" style was accepted more readily than the Chinese looking Okinawan styles. Gigo also changed the emphasis and make-up of the Tzuki techniques. No longer were they short single knuckle techniques that were powerful jabs to vital points on the body, they became long range techniques like Oi-tsuki or Gyaku tzuki used to clear greater distances and strike more general areas not associated with nerves or "triggers" in the body. The training that Gigo implemented and followed was also much harsher and exhausting and Gigo expected students to give twice as much energy as they needed to actually defend themselves into each class. He saw that over training for a situation would better set them up in the case of actual combat.

Gigo's health started to falter during the war and after classes he would often lay down in the Dojo and fall asleep after fits of coughing up blood and he would sleep for hours to come back and teach an evening class with the same tyrannical energy that he had the early days class. The conditions after the war were in a lot of ways much harsher on the weakened Gigo than on other people. He continued to train hard and push the students and developed changes to the Katas , some of which were adopted from other styles. In the cases in which he adopted Katas from other systems he would formulate critical changes in the Katas to "Shotokan-ize" them and reworked them to be more in line with his thinking and his ideas of what Shotokan Karate was. He put greater length in stances, changed the angles of movement and removed whole sections of "Detail oriented" movements and replaced them with powerful and easier to reproduce movements meant to create a more user friendly style that could be employed by many to use as sport or defense alike.

On November 24th 1945, at the age of 39 he passed away due to complications of Tuberculosis. He was training the day before this and pushing his students in the Tokyo Dojo to their breaking points, keeping pace and often pushing harder than the students. Some say it was the best work out he ever lead and that his strength, fluid movement and explosiveness was at an all-time high. Many who trained with him felt that he was trying to pass on as much of his ideas to him as he could in the last work out and he was in rare form. He went home that night totally exhausted and passed away after a coughing fit, his Tuberculosis finally catching up to his now frail body.

Gigo had been acting as the chief instructor for several years as his father had traveled north to live with his wife for a short time during the war. The north was seen as safer, if not more remote and with less comfort for those that left the air raids and the bombings of Tokyo. His father had not taught for several years and was living as a retired school teacher. Many of the changes that Gigo Funakoshi had put into place were not things that his father had seen or would have approved of in most cases. Funakoshi Senior had put Karate forwards with the idea that it was there to make a person better through harsh study of the details, it was simple and direct, straight forwards and technically traditional. Gigo had introduced Kata and made changes that in many cases were not in line with this thinking. While Gigo was the Chief instructor while his father had retired to the North during the war, it is thought that the elder Funakoshi had wanted to reverse much of what Gigo had implemented when he returned after the war, however I would say that it was more than likely the non-Shotokai members that put this forwards as Funakoshi himself would have been very old when he returned and may not have had the influence or ability to make those changes as his health and age may not have allowed him to do so.

The Shotokan (1936)

In 1936 Funakoshi, with the assistance a few of his more affluent students purchased a building in Tokyo and had a permanent training hall to act as the headquarters for Funakoshi's new style of Karate as it spread across the Japanese islands. The students searched for a name for the new training facility, they played with several ideas but finally they settled on naming the Dojo after the name Funakoshi had used in his many writings. Funakoshi was a Voracious writer of poetry and a scholarly writer who had published several books as well as being published in some local periodicals. When he wrote he used the pen name "Shoto" which means waiving pines. The students settled on "Shoto-Kan" meaning the training hall of Shoto.

Originally the name was to mean the club only, but it stuck and the style soon took on this name as well.

The actual opening of the club was a land mark in the styles history for several reasons. Prior to the opening the style was just called Karate or more often "Funakoshi's Karate" by his peers. The Karate had no distinction, much like other styles, it was somewhat generic and people often got confused thinking that all Karate was the same, then even more confused when they noted that the teachings of one instructor were completely different from another. Aside from groups like Goju that had their style referenced by their founding principles of "Hard/Soft" used to describe the type of Karate, many of the other systems used the founders name or a nick name given to them and in some cases they used different mixtures of instructors names to find the name of the system. But with the founding of the "Shotokan" the style began to be called "Shotokan" by default. Soon others began using names other than the founders to create a unique name for the unique style of Karate being taught by the clubs.

Funakoshi Senseis students collected funds and Obata Sensei, one of Funakoshi Senseis oldest active students, who had a great deal of knowledge in the business world, arraigned for the purchase of the original club in 1936. The building took three years to complete renovations and in 1939 the "Shotokan" was opened. While Obata and several other spear headed the push for this club, it is interesting that they have received very little credit for this being done. Funakoshi himself did present letters of thanks to these members, but most of the other students appeared to have not given the proper appreciation for this action.
It was here at the new Shotokan that Gigo (Yoshitaka) Funakoshi and other seniors really took the time to stylize and categorize the system into a more refined and created be foundation system that people like Egami and Nakayama took up and then used to create the Shotokai style and the JKA style of Shotokan. Gigo was known to travel a great deal to the universities to test his ideas then come back and teach the system he was creating to the Shotokan members at the headquarters Dojo. It is important to again note that the name Shotokan referred only to the Dojo at that time, the system was still just called Karate. The use of this name to identify the style that had grown at this location was not recognized as such until after the death of Funakoshi.

By the time the Shotokan was actually built the practice of teaching Karate in high schools and universities was very popular and Funakoshi Sensei was almost 70 years old. Many of the seniors at the newly established Shotokan also taught at the University club level at many highly ranked educational facilities across Japan and the popularity of training was growing. Also, many of the students of Funakoshi had moved away and out to all reaches of Japan for business and to live, they taught the style of Karate Funakoshi had introduced to new students and the need for trained instructors grew rapidly. The amount of teaching that Funakoshi senior actually did in the new Shotokan Dojo would have been minimal. However his presence was something that pushed the seniors and he guided classes often coming onto the floor to demonstrate a Kata or movement.

As Karate grew in popularity and Funakoshi Sensei and his senior instructors were working on addressing the need for instruction across Japan a structure was beginning to take form and as schools requested that programs be set up in their gyms or other facilities, Funakoshi Sensei and his seniors had the job of ensuring qualified candidates would be placed to teach at those clubs. Funakoshi Sensei and his senior members became increasingly busy with administration and development of a good instructor group to send out to different schools. As such Funakoshi Sensei handed over his teaching duties at various universities to the students.

This also meant they had to establish a technical board or group that would travel around and ensure that the instructors were teaching his system of Karate and that the quality and standards were maintained at the clubs. The Shotokan acted as the central hub for Karate growth with instructors traveling into Tokyo to train and then back out to more rural clubs and university clubs. The need for a "professional" division grew out of this dynamic. No longer was it a handful of instructor teaching at clubs and moving from university to university helping seniors teaches then moving on to the next club, the headquarters created a new dynamic and hierarchy of instructors, which left the old Shotokai members out.

Funakoshi Sensei also still did presentations and demonstrations and taught classes at several of the schools but regular classes were given out to seniors to maintain. Funakoshi Sensei was also a regular visitor to the imperial Palace to give annual demonstrations for Emperor Hirohito. All of this leads to the rapid expansion and growth of the Shotokan club and its subsidiaries. All of this for a man who was almost 70 years of age who was retired from teaching and living on a limited income. The Shotokan was pushed forwards by his students, but he was far from an inactive observer even if his actual teaching had scaled back over the years, his presence and activities were still important to the continued growth of the system and his presence was felt in the Headquarters as well as abroad.

The growth and development that was exploding in the Shotokan sphere was far reaching, took hundreds of man hours to manage and became a full time job for the seniors in the organization. This all happened outside of the University groups reach and was generally taken care of by the senior members who did not involve or discuss the business of growth with the University groups, many of which were run by esteemed seniors who would have been seen as founding members of Shotokan in Japan. The new group of managers at the Shotokan Dojo essentially took over and blocked out the other seniors who became separated from the core of the Shotokan Dojo membership.

This move set up a rift between seniors from both groups, but soon that would not matter as a new and grave issue would soon come into focus and effect not just Karate and its seniors, but the whole of Japan.

Karate and the war

One other major component that led to the huge growth of Karate could have very well killed if off completely as well. By 1941 the whole country of Japan had changed. It had gone from a feudal country led by an emperor to a more nationalistic country led by a separate government not responsible to the Emperor, but to itself and the people. The major change in the culture had changed the people and the government as well as the mentality of both. The country was no longer a separatist nation with an identity that focused on its own independent growth as well as its own reentry to the world stage.

Japan began bending it to be a nationalistic country that identified with an expansionist mentality and focused on building its resources and stretching out to gain more resources often using a new military that was growing after the Meijin restoration. To justify this they both changed their focus and use embracing the past to justify their approach…now everyone was of samurai heritage even if it was not true and people would die for the country. Japans territorial expansion much of south east Asia because the modernization of Japan meant that they had to import more than 88% of the oil and materials needed to create and then sustain the industrial base needed for modernization.

Funakoshi and his student worked hard from to open the Shotokan, but the year they opened the new facility World War two began and it dragged the whole country of Japan into the fight. The Dojo saw a huge influx of students and grew, but many of the new students looking for a system to teach them how to fight and defend themselves, many of the new students were earmarked for military service. A great number of the masters we saw come to the states and teach internationally were originally Japanese military, such as Ozawa Sensei. As much as the new influx of students was good for the growth of the Dojo, the new students, more times than not, did not stay as they were called up for active service, many of them never returned from their military service.

Perhaps the most important reason that the Shotokan was earmarked as a useful tool by the Imperial arm was the fact that when students joined the Military they had to go through a strict medical examination and physical testing, Most of the students from the Shotokan were highlighted specifically by the medical staff when they were given physicals for entry to the military. The doctors were pointing out how good a shape these students were in and how conditioned they were compared to the average Japanese recruit. This phenomenon led to the military investigating the back ground of the soldiers and the common thread being Karate training was interesting to the army commanders.

The interest of the Military in Karate training grew and finally they approached the Shotokan for instructors to teach the military recruits an abridged version of Karate. Funakoshi did not directly support the war but being a very proud "Japanese" he was sent many of his seniors to teach a stripped-down version of the style to new recruits. The system that was taught was later revealed to basically be a single punch and a single kick repeated many times with a growing spirit. Little blocking or fancy techniques were passed on thinking that the more advanced the training the less useful and the more time it would take to pass this on, time they did not have. This proved very successful and many of the new soldiers spread the word about Karate as well. The Shotokan was busy with new student and the new propaganda and nationalistic mentality meant that the students were all rolling in to learn how to fight for the country. A membership I am sure that lead to lots of excited work outs at the Hombu!

The martial arts fed a need that the new regime needed in changing the thoughts of the general population. It was a marketing tool by the new Ultra-Nationalist government that used it to warp the ideology of the masses to be as nationalistic as they were. The government of the time recruited martial arts instructors and pushed membership up. The goal was to train a nationalistic military that would grow and build soldiers to expand the objective of the government. The instructors were to teach a brutal form of fighting and often were teaching undisciplined students in the most brutal ways. Some martial arts instructors refused to participate in the new focus on martial arts, but the government did make it a popular move for many of them who saw growth out of this movement as a positive thing, this includes the Shotokan.

The goal was to create a fighting force for the government and an army that was both dedicated to the single-minded cause of the country and also controllable by implementing the mentality that it was their duty to serve the cause, or in this case they were modern Samurai and there to serve the new Daimyo or government. This mentality was passed on in the training and even parts of the uniform that the soldier wore. Senior staff and officers wore a "Samurai sword" with them into battle to show their link to the samurai spirit that the government was trying to grow in the ranks. This was allowed despite the fact that most of the officers did not have any samurai heritage and previously would never have been allowed the honor of wearing the sword in the first place.

Memberships grew quickly in the military clubs, especially new members between the age of 20 and into their early 40's. Training was brutal and discipline was violent, no control and brutally undisciplined fight training with very little actual technical training produced many army soldiers for the government and Karate was at the forefront of this training. The training was brutal and often involved training in combat boots, this lead to many injuries and a form of elitist training mentality. The military began using Karate training and the growth of Karate at the time was huge, but limited to basic moves used in the most brutal way. Those that trained in the system were taught a style that was nothing like the more technical system taught in Karate clubs not associated with the military. No ranks were awarded to the military participants as most would not be returning and the training was not seen as real training by Funakoshi Sensei or his senior students, just a means to an end.

Funakoshi had succeeded in overcoming prejudice towards his system and had finally received national recognition for his art, only to have it hijacked by the increasing war efforts. The JKA was formed to grow his art, pass on his ideals and create better people, something that he held a very high regard for, and now his system was being used to teaching combat to the troops and spread a nationalistic mentality that was focused on expansionism, dehumanizing non-Japanese (an irony because Karate was not really "Japanese") and on training men to be brutal versions of themselves. The nationalism was often reinforced with horrible racism as justification for the war on other nations with the Japanese saying that the Chinese were subhuman or the Koreans were not as evolved as themselves.

The instruction was brutal and the limited technical practices were restricted to targeting areas like the shin, neck and throat so that even unskilled students could be taught to maim or kill quickly. Obata once recalled that the training was so brutal that many of the candidates were injured and could not continue training. He did not alter the training as He thought that the training was so harsh that the military would discontinue the training and Karate could move back to its original training and building up people; however the military loved the brutality of the training and encouraged the candidates to train hard and become an elite team. The Karate instructors, who were once very excited about the prospect of teaching for the Japanese military, were not shocked at the brutality and not comfortable with the direction that the military was taking Karate training in.

The Judo people taught one or two basic throws and the Karate people one or two strikes, not enough to become proficient in Judo or karate's art at all. Many other arts, Such as Aikido, bowed out or refused to participate in the training. Sword arts were taught in a very rudimentary form and other arts were adapted as well to the military training, but the two main groups that the Army turned to were the Karate and Judo groups. The reason for this adoption of the styles was simply because Karate and Judo were more adaptable to the individual and could be used on the battle field if the soldiers were disarmed. This also lead to hand to hand training on the Allied side, and often the training was focused on dispatching an enemy in a similar way, but training was much less brutal and caused far fewer injuries on the Allied side.

While the JKA was busy training candidates for the military the war started with the bombing of Pearl Harbor and the Japanese ensured that the hesitant American forces were fully engaged in the war in the Pacific. This meant that many of the candidates in the special training program and regular students were recruited to fight the war with the Allied Armies, not just battling the military of smaller South East Asian nations. The very thing that jumpstarted the growth of the JKA now depleted its membership exponentially. As one member reported that they had to leave for duty, two more would show up to train for a week then off to the service and the war. The Dojo became a boom and bust training center that saw reams of young men sign up and then all of them leave for service. Training had also shifted to army bases with instructors being pulled out of their teaching duties to teach service men. This put a great strain on the Dojo to find new instructors and often the classes were being taught by those who were little more than novice students themselves.

Gone were the classes on Kobudo as well. Prior to the military hijacking the club Funakoshi would teach many classes with Bo staff or even Sai to the students. Now the focus was strictly on Karate. The classes became very basic and focused on repetitions and the level of technical ability was lower than ever with most of the talented instructors teaching basic Karate and little more than how to hit your opponent to put them down. Many of the stories of the "killing" or "Effective" parts of Karate being sucked out of the system came from this time. The Bunkai of the Katas were not taught nor were the Katas a focus of the training. The majority of training was conditioning and repetitions of partner work to train fighters for the war effort. Lines of students in from of Makiwara posts punching them till their knuckles were bloody and kicking the posts or heavy bags till their feet were tough and ready to impact anyone attacking them.

As the air raids from the war became more destructive and Japan became a focus for the Americans and Allied forces Funakoshi Sensei was sent north to be safe from the bombing runs on Tokyo and was joined by his wife on the island of Kyushu. His son, had Gigo, stayed behind to run the dojo and continue to run the universities. The organization grew and shrank on a regular basis as waives of military men came in and then left to go fight the war. Most of the military training was done at army bases by a select few, the day to day training was mostly at the universities and the membership shrank daily as the young men traveled to fight in the war and less and less came to train before being shipped out, woefully undertrained and under supplied.

The Shotokan was a traditional Japanese building that was built solid to with stand the earthquakes that often plague Japan, but even it could not stand up to allied bombing raids. In 1945 the allies had broken the back of the Japanese defenses in the outer islands and they had closed in on the nation itself. They had decimated the navy and allied bombers blasted Tokyo nightly. On one such bombing run the Shotokan itself was hit and destroyed.

For two years the students of Funakoshi found their way back home after the war, traveling from small islands, China and other places in the theater of war as the war effort ended and they were cycled back home many leaving the war and making their own way back any way they could. They were for the most part unemployed and looking to restart their lives. Most were looking for a place or common venture, something positive, to focus on. The whole country was demoralized from a loss that their leaders had told them could never come because they were superior to other nations. They were looking to rebuild the nation both physically and spiritually. The returning soldiers needed something to focus on, the allied troops were restricting a great deal of their normal activities and the elite mentality of Japan had been changed by the reality of having lost a war in which their leaders had said they could not lose. The samurai spirit had been tested and was battered.

The country was in chaos and parts destroyed by the regular bombing, other parts taken over by allied command and most of the industry had ground to a halt after the war effort had been squashed. Many of his students began to train again, partially out of a love for the art and partially to regain some pride in something. New training groups were formed and many of Funakosh'is older students built or rebuilt university groups and a new Dojo was founded to house the Shotokan students not in the school clubs. The seniors began growing the organization again and looked for ways to gain new students.

Funakoshi Sensei for his had part retired in Kyushu with his wife when the war had gotten bad and food scare in Tokyo. The constant threat of bombing also made the big city unsafe for Funakoshi. He arraigned for his wife and daughters to come to Japan when Okinawa became very dangerous and the family had moved to Kyushu where Funakoshi Sensei lived with his wife and his daughters, In fact he was lost their! He had moved out of Tokyo with the assistance of the students and they had setup passage for his wife and family to Kyushu, but then he apparently was lost as several went to war and many of them were killed fighting in the war or as the Allies bombed Tokyo and the rest of Japan.

While some came back and began to restart training and building the Dojos up others focused on post war rebuilding of Japan, most did not know Funakoshi survived the war. After the war Funakoshi, the Supreme master of Karate was living in a refugee camp in Kyushu while his students began to piece back together the curriculum and began to work on rebuilding the Shotokan and assembling the seniors to help. While this was happening Funakoshi lived in the camp in poverty until his wife passed away in 1947.

Shortly after his wife died Funakoshi Sensei was located by an old student of his and travel arrangements were made for the elder instructor to come back to Tokyo. The students had returned from the war and had several years to set up the Shotokan and the university clubs again after the war, but they needed the founder back to make things legitimate and to continue the rebuilding. The Shotokan curriculum at that time as a solid mix of the old Shotokan that Funakoshi Senior and Junior had introduced to the mainland, but a strong influence of the watered down, but very effective system that had been created by Obata for the military use influenced the new Shotokan. Funakoshi Sensei boarded a train in 1947 bound for Tokyo and his new organization as well as brining about changes to the style that would ground it again in its traditional roots.

Funakoshi Sensei recounted that at each train station students waited to great the old master and present him with food and presents to honor him and the numbers grew as he got closer to Tokyo. Once in Tokyo he had seen that the bombings had taken their toll on more than just the buildings and structures in Tokyo. The bombings had destroyed the once fierce national pride of the Japanese, but Funakoshi felt that his Karate could help turn this around. Funakoshi often spoke to students of the power of Karate to forge a spirit and polish ones character. This was the hope of many after the war, they were all looking for something to help rebuild Japan and find a new way forwards. This was his way of giving back to Japan as well as reforming his system with the proper intent and spirit.

One problem that faced the elder Karate instructor was that the allies had immediately slapped a restriction on any training for combat, any martial art and any program or society that touted nationalism or elitism in any way. This meant that all martial arts like Kendo, Judo, Jujitsu and Sumo were banned after the war, and this caused a great decline in their popularity and practice after the war, even after the sanctions were lifted.

Not to be dissuaded by the military ban on the training in Karate Funakoshi started planning a way around the restrictions and putting together a structure for the new Shotokan Karate system. Funakoshi Sensei was very intelligent and a good statesman, he had been trained by two government officials who were used to delicate negotiations in his instructor Azato and Itosu Sensei. Funakoshi took up conversations with high ranking officials and began his campaign to bring Karate back to Japan, first overcoming the ban to start his organization training again. He actually saw the loss of the war as opportunity to grow beyond even Japan, All he would need is a little time, and a lot of ambitious young followers, of which he had both…in spades!

WWII and its effect on Shotokan

World War Two interrupted the growth and expansion of martial arts in general but it also spurred on major expansion from the smaller groups such as Karate. More traditional Japanese groups avoided getting involved with the military directly but many, like Karate, were "recruited" by the army to help train their soldiers. The growth and success that the Shotokan saw was tempered with the fact that the training was watered down and simplified for the soldiers to use in battle with little training.
The military learned a stripped down version of Funakoshi's fighting art. Thousands of punches and kicks were thrown in full military gear. They learned the art as quickly as possible and it would not have looked much like the graceful and technical style we know today. The scaled back version of Karate was fine physically as long as it was understood that this was purely for aggressive military reasons and not for the arts actual intent. However the military had little use for the character development and actually focused the training on creating

warriors and not on creating better humans. The technically polished techniques and intricate defensive movements were replaced with spirited training that would make the recruits feel like supermen filled with martial spirit.

Thousands of young men were taught the new style of training and much of the military drilling actually affected the practice of Karate itself. This is thought to be the time when the common "Drilling lines" that we know in Karate today began. Prior to this the classes were run more individually with participants only joining together in small groups while instructors gave more one on one training. The Okinawan system of training was more intimate and called for instructors to have more one on one time with the students. This made teaching larger groups impossible and impractical. The efficiency of the new training was a result of the need to teach very basic techniques to large groups of men. This is said to be the Okinawan style of Karate. This new military style was ingrained in the minds and teaching style of the instructors who were brought in to teach the military.

During the war many of the men sent to battle died over seas! Many of these men were JKA students and instructors sent off to war to spread imperial Japans influence. They were brainwashed into battles and eventually man of them were killed thinking that they were more powerful because of their training and could muster wins against opponents with better weapons and who outnumbered them in the thousands. The Karate training had been coopted to create soldiers who were arrogant and felt that they could not lose the war because they were superior to their enemy, the training and the focus of the military at the time was to create fighting machines convinced they could not lose and if they gave their lives it was for the glory of the Japanese people and the Emperor. This type of training was counter to what Funakoshi had been teaching and lead to a lot of friction between the budding JKA and Funakoshi as well as the more established Shotokai.

Some Karate men also died performing military duty's as Kamikaze pilots. Men like Ozawa almost died flying planes into Allied ships. Ozawa Osamu Sensei was a military pilot that trained in JKA style Karate. He came from a samurai family and thought it was his duty to defend Japan in any way he could. One morning as the war was turning and Japan was losing ground to the American Navy, Ozawa was called to the airfield and told he would be serving his country and becoming a Kamikaze pilot to defend Japan. He knew that the Kamakaze pilot, or suicide pilot was sent in to the American Navy armada with planes filled with explosives only to fly their plane into the ships ending their life and hopefully taking the lives of as many Americans as possible, if not sinking the ship itself. His story has a happier ending than some.

Upon take off his old, rag tattered plane crashed after turning upside down, which kept the bomb strapped to its belly from blowing up. Near the end of the war most of the planes that were available were barely air worthy and this lead to many of them taking off and crashing. Ozawa Sensei spent months in the hospital and saw the end of the war in pretty much a body cast. He said he would have committed ritual suicide like his fellow injured officers but he was unable to because of his injuries. Of his Karate training, he said it consisted mostly of repeating a junior Kata hundreds of times, throwing thousands of front kicks and then hitting a Makiwara over and over again. This would be done for hours to forge the spirit of the military members. Ozawa said that the training and harsh treatment that the Army dealt out to the students was far harsher than would be allowed today in a Marine core training program.

Many of the masters that lived through the war saw similar situations. While the war was raging the masters needed to create instructors that could teach large masses of people, this meant turning out instructors who were only slightly trained in Karate, dumbing down the training and creating a curriculum that was easy to carry out and offered little in the way of training in any depth, actually that was frowned upon. The training was a dissemination of two or three techniques use for offence and the rest was aggressive coaching in conditioning. Then the war was failing and those instructors were put in the war theatre, and many died. As the war came to a grinding halt the need for instructors and even Karate seemed to be gone. The focus went from plans to expand to defensive fighting and much of the training that the government was pushing with the help of the martial arts was cancelled. A new approach was needed and many point to the fact that Funakoshi had retired to Kyushu for the ability of the then young JKA group to change out the training as they did, and then he was brought back to Tokyo post war and the training resumed in deeper study of Funakoshi's Shotokan and the art again began to develop.

The whole country had been bombed by American bombers by 1944. The Japanese had lost so much ground and especially the islands around the Philippines. Because of the horrible losses, in 1944 the Prime Minister Tojo resigned and new military government officials moved into fill the void. But the momentum was lost and the Allied forces were blasting the island nation. The nation was on the brink at this point, Karate training was not a priority for the general population, the only real organized training was said to be that which was still being offered to the military members. This meant that a great deal of the forward momentum in developing Shotokan by Gigo Funakoshi and others had been lost. Much of what is being taught now was created post World War II, while the Shotokai states that they teach what Gigo had taught there is no real evidence to support this, in fact most of the instructors who teach Shotokai who trained with Gigo state that the system they teach is different as much of the training that Gigo Funakoshi had been working on was lost with him.

By 1945 the allied forces had pushed the Japanese people out of most of the outlying islands; they had taken Iwa Jima and Okinawa and were pressing in on Japan Greater. In July the Allied leaders met in Potsdam, Germany and reiterated the demand that Japan surrender without condition to the Allied nations for the war they brought to the world. They also stated "the alternative for Japan is the prompt and utter destruction". As Japan continued to ignore the Potsdam terms, the United States dropped the Atomic Bomb on Hiroshima and Nagasaki. Between the two bombings the Russian forces took Japanese held Manchuria and destroyed the Japanese Kwantung Army, the largest standing army that Japan had. Nakayama Sensei had been serving in China at the time and saw a great deal of what the war had done to the Japanese people and the atrocities that the Japanese had brought to China as well.

The end of the war came August 15, 1945 aboard the American Battleship USS Missouri signaling the official end of the war, and the beginning of Karate's rebirth. It would be a year or two until many of the Japanese soldiers who were the future of the JKA would return to the nation. It was specifically a year until Nakayama Sensei would return from China as he was still overseas until May 1946. Under the American military rule the Japanese people were barred from practicing the martial arts. They were seen as being aggressive and trained military warriors to rise up against the American military. This ban however lasted five years. The ban meant that traditional arts such as Sumo, Kendo, Kenjutsu, Iiado, Judo and other arts were not to be taught or demonstrated in public. Many of the traditional schools were shuttered and never reopened their doors.

Prior to the ban there was no JKA, just the Shotokan Dojo, University clubs and many smaller groups of Karate instructors that would teach a variety of different off shoots of what Funakoshi and other Okinawan masters taught, and a lot of frauds that were taking advantage of a situation. The groups were not seen as being very organized and they were often seen as a form of calisthenics taught in the school system, almost like football or baseball in the states. Ironically much of this came because at the time the students were using Kumite drills that looked a great deal like games to the Allied military who were occupying the country at the time. This meant that the practice of Karate was still allowed under the Martial arts Ban this actually lead to a rebirth of the practice as instructors and students returned home from abroad looking for a grounding activity that would occupy their time post war.

In 1949 the military lifted the ban on martial art practice and the Japan Karate association was formed, headed by students of Funakoshi's. While the ban was still in effect the Karate masters knew organizing an official body would bring to much attention to them and could lead to the ban being extended to them. The organizations formation allowed the beginning of more organized training and a resurgence in the research and development of Karate. While a great deal of research and development was lost because of the war, the new focus that the JKA could bring to development of the art helped create a push in training again. Obata and other students of Sensei Funakoshi began officially forming the organization that was to become one of the largest and most powerful Karate organizations in the world for a long time.

By 1955 the first Headquarters Dojo was built in Yotsuya Tokyo and the first chairman was appointed; Saigo Kichinoskuke a member of the upper house in the Japanese newly formed government. Saigo was also the grandson of one of the greatest heroes of the Meiji era, Seigo Takamori, known as the last samurai. Seigo Takamori was the historical basis for the lead Samurai character in the movie the last Samurai. The JKA began teaching and training as well as working with their new political chairman to reach out to the newly formed government to engrain themselves in the newly forming modern Japan. A great deal of this did ruffle the more traditionalists' feather; however the steps that were taken created a solid anchor to build the JKA through.

As many of the American military men started to settle into their occupation of what was once the country they saw as their worst enemy, they began appreciating the culture and they began to engage in many of the normal Japanese traditions and activities. One such activity was Karate, which appealed to the Americans ideas of Japanese more romantic Samurai history. Many service men saw demonstrations and sought out instructors in the Japanese martial arts. This lead again to a new and more powerful growth spurt that saw many new generation masters come to the forefront and Karate in general began to blossom and bloom. Some of this growth was very good for Karate with the JKA and other groups building up membership and growing at a very fast rate, some was not so good with a great number of frauds teaching Karate to the service men and passing on garbage Karate to those that did not realize that the systems they were learning were false. Some service men also created their own systems and passed on the style, often creating systems out of a mish mash of systems they had witnessed and often never actually trained in. This was just the start of a issue in Karate as the growth of the "McDojo" began to take off at this point as well. Honest instructors would avoid pointing out the frauds for fear that they would.

This new growth spurt brought about the necessity for new instructors to move out and teach around the world. The war had initially pushed Karate training, destroyed that growth and then reinvigorated growth with even more possible students. The process had seen a great deal of research into the art lost and created a new system of Karate as the members that were returning from the war began to research and develop the system again. All of this made the founding and then development and growth of the JKA a possibility. If not for the war much of the changes that Gigo Funakoshi had made to the system may have stuck and we probably would have a very different system of practice, and the JKA itself may not have been founded as the seniors of the University groups were not in favor of this happening. Also, many of the instructors who traveled overseas may not have. The JKA is a result of the war and affected by the changes that the war brought about.

Karate after the war

Following the war the Allied forces banned the practice of military training or martial arts completely, however because Funakoshi found a way around this. Funakoshi Sensei had a close association with the ministry of Education as he was teaching in the universities a great deal before the war. In order for Karate training to start up again after the war he approached the ministry and the Allied forces and had Karate classified as a physical education, not a martial art. It was presented as a physical work out, a callisthenic if you like, and one that would produce stronger and healthier men. The allied powers lapped it up and allowed the practice of Karate. Funakoshi worked hard to ensure that the practice could go on and was more than happy to train his students under the heading of a physical education activity. This also allowed him to show the Allied officers and service men his art.

By 1949 the JKA was formed from the growing number of returning and new members of Shotokan Karate, they appointed Funakoshi Sensei as Supreme Master of the organization and began plans to grow even more and attract more students. The truth was that the JKA was formed not for Funakoshi but to build a professional teaching group that could use Karate as a way to find employment and equally as a way to maintain the talent base with the growing group of instructors. It was a professional division lead by several talented instructors and those that wanted to see Karate grow beyond what it currently was.

The JKA grew monthly and soon the club was unable to contain itself in the confines of the smaller training facility they had acquired after the war, a new Shotokan was purchased and the JKA grew as the professional wing of the Shotokan style. This new focus and new group opened up many new training options and new ideas were flooding in to grow and develop the style and its reach.

With a focus on having American service men recruited and taught the JKA experienced a massive growth, not just with the service men in Japan but by those that had gone home and wanted to continue training under competent JKA instructors. By 1953 the JKA saw an opportunity to grow outside of Japan and sent several of his top students and instructors like Isao Obata, Masatoshi Nakayama and Hidetaka Nishiyama to the states to teach his Karate to Americans in their home country. The United States Air force, who had been very interested in traditional fighting arts in Japan since the end of the war, sponsored several instructors from several arts to travel to the air force bases and give demonstrations all over the United States.

Soon after the trip the second round of unprecedented growth and development in the style of Karate became very apparent to the senior students and plans again went into effect to build a central office and Dojo to house and manage the growth of the organization. The new club was sponsored by some of the wealthier students and funds from the growing organization and in 1955, a short 10 years after the end of the war and destruction of the original Shotokan a new Dojo opened in Tokyo to be the headquarters for Shotokan Karate. Funakoshi Sensei presided over the opening and the Japan Karate Association was born. Different from the first Shotokan this was the JKA, Not run by seniors who were looking for a place to train other than the university, but seniors looking to grow a professional division that would see the style grow and spread.

The ministry of Education gave official recognition to the Japan Karate Association as the legal entity that was to oversee Shotokan Karate. This meant that the organization was in charge of not just growing and development of the art, but also gave legitimacy to those that wanted to teach the style. This also meant that the organization could seek to become a power house in the realm of Karate in Japan. The distinction being that they were seen as the one and only legitimate Shotokan Karate group by a government body. This angered a great many people who were still dedicated to teaching in the universities and created jealousy and a split in the training groups. The other side did not see this as a advantage and progress, but a slap in the face to their "traditional values", even if Funakoshi Sensei was going along with the growth and development of the JKA, the others were convinced it was counter to the intent of the true spirit of Karate.

On April 26th of 1957, Sixteen days after his style was given governmental recognition and legitimacy, Funakoshi passed away in Tokyo at the age of 89. A large public Memorial service was held at the Ryogoku Kokugikan (the national Sumo hall) that was attended by over 20,000 people including many famous names in Karate today. A formal funeral was also held (this we will discuss in a bit). Both sides that were formed when the JKA was established tend to hijack Funakoshi Sensei's approval when they talk about what he wanted.

The JKA States that Funakoshi Sensei was not only behind the formation of the JKA but instructed and directed the members on what he felt were the best plans. He was said to have been the architect of much of the established plans for the JKA. The JKA Stated all this while the Shotokai say that Funakoshi hated the ideas that the JKA created, and would never have approved of them as his focus was on the Shotokai's plans and wanted the system to stay small, not for profit and focused on building up individuals. Keeping in mind that the Shotokai wanted to stay in the universities and not have a professional division. It is also important to note that by this point Funakoshi Sensei was almost 90 years old and by all accounts did not manage the Shotokai or the JKA group, he had a very simple life that included teaching when he could and attending classes to watch most of the time. He passed away knowing that he had created a next generation of instructors who would carry on his dream and develop them into their own.

This small school teacher had not only created a Karate style, but he had brought it to Japan from its place of birth on Okinawa and lived through the horrible living conditions created by a world war, then Funakoshi helped bring his system of Karate to the world by sending his students out to teach in American and Europe and eventually Shotokan Karate became the most practiced style of Karate on the planet. All the bickering and issues aside, this system was created by a well-read school teacher with the idea of making better people, he worked hard and thought of his system and students first, helped generate perhaps the greatest instructors and seniors in the history of Karate and then gave them the tools to create the art that became known as the most popular system of Karate in the world. Not bad for a retired school teacher!

Funakoshi's Death.

Funakoshi passed away at the age of 89 having managed to not only formulate and synthesize a system of Karate (merging all the systems he had studied in Okinawa), bring the system to Japan and then watched as the new Karate system was sent out to the world by his students. This alone would be very impressive for a diminutive and traditionally conservative school teacher from the small rural island nation, but to add to this accomplishment he was also a prolific author and poet and published several books and in several contemporary periodicals of his time….. as well doing all of this after retiring from teaching full time in the Okinawan school system. Upon his death he was also the supreme master of two very different groups. The Japan Karate association, the professional division dedicated to teaching the public Karate, and the Shotokai, a university group once called the Dai Nihon Karate do Kenkyukai. Both of the groups were radically different in their views as to Karate's place in society and how it should be managed and to what the goals of Karate should be. Both sides were extremely passionate about the growth and spread of Karate, despite both having very different views of how to achieve this.

This Shotokai group was a university group that was formed in 1936 to run the university based clubs and the JKA was the professional division that grew out of the graduated members of the universities. While both sides taught the system that Funakoshi had created, they both had moved along and been influenced by different sources, the Shotokai by Gigo Funakoshi and especially Shigeru Egami, an eccentric that practiced a very different technical system than was taught at the University groups clubs. Egami Sensei had been a student of Gigo Funakoshi mostly and had trained under Takeshi Simoda and Isao Obata as well. The Shotokai system was based on the experiments in movement and technical developments that Funakoshi Gigo had been doing to expand the Shotokan style and make it more Japanese as well as the vast shifts in technical applications that Egami was making on his own. Egami was training a great deal with Funakoshi Gigo at the time and formulating changes based on what they were doing in private work outs. Egami had also been influenced by his time studying Aikido. Egami was the polar opposite to the JKA founders with his point of view being that Karate should never be used for sport and he avoided all aspects of sport-oriented combat when it came to Karate and the JKA focusing more on the Shotokan that Funakoshi

Gichin had taught and adopting the training and techniques to a more marketable tournament system.

The other group was influenced by Masatoshi Nakayama, A young and highly intelligent and gifted instructor who brought a lot of Kendo/Kenjutsu influence to the formation of the JKA's style of Shotokan tournament style. The JKA was also influenced a great deal by Isao Obata, one of Funakoshi Sensei's original students and a businessman who had sunk a great deal of his family money into helping Karate grow. Much like Nakayama he also had a Kendo and Judo back ground and was well versed and trained in both sports before he even took up Karate. Obata had come up through the university clubs, much like Nakayama, so they both had strong ties to the clubs (Obata having graduated from Keio University and Nakayama from Takushoku University). The JKA was formed to grow the Karate system and it was well known that they were playing with the ideas of sport Karate. The JKA was also formed to manage and provide a platform for students to continue training after they graduated from the University clubs that Funakoshi helped establish.

In the days after Funakoshi Gichin Sensei passed away there were many meetings between seniors in the JKA and the Shotokai. Most of them started off with conversations about how to properly and respectfully put Funakoshi Sensei to rest. However, it became apparent that the issues of respecting Funakoshi and running his funeral was taking a back seat to political issues such as who would run the System and who would be the new chief instructor, thus running and holding the traditions that Funakoshi had brought to the mainland, the Kyokai behaved as if they were the default Heir to the Funakoshi system and the JKA fighting to show that the system that was reshaped under the JKA seniors was to be the legacy system that Funakoshi left, so they should be the inheritors of the mantle. The JKA wanted to respectfully bury the master and show the utmost respect for all that Funakoshi had done for all the members, while many in the Shotokai had this interest as well.

The groups came together for a meeting and while the JKA was interested in planning out a proper and respectful funeral it has been shown that the Shotokai group brought up issues and items that were unrelated to the burial of Funakoshi and more along the lines of who is running the organization now that Funakoshi had passed, keeping in mind that the separation of the two groups had already actually happened at this time and the JKA was running as a separate entity, if not on paper then a natural separation existed as both groups had a management team and seniors who were put in place as presidents and senior instructors separating the groups along political and management lines.

During the meeting to address the plans for the funeral some of the Shotokai argued that the original Shotokan had burned down and that Funakoshi remained the director of the Shotokai, he did not hold such a title with the New JKA Dojo, they failed to address his title as supreme Master of the JKA and took the "Shotokan" name as a litteral reference to the burned out original Dojo. The argument tended to ignore the fact that the JKA was a organization and not reliant on a single old Dojo, they now had a headquarters to work from and were for some time now a "business" that was growing , developing and a legal entity.

This back and forth arguing apparently went on for hours and bogged down the meeting. Many of the men present at the meeting were apparently upset with this petty arguing and the meeting was said to be tense and uncomfortable for those present. Arguments and emotional outbursts marred the gathering and caused various important and influential seniors to leave as no traction was being gained in planning out the funeral.

Adding to the issues was the fact that Funakoshi's eldest son Geie, had insisted that the Shotokai be in charge of the funeral and had been specifically requesting this through an official letter. This ignored the fact that the JKA had just wanted to participate and help with the funeral, the Shotokai had done everything in its power to make the JKA look illegitimate and pushed the narrative that they were the true lineage of Funakoshi over the JKA. Furthering the issues around the request from Giei Funakoshi was the fact that Giei was an employee of the Shotokai and also that he was not in good favor with his father at the time of his father's passing.

Giei had caused his father a great deal of embarrassment by racking up expensive gambling debts and then shunting them off on students and borrowing money he could not pay back from the Shotokai and many of its members. Funakoshi's daughters had left the funeral arraignments in the hands of all the students and felt that equal participation was needed to respect what they felt would be their father's wishes. However because of social norms in Japan at that time their input was not seen as having authority nor being important to the situation and Geie had more input than the rest of the family had as he was a male child and seen as having more authority in these types of situations. It is said however that the sisters were not happy with the outcome of the planning, the fighting and the situation created by their brother and they were not very happy with their brother's actions or the actions of the Shotokai in this sad time.

It is also important to point out that the JKA also had several large clubs in big universities in its membership as well as the towering membership of the JKA, while the Shotokai existed only in the smller universities like Chuo, Noko, Seijo, Gakushin and Senshu universities, their membership being much smaller than the JKA and they had less senior members as well. The JKA had huge clubs in Takushuko, Asai, Komazawa, Hosei, Taisho, Dokkyo, Chiba, Teikyo, Kyoto Sangyo, Aoyama Gakuin, and the professional Dojo backing them up as well as several other smaller clubs in other universities. Most accounts of the meeting suggested that each time the JKA would request to assist or would start to speak and offer suggestions the Shotokai members would bring up that Geie had insisted that they be in charge of the Shotokai was in charge of the funeral and then, many suggest, they would continue to insult the JKA and state that they were not teaching according to Funakoshi Sensei's wishes. This went on for hours, and both sides stating that the other was to blame for the chaos and bickering. The meeting was chaotic and deadlocked with very little getting agreed upon...ending finally only after the Shotokai rolled out a plan they had worked out and one that they intended to go forward with prior to the meeting regardless of the input that they were going to get from the JKA.

The Shotokai took the opportunity to argue that the use of tournaments was against Funakoshi Sensei's wishes and also complain that the JKA would not recognize the Taikyoku Katas. While the Shotokai continued to press these matters that had nothing to do with the funeral the JKA refused to engage in such bickering on such an occasion .The JKA took the stance that they would not recognize the Kata because they were not Kata that Funakoshi Sensei had recognized or included in his teaching when he was alive. While the Shotokai pressed for the JKA to bend on these matters and abandon training in evolving tournament rules and training.

After hours of bickering many of the university representatives for the JKA leaders left the meeting in frustration. The planning had devolved into spats of shouting and arguments about subjects that had nothing to do with the funeral or honoring Funakoshi Sensei and the meetings had turned into a chance for the Shotokai to embarrass and berate the JKA seniors, who for their part were not engaging in this behavior. The JKA was trying to honor their departed master while the Shotokai seniors were attending the meeting with the intent of breaking the JKA and subjugate them.

The meeting proved that the Shotokai was much more interested in arguing about technical issues than respecting Funakoshi and allowing his students in both organizations to plan out Funakoshi' Sensei's funeral and burial ceremony. In the end the JKA seniors all left the table and officially protested the funeral planning being set up and orchestrated by the Shotokai, as it had been made very clear that their official involvement would not be granted without provisions from the JKA, all of which had nothing to do with planning the funeral. The

JKA was being forced to look at changes to how they were training and how they expressed the Karate Funakoshi had taught them; this was just not something they could accept.

The Shotokai, for their part, insisted that the JKA was trying to use the size of their membership to dictate changes in the plans they had laid out. They felt that the JKA was overbearing and pushing their own agenda at the meeting. There is probably some truth to both sides argument; however the truth is that in the end they both participated in the event, just the Shotokai made the arrangements while many members of the JKA performed important duties at the event.

The Shotokai did not ban members from attending and many of the JKA greats, and soon to be greats did attend the funeral. The Shotokai made a big show of making the funeral an overly decadent affair, and they had their school flags out to show who was honoring Funakoshi and present to support. The group went all out and the funeral was held in the most expensive and expansive way possible. The show of all of this would have been something out of the ordinary for such a simple school teacher, and many suggest that Funakoshi himself, being a very humble man, would not have enjoyed the spectacle of the event at all.

One of the biggest stories in the Mythology of Shotokan was that the JKA banned from participation and attending the funeral. Yes they were removed from planning and executing the funeral, and they did not have official flags at the funeral to show their displeasure at the outcome of the meeting, but they did have many members attend to pay their respects. And from one story I was told by a very high ranking instructor, this included Nakayama Sensei who did not make a big deal about his presence at the funeral and even acted as a pallbearer. Despite the issues, arguments and spats, the JKA was not only present but very active at the funeral. They paid their respects and while they had pulled out of the planning they had a huge presence at the funeral to commemorate their chief instructor and founder. Because the JKA was barred from assisting in their own master's funeral they also held a memorial at Ryogoku Kokugikan (the national Sumo hall) that saw the largest turn out for a memorial to date. They also assisted in building the memorial at Engaku Ji temple in Kamakura. All of this inadvertently served to embarrass the Shotokai and worsen the rift between the two groups.

The stories about the meeting and false stories about how the Kyokai (JKA) had behaved began to be told by the Shotokai seniors after the JKA had created the memorial and held the event, which exacerbated the embarrassment that the Shotokai had felt. The outlandish and silly stories were meant to embarrass the JKA but many of them back fired as the truth came out and saw members of the Shotokai leave to join the JKA.

For the most part the JKA and Nakayama Sensei kept quiet about the meeting and the events prior to the funeral, only when the Shotokai began talking about the meeting and members began to spread false statements about the event did they even mention the meeting. Nakayama for his part never spoke of it further than saying that the meeting decided that the Shotokai and Geie, who was not actually present, ended up planning the official funeral.

Funakoshi Sensei was known as a humble man, he almost single handedly brought Karate from Okinawa to Japan and facilitated the growth clear across the pacific to the world, but he took little credit for this and preferred to simply teach his 15 Kata that he taught and be known as a man that loved Karate and as a traditionalist. All of the things we know about him would suggest that a simple event would have been his preference for his memorial. He would have been touched by the number of people and the simplicity of the JKA event and probably greatly embarrassed by the arguments of the funeral planning and the opulent funeral that the Shotokai held. And in the end, I would suggest, he would have been saddened at the split that came out of his passing. What is most sad is that so many men with a passion for Karate could not get along for such an important event, somewhat of a theme as we will see.

Who taught fighting first?

Putting aside some of the history that was going on at the time there is another dojo "story" that is often retold to new members and has in itself become a bit of Dojo Dogma that is simply not true and at best misleading. The story is how Nakayama sensei (or other post WWII instructors) made up or started doing Kumite when no one else had been doing this. Kumite is the art of sparring, a physical exchange with a partner that is much more fluid and freer than doing conditioning drills or Bunkai. A lot of senior instructors from different factions, systems and styles have taken credit for this and it's simply not true. While Karate during Funakoshi Sensei's generation was greatly limited to Kihon drills, repetitions and all the areas of Kata study, along with an impressive amount of conditioning it also included Kumite. While the art that Funakoshi taught limited this type of brawl like training when he first brought the training to the mainland, Kumite was not totally unheard of and it was practiced by many.

The JKA was formed in 1957 to organize the professional division of the Karate students. This however is often noted as the start of Kumite training and tournament preparation. The story goes that the JKA was formed to help grow the Karate base and the genius that was Nakayama Sensei went against Funakoshi's wishes and set up Kumite training as part of the tournament. It was said that this was part of his master plan to expand the training and bring in new members, younger members, from the universities to the tournaments. He intended to make Kumite the exciting center piece of tournaments and really push the participation up. A myriad of instructors have stepped forwards and said they created the rules of the tournaments and that they single handedly pushed the JKA into creating a Kumite training plan to attract members. While Nakayama Sensei did make plans to build up tournaments officially, something that Funakoshi Sensei did frown on, and rules for the participants were accepted, there were multiple systems of Kumite that existed already for members to use in tournaments and Kumite training was actually very popular and common in clubs at that time.

Nakayama Sensei used the work of junior instructors like Shichi Tokudo, Miki, Bo and Hirayama to formulate the rules and to view the idea of Kumite as a potential boost for the JKA. These instructors were all Karate students and Kendo instructors who had experience officiating and participating in Kendo tournaments. They had practiced with different rules, different safety equipment and had been doing this since 1927. These instructors had paved the way for Jiyu Kumite to be accepted by the JKA.

It is very important to note that Funakoshi was irritated with these seniors, but it probably had little to do with the act of them doing kumite....it was HOW they were doing it. He had been told of their training and he sent members to watch the training. The training session was very basic, they "gloved up" with Kendo safety gear and went at each other with no control. One story is that the Bogu could not handle the full force strikes and one student actually injured the other when they punched through the Do, or chest piece. The lacquered wood could not hold up to the Gyaku zuki of a trained Karate student and shattered. The damage that was done to the receiver of the blow was fantastic and sent him to hospital with broken ribs. The truth is probably much less spectacular but I think it illustrates the potential for injury and that was the point of that little story.

Funakoshi was said to have felt that the spectacle of it all and the over use of protective gear belittled the art and that the use of full contact with safety gear was for thugs, his vision was of better control and a focused training that showed the beauty and control of Karate. It took a great deal of persuasion to get him to allow any form of sparring after this, but he did and it began to grow. His focus for Karate was to make better people, not a human "Dog fight" and he felt that this kind of training was well below his noble art.

Ironically Funakoshi was not against public spectacle, just bogu (gear) style tournament Kumite. He felt that they created thugs like Motobu, whom he had a long standing rivalry, and that this type of circus spectacle took away from his ultraistic focus for Karate. But Kumite was still part of training back then, just not as we know it today. Early kumite was more like Yakusoku Kumite or agreement Kumite. The whole thing was formal and the participants trusted each other to not harm the other. They trained mostly in a type of slowed down drill that would hone their skills and polish technical ability with a focus on perfecting form and technique over using the *Waza* to score points or win a simulated tussle.

So, we know that Funakoshi did not really like Kumite, he hated full contact Kumite with gear on….but as it the first last and only time that Kumite was introduced to Karate training…In a word….No! I have read accounts of Kumite training and such that would indicate that the practice of Kumite had gone back to when the style was formulated from Chinese training back in Okinawa and some form of Kumite was being practiced pretty much from day one. Many famous peers of Funakoshi Sensei dabbled in Kumite and some in street fighting outright. Funakoshi seems to have taken a dislike to Kumite training when he came to Japan, one explanation may come from his rivalry with Motobu Choki.

The story of the rivalry between Funakoshi Sensei and Motobu Choki is a famous one in the Karate world. Both sides tend to roll out different stories to illustrate the reason that the men did not like each other but the truth is that the men were simply very different personalities and had different focuses in Karate and life. Funakoshi was a Upper middle class school teacher from a upper middle class family. He was raised to be respectful and traditionally aristocratic, perhaps a bit snooty and uptight but he was a hardworking and intelligent person. Motobu was the younger son of an aristocrat of upper class status in Okainwa. He was raised in a great deal more lavish life style that Funakoshi was, yet he rejected the education that was available to him and was known to be rude, a drunkard and bragged a great deal. He never had to actually work and lived off the family income he had.

Both men were also physically opposites. While Funakoshi was smaller, quick for his age and used snappy movements, Motobu was larger framed, not as fast but very strong and two years junior to Funakoshi Sensei, in Japanese society that would mean that Funakoshi was his senior and should be afforded some level of respect. It was a source of great stress that Motobu did not afford Funakoshi the respect he felt that he warranted with the amount of work he had put in for Karate and the age difference. However Motobu came from a higher class family and while Funakoshi felt hat he deserved respect because of the age difference, Motobu held fast to the mentality of the old cast system and felt that he did not owe this lower level school teacher any additional respect.

The story of the rivalry also illustrated the difference in the two men's views on Karate. Funakoshi felt that the art was noble and that the training should be such that it helped the student become a better person while Motobu felt that the art was one of fighting and aggression. He was a real "man's man" and he would often engage in testing his mettle against others in wrestling and fighting and felt that Kumite was the corner stone of Karate and its training. Motobu felt that Funakoshi was soft and his Karate was not representative of what the fighting art should be. He felt that the Training was flawed and did not give the students the correct systems that he had learned traveling around Okinawa as a youth. Motobu had tested his skills with live fighting and often found his way into street fights and brawls that put his fighting skills to the test. While Motobu felt that this was the best training he could actually find, it turned Funakoshi off of him as a person and Funakoshi formed a view of Motobu that included him feeling he was a thug and a spoiled aristocrat's son with poor form and technique and someone that should not be emulated as a person.

It is interesting to note that even with the harsh differences and the horrible dislike that each man had for each other, they still found occasion to train with each other. On one such occasion a altercation occurred between the two when Funakoshi Sensei was teaching drills and Motobu felt a need to challenge him. Why Motobu was present at a work out in which Funakoshi Sensei was teaching is a bit of a mystery but the fact that they did interact shows that they were not separated by their dislike and on occasion still worked out together. Motobu had questioned the techniques or the application that Funakoshi was teaching, to which Funakoshi invited Motobu to show him how it should be done. This was more than likely a curt response to Motobu being a bully during a class work out and not a friendly interaction from what we have come to know about the two. The story goes that Motobu swept his rival several times and used his weight to push the smaller man down several times. This upset Funakoshi greatly and he leapt up curtly telling Motobu to try that again when he was ready for the attack. The total distain and behavior that Motobu showed to Funakoshi reinforced the loathing that Funakoshi was said to have had for Motobu. And the fact that Motobu so easily tossed the smaller man around did nothing to garner respect by Motobu for his smaller peer.

Motobu had honed his true fighting skills on the streets and by fighting as many of his students and peers as he could, while Funakoshi focused on forming perfectly executed Waza. This shows that the art and act of Kumite was well used prior to the JKA adding it to their curriculum. While the JKA was not the first to introduce Kumite training to their practice, they were one of the first to introduce rules and to formulate a system for doing kumite that was much safer and not just a free for all like Motobu and his training partners would perform. However, even with this, they were not truly the first. Many different college clubs were set up in Japan when the Okinawan masters brought Karate to the mainland. The young men were sport minded and enthusiastic to test their new skills. To be safe general rules were set in place and enforced during classes to make the practice safer-ish, even if the rules were very basic and the stylized training was not common amongst the masters, the students did do Kumite, often hurting each other in the process.

One such story is from students of the Takashuko University. In the beginning of training in Japan the universities were the key to the growth of Karate. Different styles landed in the universities with the majority being Shotokan, but others also found homes in the clubs. One such group was the Goju students of Ritsusmei University in Kyoto. They had a reputation as being brutal and doing a lot of free fighting. On one occasion they visited Takushuko for an exchange and all members lined up to do Kumite with a focus on a round robin style of Kumite. The story goes that no control was offered by either side with broken ribs, teeth and lots of broken noses and blood spilled with the perspiration. The Takashuko University came out on top, but by a thin margin and both sides garnered both respect and fear from the performance of the top fighters.

So the answer is everyone was "kung fu fighting" and it was common place, so to be fair the question should not be how was the first to introduce Kumite to Karate, but rather "was Karate not formed with some kind of Kumite already imbedded in it"? The answer would be a resounding yes! Chinese martial arts have drill sets, two person sets, basic and forms like Karat and most of them also have some form of free fighting or stylized partner training. Seeing as Karate was heavily influenced by Kung fu, it should be no shock that Karate has always had some kind of Kumite training component to the training that they did. Maybe it was not as evolved as we have today or maybe it had a different kind of practice and focus, but I would venture to say that it was always part of Karate's curriculum and no one person should honestly be taking the credit for inventing any part of that training.

The first big split (1957)

When Funakoshi passed away in 1957, his students were already starting to split into several factions. Splits were normally based on the leaders interpretation of what Shotokan practice should be, technical changes and more times than not political arguments and infighting caused the chasms that were created. In this case the first big split was the formation of the Nihon Karate Kyokai or the JKA and the Shotokai group. The issue in question for this split was on the formation of a professional division as well as the development of competition rules, meaning that competitions were going to be implemented. The JKA was essentially set up to be a professional division, and the Shotokai group was opposed to this very idea. Then the JKA was working to develop solid tournament rules, again something that the Shotokai was against. This was simply the "used" reasons for the split and the reasons that were shared in dojos around the world to explain the split. The real reasons were far more personal and embarrassing to the Shotokai.

Right after Funakoshi Sensei passed away (April 26, 1957) the Shotokan world split into four separate groups; the University groups, the JKA, The Shotokai and the overseas Shotokan group made up of small groups of instructors loyal to Funakoshi but not really part of any other group. Originally the Four groups were made up of three University groups that were under Master Funakoshi, the oldest was at Keio University team, which remained the figure head for the University based groups while Wasada split into three essential groups; the Shotokai group, the University only training group and a large contingent of overseas groups that later formed the SKA under Oshima Sensei. The third group was the Takushoku group which began to turn out professional instructors as they formed the JKA administration. The Takushoku group or the Takudai essentially became an extension or recruitment arm of the JKA. One could argue that the Takudai receive the most attention, the most arduous training and the members took a deep dive into Karate, more so than the other groups. They focused on turning out future instructors and tournament champions while Keio students were training in a different kind of Karate focused more on esoteric and spiritual Karate that Egami Sensei brought to the table.

The groups were all loose knit under Funakoshi Sensei but upon his passing a great deal of turmoil split them up, not only the funeral, but essentially different ideals that had formed and created fishers in the differing training focus for each group. The JKA or Takushoku based group relied on the 26 Kata and a very specific and scientific approach to Kihon development, athleticism and Kumite training that favoured athletic people, while the Keio university group was more focused on development of spirit and Ki in training and ushered in new training ideas set forth by Geigo Funakoshi and Egamin Sensei. The Wasada group tended to be more of a balance between the two; terribly traditional but more open to "modern" training ideas and participation in different competition style events. These splinters created the first real split.

The funeral of Funakoshi Sensei created an opportunity for the different groups to voice their displeasure with each other. The issues had been building but with all the groups not wanting to upset Funakoshi and fall out of favor with the Master they held their issues until this opportunity presented itself and then they all dove in. When the Takushoku University and the newly formed JKA were removed from the funeral arrangements committee and essentially banned from brining their university flags to the funeral the other groups saw their opportunity to pounce. First Hironishi Genshi and Egami Shigeru resigned from the JKA officially leaving the entity that they had so many ideological issues with, which I would assume did not come as any surprise to those in the JKA. Neither man had played much of a part in the JKA but unlike the "written" history books may suggest, they were active members of the early incarnation of the seniors council and made big contributions to the organization, mostly supporting their clubs and their ideas as one would expect. Most people would suggest that the Shotokai leadership were never involved in the JKA, it's a comforting thought that they were never part of the group. But the truth is they were founding members.

Egami and Hironishi Genshi both left and made the Shotokai an official organization. Prior to this the Shotokai was a loose knit group of University based students only. It was an idea or feeling that the university groups not associated directly under the JKA were somehow a group, now it would be official. It must be noted that the Shotokai at that time knowingly told others that the Takushuko based group and the JKA left of their own free will and did not participate in the Funeral, which was known to be categorically untrue. They also erased most history of them participating with the JKA to mold the story that the JKA was a upstart off shoot of the Shotokai and the university council. The truth is that Egami and most of the Shotokai leadership were not only on board with forming the JKA they were energetically involved. It was only when they realized the scope and purpose of the group that they started to back away and formulates the Shotokai.

Until this point Hironishi Genshin was a fairly unknown entity in the Karate world. He had not really been a big player until he backed Egami and the Shotkai group. He had not served in the military during the war and had remained behind to train in the University Karate club and attend school. A known communist he was not drafted by the Japanese government as they were very suspicious of the communist group. During this time he cemented his relationship in the Karate world by training with Yoshitaka Funakoshi and others who remained behind during the war. After Yoshitaka passed away Genshin began forming a relationship with Funakoshi's eldest son and ushered him into the political Karate world. While Geie filled a vacuum left by Yoshitaka in the political sense he was never going to be a Karate instructor or make any kind of impact in Karate other than negative political and social ones. However Hironishi Genshin did not see this, he saw the eldest son of Funakoshi Sensei and a person who could assist the "cause" that the newly forming Shotokai needed help with and one that would establish their rights as heirs to Funakoshi Sensei as well as solidifying their survival.

When Geie Funakoshi stepped into to scuttle the talks about who would be running Funakoshi Sensei's funeral it was at the bequest of Egami and Genshin that this occurred. At this point the split really was a three way split with the Shotokan (JKA), Shotokai and a small cluster of overseas instructors all cutting ties and going their separate ways. The split was along many different lines, while one group says it was them being disrespected that led to the split, another would suggest it was the technical changes that the JKA was making and others would suggest it was the infighting that they saw as disrespectful of Funakoshi and his memory or political issues that forced the split, the truth is…it was all of them and more. It was groups fighting for the right to suggest they were the next "owners" and heir to Funakoshi Sensei. It was about political power and it created a theme that we will see again and again in the Shotokan world.

The JKA was led by enigmatic and intellectual Nakayama Sensei, the Shotokai by the spiritually enigmatic Egami and strict disciplinarian Genshin Hironishi and the overseas group being a well spread out and diffused group of seniors who had loose affiliations at best with different University groups. The smaller groups all splintered away like shards off of a block as it splits in two. Two giant and healthy groups formed while many smaller instructors, feeling ignored and watching as the childish fights waged in Japan, simply took what they knew and moved on. They continued to teach what they had learned and ignored the bigger groups as they battled for superior position.

To truly understand what happened next to the JKA and its export of Karate to the world some back ground will be useful to understand how this occurred. Both ancestry and wealth contributed to a man's position within the Japanese class structure, and within Japanese institutions, especially the colleges and universities. As it turns out this would be very important in how things played out after Funakoshi Sensei passed away. The different social and economic levels of the members created a cast system as it were with some universities feeling superior to others, and the members of the Karate world who attended the schools deemed socially stronger had more push and power in the politically charged world of Karate or at least they felt they did.

Even today, a family's wealth and position in society determines to a large degree which university the child will attend in Japan, and graduates chances for success are influenced by what university they attend. The big three universities, in terms of social and political prestige, are Keio, Wasada and Hosei. After the big Three there is Takushoku as far as big Karate clubs, but the Takushoku is not part of the "Establishment" of Colleges in Japan that made up the big three prestige universities. Karate participation in the university world however started at the Takushoku University and Karate was seen as strongest at the Takushoku group. The group was created prior to the war (WW2) and many of the world's best Karate athletes came out of this group. Takushoku men were typically majoring in Economics, Import and export and international law as they expected to travel internationally to teach Karate as well. Members at the "Big three" were expecting to stay in Japan and this greatly affected not only their University education but also their training and outlook on Karate.

As the Takushoku men expected to leave Japan and lead the charge in internationalizing Karate, which lead to an attitude that they needed to be the best at Karate, and this rubbed the other clubs members the wrong way. The Takushoku students were known to go into Karate training and take class every day…two class often….and the classes were 3 hours long. They did not take breaks to go home on holidays but doubled up on training. The training was harsh and often students would do a kata for hours working on form and technical perfection and leave broken only to report to the evening class to repeat the same training. Hours of doing just Mae geri or a combination repeated ritualistically for the full three hours are stories I have been told. One instructor told me of a time in which they were told to repeat stepping punch up and down the hallways of the club for hours while others were doing Tekki Shodan for three full hours, if they failed to do the movements all at full speed and power they were struck harshly with the Shinai till they were unable to walk without assistance after class having had their ankles battered and legs smashed. From what I was told the Keio and Wasada university groups were led by "Captains" and the work outs were mostly calisthenics and theory with an hour of training, nothing that stood up to the crazy, high intensity, work of the Takushoku clubs.

The types of jobs that were available to Takushoku graduates were not considered prestigious by the old mentality as well. The university specialized in Commerce, political science and Economics. They also had a strong foreign languages, international studies and engineering faculties. Keio University however was more a Law, Business and medicine university that captured to these faculties but also had faculties in Science, Policy management and letters. Wasada has been ranked as one of the best universities along with Keio as well, but is more of an open scope university with over 36 departments and 23 graduate schools. It was still seen as a upper level university, but as a private research university it was much more liberal than Keio and as such the Karate group was set up very different than Keio and other Universities in the Shotokai scope. Ironically Egami graduated from this school as did Kazumi Tabata and Tsutomu Oshima. While Egami became very entrenched in the Shotokai Tabata and Oshima left Japan and were part of the overseas instructors who became part of the smaller splinter groups that moved away from the Shotokai and JKA groups when the split occurred.

A great deal of Class friction was becoming an issue as the JKA was forming. The "old boys" of the big three University clubs saw the JKA members as lower class in unofficial cast system that was the norm around WW2. This and the disputes arising from business practices, philosophy and training methods all made for a very uncomfortable peace in the Shotokan world at the time. Add to the fact that the Shotokai had made it very well known that they had an issue with the JKA staff of instructors being paid to teach and run the Shotokan dojo, chief among them were the head instructor Nakayama and Takagi who ran the staff. The Shotokai, from what I have been told, did not pay their instructors. They all had day jobs that were very lucrative or inherited companies and fortunes that allowed them to run their Karate clubs as volunteers. The JKA however was run by "middle cast" people who could not afford to not get paid for the enormous amount of time they put into setting up and running their clubs and the greater JKA.

In April of 1955 the JKA had opened its first commercial Dojo; note not the first commercial dojo for Shotokan but the first JKA Karate Dojo. The dojo was at the old Kataoka movie Center and was the first real professional JKA headquarters. This meant staff and a need for a manager. The Shotokai was aghast that someone would charge to run a Dojo that they felt was in existence to teach their pure style of Karate. Regardless of the feelings that the Shotokai members shared, a marketing program was set up to aggressively market the new facility and

Karate training and a push to grow the new facility was undertaking. This also served to upset the Shotokai membership and seniors and caused a great deal of friction with them and the JKA seniors.

Many of the old line masters, Isao Obata of Keio among them, felt that it was immoral for a man to accept money for teaching Karate. That and they had all contributed financially to the growth of Karate and they were not being paid back for their contributions. The seniors who were upset were mostly from Keio and Wasada and felt that they were senior to Nakayama and his Takushoku group. They felt that the members of the JKA were stepping outside their preview and making big moves that they should not be making without permission and direction from the Shotokai or at least more senior members like Obata. The formation of the JKA and the marketing of Karate were exactly the divisive action that the Shotokai groups needed to start the actual split of the Shotokan groups. The Hosei group was the first to leave the group as a whole. The next was the Keio group lead by Obata. The two University groups may have felt that their leaving would scuttle the plans of the JKA, but it actually freed them to focus on growth and expansion plans without worrying about stepping on others toes or upsetting seniors that were set in their ways. Unburdened with the conservative "old boys" group the Takushuko and JKA men pursued the development of Karate in their own way; not surprisingly, with respect to training, they choose to internationalize the art and focus on growth and development outside of Japan. This move proved to be genius and helped them grow astronomically.

In order to affect the international growth of Karate the JKA group focused on creating a solid sporting aspect to the training and continue to focus on development of instructors with strict and harsh training that would foster the instructors understanding, skills and teaching skills. They turned to sport rules that had existed for some time as **Kokangeiko** (Exchanges of courtesy and practice), in which they had tested their techniques against each other in free style Kumite. While the "old boys" had refused to acknowledge these **Kokangeiko**, being as they were often unsupervised bloody events, feeling that they were Shenanigans and in direct opposition to what Funakoshi Sensei had taught. The truth is that the **Kokangeiko** served not only as a test for Waza (techniques) but also as a fertile testing ground for future training and sport development.

At this time the Shotokai group suffered low enrollment and saw members who attended University classes at their club locations actually travel to schools that were aligned with the JKA so they could participate in these events, all while the JKA enjoyed a huge enrollment and growth. This was a trying time for the Shotokai as they were refusing to change or capitulate and rejoin the JKA and yet they were suffering severe drops in membership and watching seniors and talented Karate members jump ship to join the JKA.

By 1950 virtually all the major style of Karate in Japan were practicing some form of Free style sparring and engaging in tournament training as well as participation in the events. The JKA contest rules were comprised of 16 articles that specifically laid out competition, making it much safer to participate and kept the focus on good technical training. These were completed and codified on August of 1956 offering a legitimate and safe but still traditionally focused avenue for sport training and technical improvement that attracted the seniors and new members of Karate. Collegiate clubs and branch Dojo immediately commenced staging a staggering number of tournaments to try and improve skills and to turn out better judges. The membership were hard at work creating training curriculums that would improve explosive and dynamic movement skills, training in the new rules they were encouraged to focus on spirit, skill and the idea of the single perfect technique to score a "killing blow" with. The flurry of activity culminated in the All Japan Karate Do Championships in 1957.

To this day the All Japan Karate Championships are still held and still host the best of the best in young competitors. Men like Kanazawa Hirokazu, Mikami Takayuki, Asai Tetsuhiko, Shirai, Hiroshi, Enoeda Keinosuke, Ueki Masaaki, Ochi Hideo and many others all were champions in the Kumite and went on to be JKA instructors or found their own organizations. The participants are selected from the best university student Karate members and the events are often super exciting. I make a habit of watching them on line and guessing which of the champions will be making big waves in Karate in the future. The championships bring out the best and most hungry competitors as they work to become part of the JKA instructor program or make a name for themselves internationally. Shiina Mai, an instructor in with the JKA is one of my favorite women's Kumite Champions winning the 2011 Kumite event at the 54th JKA All Japan Karate Championships. Her success as an instructor can be traced back to the work she did and her performance in this event.

Concurrently the JKA made another move that was a master stroke in their focus on expanding and becoming a truly international body. They set up the now famous and prestigious instructor training program that focused on training and developing members who would travel to other countries and build the JKA structure across the globe. The JKA ensured its success by allowing only the most talented of young Karate students were admitted to the program and only the graduates of University were to attend. They were also all Nidan ranking when they entered the program and only upon recommendation of a senior in the JKA. The intensive years of study included not only Karate but basic Psychology, physics, anatomy, business management, history and philosophy of physical education and sport, and many other subjects. The goal was to turn out the best instructors who could spread great Karate and improve the JKA standing abroad. The true focus of the program was to create a elite level instructor who would show that the JKA was truly the best Shotokan organization on the planet.

Eventually the program focused more on training and studies that would help the students grow their skills and understanding of Karate and teach solid Shotokan and several of the original studies dropped off. Upon completion of the training program (with fresh Sandan certificates) the newly minted instructors were assigned to a year of teaching internships abroad. The results of the training, apprenticeships and harsh conditioning that the program foster was a handful of highly proficient Karate instructors who were well prepared to plant and nourish the JKA flag overseas. What started off as a super harsh extension of the old Takushoku university training also transitioned into a professional instructor training program that still has hints of the harder and more aggressive instruction that once was the norm. It's also important to note that this was not the only venue for becoming a JKA instructor. In fact many of the great instructors that went abroad and many that teach in Japan still did not graduate the program; many of them also attended these classes and trained just as hard but never became graduates.

The first instructors to arrive in the states from the JKA were Nishiyama Hidetaka in Los Angeles and Okizaki Teruyuki, who landed in Philadelphia, both arriving in 1961. Others soon joined them and the expansion of the JKA in the United States and abroad started off like a spark as it turned into a wild fire. Others who followed in rapid succession included Mikami Takayuki, the 2 time all Japan Champion who first went to Kansas city then on to New Orleans; Yaguchi Yutaka was assigned to Denver after a brief stint in Los Angeles; and Kanazawa Hirokazu, also two time All Japan Karate Champion was brought to Hawaii. Kanazawa was brought in to replace Mori Masataka who moved to New York. Hawaii was then seeded to Asai Tatsuhiko. Sugiyama Shojiro , also a graduate of the instructor training program landed in Chicago and then Ueki Masaaki and Takashina Shigeru landed in Florida, Ueki moving back to Japan sometime after. Kisaka Katsuya was place in New Jersey and Koyama Shojiro in Arizona. By the mid 1970's American students were themselves achieving instructor status and most of the senior JKA men had either settled in or cycled back to Japan, as well as a few leaving the JKA totally. The founding JKA masters had developed great Karate men like Robert Fusaro of Minneapolis, Robert Graves of Oregon, Greer Golden of Ohio, Ray Dalke, Frank Smith and James Yabe of California and Gerald Evans of Philadelphia, a Tone of British and south African instructors and a others all over the world. The growth of the JKA in America was exponential and only pushing faster as time moved on. But with growth...came splintering and separation.

By the late 1960's a growing turbulence was forming in the states. A great many instructors felt that they should be heading the Single group that was to lead the arm of the JKA in the states. Personality clashes and a feeling of mistrust that had been put in place when several instructors stepped on each other's toes lead to infighting and loss of cohesiveness set in, most of this was in the united states, but abroad in Europe this petty jealously and total lack of cohesive participation began to grow personal issues and political tensions that were about to open up the seams of the international program.

Instructors left the JKA and formed new organizations that rivaled the existing JKA organizations locally; some formed subgroups in the JKA American groups and competed with each other for students, prestige and control of the JKA in the united states. Okizaki Sensei began spreading his ISKF organization across both the United States and Canada trying to unify members by giving the senior student's control of their areas, as long as he was brought in for grading and events. The approach of Okizaki Sensei was very different from Nishyama Sensei, who had his ITKF organization set up prior to the ISKF being created and the two groups separately developed students and competed for control of the JKA name in the states. It was generally accepted that Nishyama was seen as a rebel and off shoot of the JKA while Okizaki was one of Nakayama Senseis seniors and it is reasonable to assume his organization, hosting a who's who of seniors, was seen as the true representative of the JKA in the US and Canada at that time.

Outside of the US the JKA had a stronger and more internationally cohesive structure that lead to huge expansion and more fluid control of the groups. Kase Taiji ran most of Europe from France, Ochi Hideki held his sway over Germany, Shirai Hiroshi was sent to develop Karate in Italy, Enoeda Keinosuke ran a solid and successful team out of the UK, Miyazaki Satoshi pushed his rugged training system into Belgium and his students found great success under him, he also played host to many young JKA instructors as they had to do apprenticeships abroad. European Karate became a model of success by creating pockets of influence that were given to instructors who kept them clear of competition from other seniors. Also men like Kase ran their areas with a sense of respect of others "spheres of influence" not opening clubs in others locations. Other instructors all respected each other but looked to seniors like Kase for keys to success and for ideas on how to run their areas properly. The competition and issues that the US had were limited in Europe because of the respect that men like Kase commanded not just from their students, but their peers. If an instructor would create issues it was quickly and respectfully dealt with. The issue was never let to fester and create issues. Also, each country was smaller than the US and as such it was easier, ego wise and logistically. An instructor could be in charge of a whole country and know that they held court over the entire nation…and it would be the size of New Jersey.

The JKA established foot holds in other areas of the world by sending out instructors or by training and developing locals to help spread the JKA around the world Men like Higashino Tetsuma in Brazil, Ishiyama Katsuya in Venezuala, Okamoto Hideki in Syria , Tanaka Masahiko in Denmark, Sasaki Kunio in the Philippines, Matsumara Hiroshi in Mexico, and men like Stan Schmidt in South Africa all contributed to the stability and growth of JKA Karate worldwide. The common goals and focus of growing the style and organization was so strong that the men who represented the JKA in these nations worked with the JKA to build and not to take their own piece of the pie and leave. They were given the sense of ownership but also the sense of belonging. The JKA grew rapidly and today is practiced by approximately 5,000,000 people in almost every country in the world. It is seen as the biggest single organization in the world and the Shotokan style grew alongside the lead organization to be the largest, most practiced style of Karate in the world.

While the JKA was spreading, creating the innovative instructor training program and expanding the "old boys" of the Shotokai in Japan were also trying to make moves. Obata Isao of Keio University organized the Zen Nihon Gakusei Karate do Renmei (roughly meaning a student's perspective of Karate) hoping to unify the collegiate practitioners of all styles. Ultimately however it evolved into a loose structure sheltering disaffected Shotokan students who wished to pursue Karate but not follow the JKA or other Shotokan groups or the JKA and the hard line groups. This development would be enveloped and absorbed by the Shotokai, led by Egami and Hironishi of Chuo University, Hiroshi Noguchi of Waseda and a few others. While not Obata's original intent, his group shifted its alliance from JKA to a more independent group and finally fell under the Shotokai banner.

The Shotokai saw its share of splitting as well. The principle leadership of Egami and Hironishi tried to maintain the old style of spirit driven training with no tournaments and expansion was the last thing on their minds. Oshima Tsutomu from Waseda University, and a student of Obata, was the first to expand out of Japan and arrived in Los Angeles in 1956 to start teaching. Founding Shotokan Karate of America Oshima Sensei stuck to many of the old Shotokai rules and traditions, such as halting the Yudansha ranking process at 5th Dan. He also taught and interacted with established JKA instructors for some time until a conflict between him and Nishiyama put an end to this practice. Oshima is still listed as a Shotokai master but the connection is tenuous at best, his organization is larger and much more powerful as a separate entity and his focus on training to develop students and participate in tournaments makes him very unique compared to the purest Shotokai groups.

By the 1970's big names like Kanazawa Hirokazu broke from the JKA over style and training differences, as well as a great deal of financial issues. Kanazawa helped found the Shotokan Karate International with Asano Shiro. The JKA however remained fairly calm and lost few members while Nakayama Sensei was alive. Reaction to splintering's was consistently very subtle and never excessive or over reactive. The JKA lost very few groups to the splinter groups because of this.

While the first big split was the JKA and the Shotokai splitting its important to acknowledge that instructors like Kanazawa leaving did have an impact as Kanazawa was a very important part of the JKA marketing machine as the first real champion of the JKA along with Mikami. The split with the Shotokai had much more tangible impact simply because it was not amicable and the two sides showed a great deal of stress and infighting with the failing relations.

The reality is that the technical gap that developed between the two groups was very narrow. With a few differences in Katas practice and the fact that the Shotokai still participated in relatively little free style sparring in their Dojo's. From the 1960's forwards the JKA pursued the study of Karate from a very scientific point of view and focused on body mechanics, kinesiology, anatomy, physics and modern psychology while the Shotokai focused mostly on content that Funakoshi Sensei had taught and some of the practitioners drifted slightly into more esoteric styles of practice. Each group continued to insist that its practiced Karate exactly as Funakoshi had intended however the JKA's argument may hold a bit more water as the writings of Master Funakoshi suggested that Karate was an "unfinished art" and it should continue to grow and change, to develop and build. Funakoshi had said that "Mans knowledge and circumstances grew and changed" suggesting that the practice of Karate should also change with the advent of more knowledge. However it is still a traditional art and the roots should only be strengthened by innovation and advancement.

Second Generation students and boom of Karate

When Funakoshi Sensei retired from teaching he focused a great deal on ensuring that the style he created was in good hands. Upon his passing he left a strong willed group of individuals to grow his art. The fact that people like Egami Shigeru, Nakayama Masatoshi, Nishiyama Hidetake, Kase Taiji, Obata Isao and Harada Mitsusuke could not get along is not a shock at all! Strong willed and bull headed is how some were referred to. None of this is a bad thing at all! It would be very difficult for these men to grow an organization the way that the Shotokan system did if they were not very strong willed men. The accomplishments that each man made in advancing the system would never have been possible if they were not all individually strong and wanted to build something great.

These men were all taught at different times and represented different eras and ideals even though they were mostly in the same generation of students. The second generation that Funakoshi had taught mostly after world war two included many of these men who would have been juniors before the war and came into their own after. Men like Kase Taiji, who was a student of Obata Isao at Senshu University. His training was greatly influenced by Gigo and Giching Funakoshi and Nakayama Masatoshi of the JKA, but also Genshin Hironishi who was a Shotokai senior. His style was a cross between the Shotokai and JKA systems. He was representative of the cross training that actually was prevalent at the time. He took Shotokan after a lengthy study of other arts like Aikido, Kendo and of course Judo. This again was more the norm for the time than pure Karate only students. His training was also more Shotokai than JKA but he still represented the JKA in France and acted as the Dojo enforcer for the JKA prior to leaving for the European growth program.

Nakayama Masatoshi trained for a while with Funakoshi Sensei before the war, but spent the war in China. When Nakayama came back he worked to rebuild the JKA with others and worked hard to relearn and develop his Karate knowledge after the war. It is said that Nakayama learned a great deal of Kung Fu while traveling in China which influenced his training and understanding of Karate. Nakayama and the others would have learned a great deal different system from Funakoshi than was taught to the other seniors who formed the Shotokai, as they were learning and adapting more from Gigo than his father.

While Nakayama was a young experienced translator and exchange student who had a good education and was one of the Takushuko boys, Harada and Egami were trained more under Gigo Funakoshi in his experimental years. They were members of the Shotokai growth and both groups represented different training, he was also from a school that was not seen as being on the same level as the schools they graduated from and even with the pedegree of being the son of a famous Kenjutsu instructor and a doctor, Nakayamas studies at Tokushoku university put him at a social disadvantage when dealing with Harada and Egami. While Nakayama had also trained under Gigo the majority of his training came from those that worked daily with Master Funakoshi.

Obata Isaao, the son of a wealthy business man, was originally a very big part of the driving force to develop the JKA. Obata organized the original students of Funakoshi after the war to bring the group together and form a governing body for their style of Karate. He was very well versed in business practice and had a great sense of what was needed to create a solid organization. He created the frame work for the JKA and was the first chairman of the new JKA. Obata, Along with his peers Takagi Seichi, Noguchi Hiroshi, Egami Shieru and Hironishi Genshi were the senior council that brought all the members together originally to form the JKA or at least to establish a foundation for an organization of sorts. Obata Isao originally brought together members of the Wasada, Keio and Takushoku universities to form the council leading the organization, with the Takushoku group making up the majority of the instructors who would form the core of the JKA.

Obata being the Chairman offered some early challenges for the forming of the JKA. He shared several views with people like Egami and Hironishi that were counter to the actual route that the JKA was taking in its formation. Obata felt that the Takushoku group was way too aggressive in its expansionist methodology as it tried to grow and build across Japan and out into the rest of the world. He wanted to slow things down, create a more firm and smaller group first. He also did not like the training that the Takushoku group advocated, feeling that the training was far too regimented and militaristic with a focus on sport and a system that developed around the ideas he saw as foreign, which has mostly developed out of Kendo training most of the seniors had undertaken in their youth. He did not like the fact that the structure of class was starting to look like military drills, he was used to the Shotokai system of training more individually, which was great in smaller groups but very difficult to maintain when the groups grew to large, which was the goal of the Takoshoku group.

Obata was also a unique choice for the chairman's position as he was not a very dynamic or enigmatic person as the position required. He was shy, relaxed in his approach to things and a known introvert. He had a hard time maintaining control or convincing others of his vision of the group, which again was dramatically different from those who were part of the JKA push to become a professional organization. Shortly after being named the Chairman his JKA peers began to break away and go back to training the way they wanted too and for the most part ignored the chairman's technical ideals hoping his money and family would help them build while they ignored his attempts to direct the training and technical aspects of the organization.

The university groups eventually decided that this new group was not what they wanted and driven by Egami and Hironishi they broke away, never having put their full efforts behind the newly created JKA, this solidified and reunited the Shotokai officially. They placed Master Funakoshi as the President and Egami and Hironishi as the leading seniors. Obata pushed forwards and formed the JKA but he was never happy with the direction the new group was going. Shortly after Obata left the JKA as well, sighting his unease with the direction that Karate was going with a focus on sport and competition as well as harder training systems that hurt students. This is when he formed the "All-Japan University Karate League which later merged with the Shotokai.

Essentially this was the first split in the JKA, it created a dynamic that actually helped the JKA grow as students saw the options for training as a professional organization focused on sport and growth or the university based group opposed to sport and training in the old ways with a focus on the spiritual side of Karate. As Japan was a forward thinking and progressive country after the war, looking for new ways to do everything and more modern approaches, the JKA appealed to far more University students than the Shotokai did. This also gave the JKA a bit more of a free hand at changing the curriculum and developing a progressive research and development minded group. The Shotokai stuck close to the teachings and teaching methods of Funakoshi Sensei while the JKA began to alter the Kata and did scientific research to address technical methods, taught larger more structured classes and abandoned the idea of one on one or smaller group classes. Because of this the two systems split greatly and grew apart looking less and less like they came from the same source each passing year.

Other than expansionism and military style training, one of the major stumbling blocks that Obata had with the JKA was the idea that instructors would be professional and would charge for their services. Funakoshi Sensei had no set cost for classes, nor had other instructors "Charged" for services. Most of the time Funakoshi and the others were given "Donations" for living expenses, or they were provided a stipend by the facility they taught in and the facility charged. The JKA wanted to set out rates and have students pay for the training so they could have a stable income to pay rent, apply funds towards expansion and host events like tournaments. This would also entice instructors who had talents teaching to stay with the JKA or go to new locations to teach and take courses like the new instructors training program that was at the time in the works. None of this sat well with Obata who had sunk a great deal of his fortune into expanding the JKA and forming this new group to lead the Shotokan world. The new process for growth and this new idea about building a new professional division did not sit well with Obata or the other traditionalists but it was the key to expansion and development abroad and in Japan.

While Obata was the business mind behind the JKA as well as the bank roll for much of the early development, and served as the first chairman, he was joined in the organizing of the group by a bright young and very talented instructor in Nakayama Masatoshi. Nakayama Sensei was junior to Obata and had also trained directly under Funakoshi Gichin and Funakoshi Gigo. Nakayama Sensei came from a famous family of Kendo masters with deep roots in the martial arts. Nakayama was also a direct descendant of the Sanada Clan; his grandfather was Nakayama Naomichi, a surgeon and the last of his family line to be the head of his family style of Kenjutsu. Nakyama's father was also a surgeon and expected him to follow in his footsteps and become a doctor or more specifically a surgeon.

Nakayama Sensei had grown up in Taipei, as his father had been stationed there as a military doctor during the occupation of Taiwan. Around 1935, the Japanese government began an Island wide assimilation project to bind the island of Taiwan to the Japanese empire. It was during this time that Nakayama was growing up on the island nation. In 1938 Taiwan had close to 309,000 Japanese settlers on the main island, most were business men and farmers who owned cash crop producing farms that helped support Japan. Apart from academics, Nakayama participated in Kendo, Judo, swimming, tennis, track and field running and Skiing.

Nakyama had entered the Takushoku University in 1932 to study Chinese against his fathers wishes, as he wanted him to follow him into medicine, and accidentally stumbled into a Karate class taught by Funakoshi Sensei and his son, which started his passionate love of Karate. Nakayama Sensei had misread the schedule for the Kendo class and arrived several hours before. He watched the class for a short time and was fascinated with the art; he once said that he began training the next class and never did make it out to the Kendo program.

Nakayama graduated from the Takushoku University in 1937 with a Second Dan in Karate and took a post as an interpreter in China, he did not come back to Japan until after the war. By all accounts Nakayama was not a physically gifted student and his ability was average, but his mind was incredibly acute and he picked up things fast. He studied Karate from a very scientific point of view and worked to understand physically how to make his abilities better. He was also a great instructor and a very dedicated student.

Having been part of the restoration of Funakoshi's students post world war two and having been seen as a fairly advanced student he took up the job of assisting Obata in organizing the JKA early on. Because he was seen as a senior student who could teach well and had continued training to some degree while in China the group elected him the head instructor when the JKA was established in 1949 and he was promoted to Sandan or third Dan in 1951.

Four years later the organization promoted him to fifth Dan, the highest level that Funakoshi himself had ever promoted someone to, and helped establish the first instructors training program based on the sport science he was infusing into the training protocols and technical changes in the JKA system. By 1961 Nakayama had accepted a promotion to eight Dan and finally he accepted ninth Dan. Nakayama was officially the highest ranking Karate master in the world....actually he was the highest ranking master each time he was promoted, which also lead to issues in the Karate world as Funakoshi himself was only ever appointed a fifth Dan and only ever gave out a fifth Dan. Many said that the new ranks were grandstanding and that Nakayama was not deserving of such ranking. He was a small man with good teaching skills but most felt it was political in general and that rank should not be used in such a way. When Nakayama Sensei passed away he was promoted posthumously to Tenth Dan, this was originally the highest rank and supposed to be granted to those who had rank an organization and passed away. The JKA also promoted Funakoshi to Tenth Dan upon granting Nakayama his rank.

Nakayama Sensei rested control of the JKA from Obata and along with men like Nishyama, Kase and others to form a solid organization that was very progressive. While students like Kanazawa and others left to form their own organizations, the JKA continued on focused on the promotion of the new Karate that Nakayama and his JKA had researched and developed. The new system had one foot firmly in the new age of sport Karate but the other firmly planted in traditional values and thinking. They all worked very hard to spread the JKA outside of Japan and pushed to create one of the strongest organizations in the world with a dynamic system of Karate that would be seen as the standard for all organizations and a body of instructors able to push forwards and create what we see today as Shotokan's premier organization.

Nakayama Sensei Era

Post world War two saw JKA Karate began to grow and its popularity took off in Japan and abroad. It took a lot of hard work to turn around the popularity after the war, most martial arts were viewed as militant and part of the populist wave that had swept Japan into the war. Karate was partial exempt from this as their part in training the military was relatively unknown and they were a newer martial art that was actually strange to the Japanese as much as it was to the rest of the world.

After the war the seniors had a great deal of rebuilding and organizing to do. The hard work began to pay off as the JKA and Karate in general began to rebuild and grow again, and in October 1957 the first All Japan Karate Championships were held in Tokyo to help push Karate to the forefront. The tournament was limited to 4 categories; Mens individual (general) Kumite, Men's Kata, a group (Prefecture) Kumite and a Team Kata training division. The Men's Kumite (General) was won by Kanazawa Hirokazu with Tsuyama Katsunori as second place and Nakaumura Masahide as third place winner. The success of the tournament led to a huge increase in the popularity of Karate amongst young University students and the JKA began to boom again. The tournament was the brain child of Nakayama Sensei and it really helped kick start the process of growth.

Once the annual tournament system was established the JKA branches in towns, schools and as many as 40 University and college clubs in Japan began to fill up with new members. This mean that the JKA needed to reorganize and become more of a unit organized like a company. In 1958 Master Nakayama was appointed the Chief instructors position to oversee the growth and development of the organization he helped found. By this time the tournaments were a hot commodity for anyone wanting to prove themselves in Karate. Kanazawa Hirokauz and Mikami Takayuki shared the first place position after a great battle in which no one was appointed a clear victory over the other. The tournament was a historical moment, the tension created by the match and the drama of not having a specific winner drew people into the sporting aspect of the event and the flood gates to the dojos began to spill over as memberships doubled and the redoubled.

The following two years saw an unprecedented growth in the JKA and men like Shirai Hiroshi, Sato Masaki, Iwaizumi Toru and Asai Testuhiko shared the stage with Kanazawa and

Mikami in the tournament's most popular Mens Kumite division. The Tournaments that were once seen as a terrible affront to the Karate training by the old boys in the Universities were now the reason that the JKA was growing and membership skyrocketed. The popularity of local tournaments aided in the growth and the JKA all Japan tournaments were seen as the pinicle of perfection when it came to the competitions and those that trained and competed were the superstars of the JKA, and thus the superstars of Karate.

In 1961 Asai Tatsuhiko was crowned the grand champion and came in first in the tournament and Shirai Hirosi came in second with Enoeda Keinosuke and Mikami Takayuki placing after them. More importantly for the development of Karate…. the crown Prince of Japan (now Emperor Hirohito) attended the 5th annual event, which was a huge boost to the event and saw attendance grow and swell the crowds numbers, the event was now an annual event that was growing beyond imagined numbers and helping Karate Dojos swell with new members as well. The new notoriety that the JKA was getting helped build membership and with that came new divisions in the tournament including women's events and youth events. Over the years the event has grown to also include a separate University event, High school events due to the increase in participants. The event is also now only seeded with participants who have earned a spot at the national level by doing well in regional events.

During this period the JKA further developed its Karate Instruction system as well, and greatly expanded its branch Dojos through Japan. The organization had been sending out its most accomplished students to the world as a professional instructor base. Between its inception and 1961 the JKA instructor training program graduated men like Mikami Takayuki, Kanazawa Hirokazu, Yaguchi Yutaka, Sato Masaki, Saito Shigeru, Mori Osamu, Miyazaki Satoshi, Enoeda Keinosuke and Masaaki Ueki. These men, along with others, went to the Americas, Europe and the Middle East to teach and expand the JKA's influence and organization around the Globe. Establishing Dojos and developing great Karate men themselves the first wave of masters sent out helped to build the JKA organization overseas and establish well known clubs like the Red Triangle club of Enoeda's in Liverpool England that turned out the well-respected English Karate team. Karate was quickly becoming a big hit outside of Japan and growing as quickly as it had inside of Japan.

In 1975 there was some talk of Karate being a prospective event to enter the Olympics, which unto itself is a huge indicator of the success that the art had found after the war. With this possibility in mind the IAKF (International Amateur Karate Federation) was formed by Nishyama Hidetaka Sensei and the first world cup was held in the United States to help build interest and to show the IOC that Karate was a viable event for the Olympics, putting it a full decade ahead of Tae Kwon Do for consideration into the Olympics and only 7 years behind Judo.

The IAKF held the world cup several times over the next few years, however the event veered away from traditional JKA style events to try and create some hype and sensationalism around the Kumite which soured the JKA on the tournament, however the event continued to be very popular in North America, it began to see lower participation by the JKA athletes from Japan. For its part the JKA, wanting to maintain the spirit of the JKA Shobu ippon (Downing the opponent in one blow) system, as such they created the Shoto world cup Karate tournament. In 1985 the first international Shoto world cup was held in Japan and this was attended by over 50 countries, a testament to how international the style had become. The very spirit of the tournament made it electric and the IOC showed greater interest in the Shoto cup than they had the World Cup, creating issues between the JKA and Nishyama.

This period was witness to a spectacular development phase in the JKA and in the art of Karate in general. As a result of continuous training amongst the senior instructors and an environment of cohesiveness under Nakayama Sensei the Karate technical level grew and developed throughout the entire system and with all the groups around the world. For the first time there emerged a clear, scientifically based, practical "Best" form for real Kumite, technical advancements and understanding of how to train and apply Karate. Scientific research was put forwards towards how to move, why things occurred, proper technical advancements in Kicking, punching and even stance work was presented to the JKA with a basis in science and general best practices to avoid injuries and get the most potential out of the athletics of Karate. All of this advancement was because of Nakayama Sensei's drive to modernize Karate and break away from the old Dogma and reliance on mystical, unscientific explanation that the Karate practitioners had first put forth to explain movement skills and technical application. Along with the progress in sending instructors out internationally the new focus was more acceptable to the Western students and this new focus contributed greatly to the advancement and growth of Karate in the west.

In 1986 Nakahara Nobuyuki, a very distinguished business leader and former Tokyo University Karat club member was appointed the 8th Chairman of the JKA. Directly linked to big businesses and the bank of Japan, Nakahara Nobuyuki gave the JKA a new level of prestige and helped grow the organization into its current home. Unlike previous chairmen/presidents Nakahara did not rely on family money or personal finances to build up the prestige of Karate, he made Karate a business and created a solid program for development in this direction. This was the first phase of the JKA really taking itself seriously as an international business and organization. Nakahara served until his resignation in 2015. However his involvement allowed for even greater spurts of growth for the JKA. The membership grew, the new club was purchased and rebuilt to suit the JKA needs and an international instructor's format was created so that the JKA could maintain control over the technical standards of the Karate taught in their name. While the majority of the technical growth was directly related to Nakayama and other seniors, it was Nakahara Nobuyuki who took the format and presented it as a business model to others and made the JKA the business that it became.

Sadly, in 1987, at the height of the JKA growth phase that he had pushed so hard for Nakayama Sensei passed away at the age of 74. Nakayama had been the driving force behind the JKA's technical advancements and growth for many decades and saw the advancements of the system that the JKA put forwards for instructor development, he modernized the organization and made the sustainable and formidable association grow and faced many splits and issues that had challenged the JKA and he pushed to create his dream for a Karate organization. The one thing he did not do when he died was leave a set plan for those that were to take over. The lack of an heir led too many issues we will look at in a while.

The one thing that must be taken into account when you talk about Nakayama Sensei is his passion and genius in creating and developing a system of Karate that would become the largest single organization for Shotokan and even Karate in the world. The JKA is well respected, and seen as the golden standard for Karate organizations to live up to. It's centralized Honbu and strict adherence to the rules laid out by the Headquarters makes this group a well-controlled and long standing organization. However the seniors are all given a great deal of latitude in the way that they teach and the twists that they put on their Karate. Nakayama knew that the organization would see hurdles and challenges, but he also had faith that Karate had to grow, and with it he remembered his roots in Karate and how his dream came to be. The true genius of Nakayama Sensei may have been in the way he dealt with his membership and how he dealt with individuals and make everyone feel like he was offering them something special and specific to them. He was also a great organizer and presented his system of Karate in such a way as anyone could understand and work towards his systems highest levels.

Nakayama Sensei, the blue prints for Modern Shotokan

One more "Dogmatic false truth" is that early training in Shotokan Karate was based on work outs that were about 80% Kata work and 20% Kihon work on average. Very little training of any kind was done with partners and the training in Kumite (Especially free style) was unheard of in clubs that Funakoshi Sensei ran. It is also suggested that training was grounded in Kata work and the little bit of partner work that was done was normally scant and based on Bunkai training only. As you can imagine, this also suggested that there was a large turnover rate in most of the clubs early on.

The suggestion further goes that most of the early student that stuck around and continued to train with Funakoshi did so out of dedication to the arts and spent countless hours practicing Kata, Kihon and Bunkai exclusively, the hours of training created strong technical skills but not a great deal of practical use time. The members lacked the real world application needed to make Karate applicable. It became an esoteric activity that build up the character of the person but did little to generate an art that could be used for sport or even martial skill development.

It was said that Funakoshi had outright banned Kumite because of bad experiences he had in Okinawa or when he first came to Japan. The truth however is that you do hear about University clubs doing Shiai's early on and involving crazy free style Karate that left a lot of people injured as the rules were….well the rules were not existent. Because of the brutal nature of early Kumite it was said that Funakoshi Sensei felt Kumite was not in the true nature of Karate and that the practice of Kumite would create bullies and thugs. While this plays well with the whole "Evolved Kumite" idea, this is not true at all and the story is made up or an over simplification of some facts that don't really support this.

Funakoshi Geigo taught various forms of Kumite and Funakoshi Sensei did not raise an eyebrow when his son was teaching this. It is more likely that at his advanced age Funakoshi Sensei did not participate in Kumite anymore, which led to the story that he banned it or did not like it. Also, the turnover rate in Universities was pretty much non-existent with students training till they graduated.

However, Nakayama knew that Karate would grow quicker and develop a following if it had a dynamic training method, solid base in science and if he formulated a safer way of doing Kumite he could tap into the excitement of sparring that drove other arts like boxing. Essentially Nakayama had to do two things to create the wave of excitement that would transform the university based practice to a business that saw members join from all walks of life. First he had to modernize the approach to Karate training. This meant creating a sport aspect and brining in a great deal of sport science that got rid of old mythology and folk lore-ish training practices and ideas. He also had to introduce a stylized system for teaching Kumite to students. This was accomplished by creating the 1/3/5 step Kumite, and semi free Kumite as stepping stones to free Kumite. This created a safer practice to build up your skills and abilities in partner based interactions. He also had to research how to protect the people doing Kumite, be it stronger rules or sparring equipment.

The Kumite system that the JKA adapted took a great deal of time to design. It's very important to note that many instructors have taken credit for the free style rules that became the Shobu Ippon rules and many state that they were the ones to formulate the system that was finally used, but the truth is that Nakayama formed a committee and studied things like Boxing gloves and other safety equipment to find the acceptable equipment for Kumite. He also studied Judo, Kendo and other arts to formulate the rules and regulations for not only tournament Karate but Kumite in the Dojo. He then took all the information that was taken in and discarded a great deal of the suggestions, threw out whole sections of ideas and refined those that were set aside for him. Finally what he came up with was something that was unique and his, but he always gave credit to those that had helped out, even if all their suggestions were turfed out at the end.

All of these innovations led to the popularity of Dojo Kumite as well as a new form of "traditional" sparring to be adopted that looked new and was much more athletic than the older forms of Kumite that people like Motobu Choki would engage in. In the end, many would take credit for "creating" the new rules, and many who did had little to nothing to actually do with creating the rules for Kumite, while others were part of a group that Nakayama used to test his ideas and to work out the specifics of his Kumite practice.

Nakayama Sensei worked very diligently to remove a great deal of the old useless Dogma from the training that had been common place in the Karate systems of the time. The system he developed was much more linear and explosive and used a great deal of his Kendo experience to develop the trained movement skills and he worked on creating a very science based influence to the training. Now fully modernized with the new practices of Kumite and the sport aspect engraining itself in the organization his influence was creating the system and style we know today. With the advent of his different administrative (expansionist) styles and his ideas and influence on teaching the JKA began to spread far outside of Japan and the JKA started to become the Empire we know it to be now.

One story I was told a long time ago had to do with a senior, unnamed, master being challenged by a Motobu black belt to show him the "new" system. The idea of the challenge was that the Motobu black belt felt that the new JKA Kumite system was a farce and could not be used to defend one's self. The instructor from the JKA (who I suspect was Kase Taiji) politely turned down the suggestion to "show" the new system several times before lamenting and lining up with the Motobu-ryu instructor. The whole thing was over in seconds from what I was told. The JKA instructor (Again, sounds like Kase Sensei) first swept the Motobu representative and the launched a Oi Zuki at the face of the instructor that was not blocked. The whole engagement was seconds long and the Motobu Ryu instructor did not have a chance to defend himself let alone attack.

Now this story MAY be wishful thinking and hyperbole that has transformed into a story, but seeing as the suggestion was (on several occasions) it was the gate keeper and Dojo guardian Kase Sensei and he had, on several occasions, been called up on to represent the JKA in street challenges it is not something I easily dismiss.

Nakayama and the modern JKA

The Modern version of the JKA was built around a focused vision of what the JKA should be and how it had to be different from other systems that existed to grow. It had to be a modernized, scientific based program that grew and developing into a professional company. Gone was the need to go to other Karate groups to relearn Kata or get advice on Karate, now the masters were going to use kinesiology experts and scientists who specialized in modern sport to help develop better speed and power in their form. The instructors training program was set up to develop the very best instructors that could then be challenged to be better, and learn the depths of Karate so they could travel and teach, and the advent of the Shiai Karate program was in full swing with major events happening several times a year. The system was logical and scientific, explosive and made up of very basic but dynamic movements and rooted in science with its feet also planted in tradition. This was the Nakayama Era of modern Karate.

During the period of expansion the JKA did not slow down on development and modernization. This was part of what attracted the youth crowd in the universities and drove up the membership in the College clubs. A modern approach to an ancient art was a very exciting approach that saw not only the stands fill with spectators at tournaments, but the Dojos filled with members as well. Many new teaching elements were developed to modernize the instructors program and sent the program saw its graduates travel to the Middle East, Europe, and North America, and all over to spread the system of Karate that the JKA was teaching. They reached out to all corners of the glob and while expanding quickly the organization did so smartly with senior instructor and retired competitors teaching their brand of Karate to help build the JKA internationally, which in turn brought international competition to the Japanese. By winning most of the international competitions and only sending their very best to challenge at tournaments the Japanese created a mystique of invulnerability at the tournaments.

The JKA undertook a huge program of expansion and put a great deal of effort into research and development of a more scientific approach to Karate training and its techniques under Nakayama Sensei. They used modern science and equipment to measure force production, studies of Stance, posture and movement all turned to newer sciences to help build a more solid technical understanding of how to improve these points. Biomechanics and Kinesiology were used, not hyperbole and Pseudo-Sciences as in the past, based on observation alone. The end result of this effort is that many books on the subjects were written by Nakayama and members of the JKA as well as a system for training athletes and layperson alike that would produce the best results in movement as well as helping with health and self-defense. The true essence of JKA Karate was developed, refined and introduced by instructors of the instructor training programs to instill the new art to a new generation of students around the globe.

The advent of professional Karate instructors cannot be understated in importance when referencing the growth of Karate around the globe. Prior to the program most Karate instructors were simply senior student that had trained in the University clubs and maybe had reached a "team captain" level for the club, so they got to lead classes. When they left school a few of them would open small clubs or come back and teach, none of them were well trained beyond the strict military style training from what I was told. Admittedly they were talented students, and talented team captains as well as competitors, but they lacked refinement and insights that the program offered.

This old system had many stumbling blocks, like limited time to train with the instructors between family, school and possible work responsibilities and this lead to different methods of teaching the same technique, which served to confuse students. Also, each year the "captain" would graduate and go into the work force, leaving less time for him to visit the school to help out. This caused little continuity in teaching the different skills needed. The students leading classes often supported other instructors and had only a few years of training themselves. The official instructor coming in to teach once every few weeks had to correct issues and spend time correcting issues and had little time to teach more advanced skills

This modern JKA built itself on first researching and finding the best ways to perform techniques, and then altering Kata to mold it to the training needs and using science over mythical methods, working with experts in movement skills to improve and standardize movement requirements and most of all on teaching instructors to teach these techniques all the same way. This meant that the JKA uniformity in teaching and practice, the only way to create a brand that made sense and could be marketed to the masses. This also meant that the JKA now had clubs that were not vastly different in their approach to Karate, ideas did not start to clash in clubs and different approaches were not formed, but rather all the clubs taught Karate the JKA way and in similar ways. The qualified instructors were then assigned posts that would help the JKA expand. Only a few instructors started to move away from the core values of teaching and standardized teaching methods that the JKA was teaching and while a few were big name people the general body of the JKA recognized the system that was being laid out for them, they were behind the chief instructor and all helping to develop the JKA.

The first seven chairmen of the organization were selected for their ability to bring prominence to the JKA and to help create a structure in the business end of the organization that meant growth and expansion for the new, young JKA. The first Chair was Seigo Kichinosuke, who was selected as chair because he was seen as an honorable man and a person that could bring an air of propriety and legitimacy to the JKA. His job was to provide a presence to the JKA while it was forming. He allowed the JKA to create bonds with government groups and agencies as well as investors in the JKA's future. The organization knew that they needed to focus on looking legitimate and creating a feeling and image that they were a legitimate martial arts organization to grow and be accepted.

A string of government retired ministers like Second Chairman Iwao Yamazuki and Masutani Shuji then were elected to provide a political stability to the group and oversight that allowed the business end of things to smooth be run while Nakayama Sensei build the structure of the JKA and developed young talent in teaching Karate. Kakuei Tanaka was raised to the post of chairman and elevated the level of the JKA in the government's eye as he was the former prime minister of Japan. Under him the JKA made huge inroads in gaining support by the government for their planned events and exposure. All of the chair people and the board created a lot of success and gave Nakayama Sensei the freedom to focus on development of the organization. It also allowed the JKA to raise and save funding for a future project.

In 1972 the JKA found itself in a unique situation that needed rectifying to continue seeing the growth they were enjoying at that time. The facility they trained in was not big enough and needed to be fixed up a bit. Instead of investing big money in an upgrade of their current facility the chairman, Kosaka Zentaro, whom had been the minister of foreign affairs and minster of construction, moved the JKA to Ebisu. This move to the new location opened up more opportunity to train and grow the tournament training aspect by opening up space for extra training classes and creating a more modern facility for the members. The new Dojo was in a great location and had a newer building that had been a bowling alley. The money was invested and the building was renovated to make it useable by the JKA.

The Group stayed in that facility focusing on growth around the world until the appointment of Nakahara Nobuyuki, a distinguished businessman and banker, who lead the JKA into a new and modern facility, sadly however Nakayama did not see this as he had passed away prior to this.

Nakahara and Nakayama Sensei worked well with each other. The growth and development focus of Nakayama was complimented by Nakahara's business sense and ability to raise capital for different functions of the JKA. This included a world tour that saw the 74 year old chief instructor visit even my little area on the map in Canada. The tour was his way of raising the spirits of JKA instructors and creating a common focused goal for all the instructors around the world, the focus was to be on the growth and development of Karate. It was a unification tour that proved a huge success! The unification of groups and the idea of pushing Karate to be bigger and not just Karate but JKA Karate was his main purpose at each venue as he traveled across the world. He felt that the only way forward was a unified Shotokan Karate focus, the splits had to end and the work had to begin. The monumental effort that he put forwards to grow the JKA paid off and the organization was growing and growing at a incredible rate. The JKA was seen as a power house of Karate in Japan with other organizations and styles playing catch up and not seeing the success that the JKA was having. However, Nakayama's health was starting to wane and he often had to rest long periods after teaching and his travels were taking their toll on his ability to teach for long periods. Nakayama Sensei had been in a major Skiing accident years back and injuries and the taxing schedule for teaching and travel were starting to weigh on him.

When Nakayama Sensei returned to Japan after the world tour to promote and shore up the JKA his health quickly went downhill as he could not recuperate from the stress of the travels. Years before the tour he had been teaching downhill skiing as part of his University classes, he was a full time PE instructor as part of his University Job. His students were all caught in a horrible Avalanche, but as my instructor told me one time, Nakayama Sensei had seen this accident happening and reacted immediately and saved his whole class, but he had been caught under the full weight of the avalanche and had almost died. The doctors said he would not live, then when he woke up they warned his family he would never walk again. Upon walking they told him his years of being a Karate master were over. He resumed his active schedule traveling and teaching shortly after his full recovery, however his body was still not 100%. His long battle with the ill health the accident caused him put strain on his heart and his body. After a short battle with ill health the genius and architect of the JKA passed away April 15th 1987 in Tokyo hospital.

After his passing the JKA and the Shotokan world would begin to change. His dream of a unified JKA that saw a technical growth and progress in promoting itself was in limbo. Many of his plans were abandoned and the single minded approach of the JKA to get things done was altered by fractions in the group. Most people who trained with him saw his genius and the stories my instructor passed on to me about his classes and his personality will gleefully haunt and inspire me forever. He had a powerful and commanding presence and his One of my most embarrassing and regretful decisions I have made regarding my training revolves around the grand tour that Nakayama and the JKA held in the 70's I had the chance to train with Sensei Nakayama in 1987 and choose not to, granted I was a young kid of 14 at the time and thought that he would be back to teach and I would train with him them. I was shy and honestly felt that I may have embarrassed myself and my Sensei in front of the genius of the JKA, a title that Dingman Sensei bestowed on Nakayama Sensei often in classes. Nakayama and several other instructors came to Winnipeg and my instructor acted as his driver across the prairies. The stories my instructor have told me over the years are an illustration of a man that was inquisitive, talented and honest with everyone he met. He was both intimidating and held a magnetic personality. His English was very good but he used a translator to assist and his techniques and understanding of how to improve movement skills was on the level of genius.

Del Phillips Sensei of Saskatchewan tells a story of Nakayama warming up playing with him doing Kumite. Del Sensei would attack full power and be deflected or redirected with one hand from the master in such away as he was not just unable to strike him but off balance, having to take a step to regain his footing. He once told me that he tried his hardest to strike the master after being told to do so several times and every time he came close a slight touch by Nakayama and he was reeling forwards or driven on an angle forwards stumbling and confused.

Little did I know that was his last visit to Canada, and the start of the issues within my beloved JKA. Nakayama's passing created a wave of chaos that is still being felt in the modern Shotokan world especially the JKA and its off shoots.

Nakayama Passing changed everything

I remember when Shihan Nakayama passed away. The Dojo was very quiet for weeks after the news reached us. My Sensei was hit particularly hard by the news as he had a special affinity for our chief instructor. Immediately after the news hit our club the tangible sadness rolled over the classes. Many of my seniors had trained with the master a few months before and the whole club was raw from the sad news. I remember sitting in the visitors galley waiting for the kids class to start and a lot of the seniors who had been working out were mopping around listless after the announcement had been made. The feeling of melancholy was tangible in the air. They still attended the class but you could feel the difference in the air, it was palatable and overpowered the old scent of hard work and replaced it with melancholy.

Our office manager also was "off". She was a drill sergeant at the best of times and often herded the kids into and out of the class and change rooms, keeping us all on track and keeping us out from under Sensei's feet. However Mavis just sat in the office overwhelmed with the feeling that was seeping into the Dojo. Sensei, who normally spent the majority of his time on the training floor when at the club, sat in his office reading newspapers and drinking coffee waiting for class to start. It's hard to describe the atmosphere as anything but sad. It would take a few weeks for the regular vigor and spirit of the club to pick back up again. The picture of Nakayama Sensei looking down on us as we trained became even more significant as his picture in its golden frame sat next to Funakoshi Sensei watching over us.

After Sensei Nakayama passed away there was a turbulent few years for the JKA both locally and internationally. Many people believe now that when Nakayama Sensei passed away he did not leave a successor and that this fact generated a lot of chaos and in fighting in the JKA that halted the growth and tarnished the organizations reputation. This story became Dogma internationally but it meant that we had to ignore a few major facts that have been erased from the JKA history books.

Again as the story goes, Nakayama Sensei was so powerful a man, having survived a avalanche to save his students lives, and surviving and thriving the rehabilitation to once again become the all-powerful master of the JKA...he did not see his own passing coming. None of this is true by the way, well he did survive an avalanche and he did save his charges lives, but he was never the same...struggled through rehabilitation and physically was unable to do as much as he could prior to the accident, and some people suggest he planned for the succession of power when he would retire or pass away. However, as you will see...the story has a purpose and is retold for a reason.

This story of no successor was told over and over in clubs years after Nakayama Sensei passed, and it was also told more recently at a meeting I attended as the conversation turned to our current head instructor and the splits we had with the Asai Sensei said of the group. We were discussing how the split happened and the ramifications and one of the instructors piped up and said "well if Nakayama had left a heir to the "crown" of chief instructor we would not have seen that split.....but he did leave a heir to the Chief instructors post....just no one liked his pick and after some time of the heir apparent working as the new chief instructor...an internal war civil (and I suspect not so civil by Japanese standards) developed.

At the time of Nakayama Senseis passing he was working closely with Asai Tetsuhiko, a talented younger Karate instructor known for his flamboyant technical execution and fluid Karate. Asai Sensei was, at that time, the chair for the technical committee and served as the Technical Director of the JKA. He was by all accounts the back up and next in line for the Chief instructor chair. While the JKA was made up of many great instructors, super impressive sport stars and so very many talented and smart me, Asai Sensei was the next man in charge by all accounts.

Nakayama was grooming his junior to step in as the Chief instructor of the organization and it was not a fact that was hidden in the least. While Nakayama Shihan was set on Asai becoming his replacement, upon Nakayama Sensei's passing many felt that Abe Keigo was the natural for next in line to be the chief instructor. Abe was extremely loyal to Nakayama and was known for his solid fundamentals and attention to detail, his rabid loyalty to Nakayama and his passion for the fundamentals that Nakayama Sensei had laid out.

Abe Sensei followed what Nakayama Sensei taught to a tee and would never think of making any changes to what he was taught. While some wanted Abe to be the heir to the Chief instructor Nakayama Sensei had felt that Asai was the most suitable choice, not only because he was senior to Abe but also because he had spent more time with Nakayama developing different approaches to the growth and development of the organization.

Nakayama Sensei also liked that Asai was a free thinking person that was open to change, and as we know Nakayama Sensei felt that Karate had not completed its transition and evolution, it had to be living and growing. Abe would have made a great chief instructor for the JKA if Nakayama was interested in the organization not developing past the current state and sticking to the roots and traditions that had been established, but as he wanted to see more growth his choice had obviously been Asai Sensei.

When Nakayama Shihan passed away Asai Sensei stepped in as the chief instructor and right away friction began to come up with other instructors in the JKA. As I said previously, for years Nakayama Shihan had stated that Karate should be alive and always changing and adapting, however he was also fond of stating that the JKA had a specific feel and style that the students should have maintained but that Karate was ever evolving and changing. You can see the JKA style in practice not only in the JKA but many of the off shoots of the JKA maintain the feel and look that the JKA fostered over years of research and development. When Asai took the helm of the JKA he may have looked to the first statement far more than the second caveat! Asai had a very unorthodox way of teaching Karate and he did not follow the normal JKA path as closely as some assumed a chief instructor should have.

Many with in the JKA felt that any instructor after Nakayama Sensei was a ceremonial place holder. They would be there to maintain the status quo and not make any changes, which appears to have been against what Nakayama Sensei is documented as saying, but also what most of the seniors wanted. Asai Sensei tried to radically change the approach that the JKA took towards Karate practice the same way that previous instructors like Gigo Funakoshi, Kanazawa, Kase and Egami had. He began to openly teach his system in the Hombu Dojo and he also was the biggest proponent of researching and exploring Chinese Martial arts and integrating them into his teaching and his style. He studied crane kung fu and traveled a great deal to China and Taiwan to lean from Chinese masters and incorporated their teaching into his personal training.

The JKA seniors viewed this as a large step back from the scientific approach that Nakayama Shihan had taught and many felt that this was a huge stab in the back to the master who had created the JKA system and recently passed. Further they saw a great deal of the changes that were being implemented as heresy and many refused to listen to Asai, several masters threatened to leave and the structure of the JKA was in peril as seniors who left would drag the Dojos and clubs that supported them along and the JKA would fracture.

Questions about Asai and his loyalty to Nakayama Shihan began arising and people saw the split between what was being taught and the established fundamentals that the JKA style represented were seen as being totally different from what was now being taught at the Honbu Dojo. Nakayama Shihan had worked his whole Karate life to establish the JKA as the "Keepers of the highest tradition", a slogan later taken on by the JKA, and Nakayama Shihan had labored long and hard to spread the system he had built, some seniors took these radical changes as a slap in the face to the patriarch of the JKA.

Years before Nakayama passed away he had set up a small Dojo for live in visiting students in the basement of the building he lived in. He called this the Hoitsugan and it is now ran by Kawawada Sensei. The Dojo served as a personal Dojo for Nakayama and after his passing it became a flag ship of Nakayama's Karate and still exists today serving as a special dojo for visiting Karate-ka to use the dorms and train in special classes ran by Kawawada and others. The idea of keeping static the style that Nakayama and his students had fostered contrasted sharply by the ideas and practice that Asai Sensei was introducing.

Asai's methods were "unique" and "unorthodox" and many of the old guard felt that he had strayed from what was seen as the fundamentals of JKA Karate and that he was no longer a good representative for the JKA. A movement began forming that would oppose Asai Sensei and many of his peers were going to chairman Nakahara with concerns. This is when the true issues came up! And when the trouble started to boil over! By openly attempting to introduce new ideas right away Asai had alienated himself from half of the seniors. Many of the seniors still saw his grip on the chief instructors post as being tentative and they were not impressed by his arguments that the more Chinese system he was introducing was more traditional or that his system was functionally more dynamic, many of his peers saw his teachings as arrogant and his ideas as rebellious against a much loved Icon of Karate.

It is important to note at this time that the time line of the story I am putting forward MAY be a bit off and used by some in the JKA to justify the following war that occurs. I was told by one person that Asai Sensei waited until the end of the legal battle to start making changes to the system he taught and some suggested that when the war began he used that as a reason to implement the changes he had been working on. Now that Asai has passed on I do not feel comfortable taking any one person's perspective as gospel, Rather I will put the story together the way I was told it with a caveat that while it did happen…maybe not in this chronological order.

I was once told by an instructor I trained with that Asai Sensei was good friends with many of the men that opposed him now, they would socialize but when it came to Karate they were not happy with his changes and the attitude that he was in charge and unaccountable to anyone. He said it was a full out rebellion, but a friendly one. It was as if it was a family squabble more than a political or business issue. Asai Sensei himself pointed to the friendliness that he had with the JKA instructors and that they often were jovial towards each other publicly, it was just that they had differences of opinion that made it impossible to work with each other.

Around this time it became evident that Asai Sensei did not like Chairman Nakahara, the chairman of the organization and his junior in Karate. Many of the seniors were complaining to the chairman about Asai's behavior and the changes that he was setting up in the JKA. Nakahara for his part was trying to dictate to Asai what should be taught at the JKA. I was told a story about one suggested event in which Nakahara sat in Asai Sensei's office dictating and instructing Asai on the way to teach the JKA way. He went on for some time about tradition and how Nakayama had taught class. Asai Sensei sat patiently and drank some tea, then went out on the floor and taught a class 100% the opposite of what Nakahara had told him to….while Nakahara sat angrily watching. The chair then got up and left the Dojo, this was supposedly the episode that started the war. Again, this is hyperbole but may have some truth in it.

Chairman Nakahara was also in charge running the business end of things and working to expand the JKA, on other words he held the purse strings. Many of the business choices made were less than popular with Asai Sensei and he often voiced his displeasure with others about Nakahara and the board's financial decisions. Asai had felt that the Chief instructor should have more sway over or complete control of the bank and should make any decisions that the organization was making regarding spending the JKA money, while this had never been the case under Nakayama, Asai felt that it was only right that the head of the organization should be signing the cheques.

While it may have seemed that the arguments were purely over business to some or as a reflex by Asai to the questioning of the juniors and his peers, this was more of a loyalty issue. Asai was new to the post of Chief instructor and while he had loyal followers, most of the JKA saw him as someone coming in to make changes and someone that they hoped would be a place holder after Nakayama Shihans passing. However Asai began making changes immediately after taking office and this caused a great deal of stress with some of the members who were seniors and who had been loyal to the previous master for years. These disagreements with Nakahara grew over time as more and more of a divide began to form.

For many of the seniors Asai Sensei's views and training were not in line with what Master Nakayama had taught but more of an advanced training process and some of the changes and new techniques that Asai had tried to introduce was simply "personal training" or his interpretation of Nakayama Karate. Several of his supporters simply trained the old way while supporting the founder of the "new Methods". Asai was introducing new ideas and practice and his demonstrations that he gave were touted as the "New JKA" or "New methods". To some traditionalists that was a total affront to the traditions they had come to love and were seen as Asai grandstanding and seeking to rest his control over the JKA by putting his personal stamp on the organization far too soon after taking the position of Chief instructor.

While this chaos was going on many of the seniors were asking him to step down so that the JKA could remain on the current path and honor Nakayama Shihans vision of Karate. I can remember my instructors Sensei coming to Winnipeg to teach a seminar and discussing openly that the issues were bad in Japan. Many of the masters were not happy in North America as they felt passed over for the head man's Job and a few were very unhappy that Asai was selected as the replacement. While my instructor sat and listened to his Sensei talk and nodded his recognition of the issue I sat near with my back to them so they did not know I was listening. The conversation was an eye opener that our organization was in trouble at the highest level. But, as we were ISKF at the time, it was obvious that Okizaki Sensei and the other seniors in the JKA and its branch organizations would not let this issue continue very long. The board would meet and clear up this issue to save the JKA.

As an aside I have always felt that Asai was a unique choice for Chief instructor, one that was destined to cause turmoil in the end. He was a visionary and wanted to create his own system. As evidence his system of Shotokan was created when he left the office and as part of his personal training he created many Kata (like 60 plus) to help his students master his movement patterns and ideals. I have felt that someone like Abe or even Kase would be a better suited candidate for the position. Abe would have been a staunch traditionalist and also held high posts in the JKA and Kase, while still a bit of an old school guy, would have served as a valid choice because he had been the JKA enforcer for many years during the early "Dojo war" era and commanded a great deal of respect. I could even see the JKA recalling someone like Okizaki, Mikami, Nishyama or others to Japan to take over, but that's a bit of a harder sell as they had a huge group he ran in the Americas and it would mean giving up or altering that relationship greatly. Also, some of the more seniors had stepped on some toes on their own.

The sides were drawn and on one side was Asai's loyal group of seniors including men like the dynamic Yahara Mikio, Abe Keigo (a loyal Nakayama Stalwart), Kagawa Masao (the incredible kicking machine), Yamaguchi Toru (the tiger!) Isaka Akihito (a unique Karate person himself) and Pemba Tamang (an Indian Karate student). I have been told multiple times that all of these loyal men worked hard to convince Asai that fighting for his position was the right thing to do. They felt that he was the heir that Nakayama had wanted and his new vision was the way to go. These seniors had mostly trained under Asai Sensei coming up in the ranks and were loyal to their instructor. While some, like Yahara and Kagawa, were not changing their training, they were still supporting Asai and wanting the JKA to simply stay one group. The Katas that Asai introduced were adopted by some but Yahara and Abe stuck to the old training and did not adopt them, but they supported Asai in his research and his stake on the JKA heads position.

The other side of this chasm was the Nakahara backed group. The instructors were notable masters like Master teacher Ueki Sensei, Kumite king Tanaka Sensei, The man that Nakayama himself had said was the personification of perfect technique Osaka Sensei! Other masters also felt that Asai was not only introducing a very different version of what Nakayama Shihan had taught, but he was also trying to run the organizations business end, something Nakayama Shihan did not do himself. Most of the overseas masters were siding with Nakahara out of respect for Nakayama Sensei's system and loyalty to the JKA brand name. As Nakayama himself had recently completed his world unification tour it was a bad time to advocate change from his brand of Karate and Asai had not realized this when he started making major changes to the curriculum and ideals that formed the foundation of Nakayama Sensei's JKA system.

Those loyal to the Nakayama Brand of JKA saw the handpicked Chairman as trumping the upstart Technical director turned Chief instructor, they also felt that the JKA system was working in the right direction without the changes and that the radical left turn that Asai Karate represented was too much of a divergence from the traditional norms for them to take. None of the senior instructors, some of which outranked Asai at that time, agreed that abandoning years of scientific research, biomechanical research and use of kinesiology to analyze the movements in Karate was an acceptable choice. Nor did they favor introducing Chinese theory and mysticism ideas back into Karate after Nakayama himself had worked so hard to create the more advanced and science based style of Karate. They all asked Asai to leave his post and step down as a member of the JKA council and perhaps even leave the JKA.

From what I have read and been told what happened during the split was both unusual and uncomfortable for all parties concerned. While both the chairman led group and the Chief instructor led group went to battle in the courts for ownership of the JKA name and all that came with it, they continued to share the JKA facilities and name. The headquarters Dojo was split down the middle so to speak with several days a week dedicated to one side and then the rest of the time to the opposing group. Training opposing nights they basically evacuated the headquarters club on the nights that the other side was using the facility making the use of the training hall a major issue. To the outside world this was not seen and the groups tried to keep the arguments in the courts and act civilly to each other as much as possible. Overseas we were told a bit about the unrest but only when court cases were concluded. In typical Japanese style the drama was kept under wraps as much as possible and as a student in Canada we only knew about the big things like court cases as a periphery and normally unspoken event.

When the masters came to Canada to teach it was only spoken about to my instructor in a closed office meetings or at his home when only the master and my instructor were present. Most of what we were told was "it does not matter, shut up and train" and that was about it. The chaos and dissent that was affecting the organization was kept as low key as possible and our training went on as usual with little to no ripples reaching us in Canada. It was an unspoken truth in our club that regardless of the outcome we would not be siding with Asai Sensei and if his side won the court cases, we would stay ISKF and true to whatever the leadership of that group decided. Looking back years later it becomes obvious to me that there was a lot of issues we were never told about and things that may have affected my training and my interest in the JKA and ISKF if I had been privy to them. Thankfully I was ignorant of them at the time.

To identify the two groups more clearly they took on different names to associate them with their stances. One side was called the Nakahara Group as they were associated with Chairman Nakahara, the Asai group took on the name of Matsuno group, and this name was used as the main financial supporter of the Asai group was Matsuno Raizo. Matsuno was also one of the major instigators in a event that caused the split. Asai wanted Matsuno to replace Nakahara as the wealthy business man supported Asai and Nakahara represented someone that Asai would have an uphill battle with even over technical adjustments, and by all accounts Asai wanted the clear road for him to control the financials and technical aspects of the JKA. He wanted no checks or balances to his governance of the JKA. This signaled the first big split in the JKA. Prior to this small groups would split, normally one big name person would leave to run their own organization after having been JKA for some time, such as Kanazawa Sensei, but it had never seen a split in which the groups involved both wanting to be the JKA and use the JKA name still. This would not be the last big split but it was the first large and the most significant split the JKA was to see in its life time.

More on the Second Chief instructor and the Court.

To say that the split was not an amicable and friendly one would be an understatement! Both sides laid claim to the JKA name and its licenses and neither would relent in their attempts to cement their rights to the name and all the JKA holdings and heritage. The struggle for ownership of the name would last a decade with back and forth court battles plunging the JKA into the courts time and time again. One side would say that Nakayama Sensei would have put his faith in his style, the loyal seniors and the Chairman as well as the board owning the rights to the name, the other side would insist that Nakayama Shihan would have moved Asai to the seat of Chief instructor had he been able to before he died. They said that the fact that he was the Technical director of the group for as long as he was should be enough for him to lead the new JKA.

The Asai group also provoked a great deal of the issues by calling a general meeting of members at the Hombu dojo without a set agenda and tried to arrange it so that the students loyal to Asai not only outnumbered the Nakahara side but the voting questions were all in favor of electing Asai as the Chief instructor for the whole of the JKA and that the board would be dismantled. This would mean that Asai could form a new board, one that would give him control in all aspects of the JKA and force the others to capitulate to his new systems or suffer the consequences of crossing the new King.

The Nakahara side found out about this meeting and immediately set in motion the legal blockade of the vote that was needed to expunge and delegitimize any vote that may occur. This scuttled the meeting and Asai and his charges left the meeting knowing that they had failed in their first attempt. Failing to influence the membership and hold a legal vote in their own favor the Asai group illegally tried to change the official executive register and remove most of the Nakahara side of the group from their posts, a curious move seeing as they were previously told by the courts that they could not do this. This also did not stand in the courts. From the time that the illegal meeting was called the group was split completely and the court battle began. Asai had shown his hand to soon and this allowed the Nakahara backed group and Nakahara himself to make plans and see the type of moves Asai would be making and put up legal counters and blockades before Asai could act.

At the time of the split the Nakahara side did not have a chief instructor candidate to lead the charge against the defunct Chief instructor in Asai Sensei. The Nakahara group looked for someone that was senior to Asai Sensei in "time training" in Karate so that they did not run into an argument that Asai was senior to the Chief instructor if and when they won the court battle. The Nakahara group realized that if the candidate was junior to Asai Sensei that the Matsuno group would hone in on this and make it an issue in court and in the court of public opinion. After reviewing many candidates the group found a very unlikely leader in Sugiura Motokuni.

Sugiura Sensei was unassuming, quiet and not one to push for advancement in position in the group. He was not exactly someone that came across as being interested in advancement past his current possition and he while he had a strong history with both Funakoshi Sensei and Nakayama Sensei he was not someone that sought out the lime light or was well known outside of Japan. Sugiura Sensei began his training as a youth under Funakoshi Sensei and his son Gigo.
While most of his training was in fact under Gigo Sensei at a university he had experience in Funakoshi Seniors Karate and learned a great deal under Nakayaama Sensei as well. Sugiura had started training in Karate in University and had worked hard under both Gigo and Nakayama Sensei and while he was a smaller man he was quick and picked up the system quickly. His main influences were in act mostly Nakayama who became a lifelong mentor and friend.

By his 20th birthday Sugiura Sensei had been awarded his 1st Dan after 4 years of training at the University level. He then left and spent a year in Tsuchira Navy flying Corps as an airman. Soon after he returned to the newly formed JKA and trained under Nakayama sensei while teaching junior college in Tokyo. In 1951 Sugiura sensei was teaching at the Tokyo University sports department and was awarded his Nidan, then in 1953 his Sandan. By 1955 he was assigned responsibility for managing the instructors in the JKA. His position was seen as second in command to Nakayama Sensei as he was in charge of assignments for each instructor in the technical development program and who was teaching the program. Known as firm but fair Sugiura got along well with most of the instructors because he was not seen as someone who was overly ambitious and a person who was hard working and committed. Serious but approachable he was the perfect manager for the instructor corps.

In 1957 Sugiura Sensei received his 4th Dan and while coaching at various clubs he was appointed an even greater position by Nakayama Sensei. He was appointed the director of the Japan Karate association in general, an executive position that meant he was in charge of the whole organizations daily business and worked closely with the board to make sure that the organization was moving in the right direction. From what I have been told he developed a good working relationship with the board at this time and befriended many of the seniors and council that were in charge of running the organization. One account that I was told by a senior is that Sugiura Sensei had a good respect for Nakahara and the other board members, a great working relationship and had common views on the direction that the JKA should be going in, which greatly affected his selection as the replacement for Nakayama sensei after Asai Sensei started creating waves.

The relationship and experience as an administrator put him ahead of all other positions in the organizations hierarchy, including Asai and his Technical director position. The position was created to free Nakayama up for more research and travels. Nakayama awarded him his 5th Dan and then 6th Dan in 1963 for his service. During his work as the manager to Nakayama's Architect Sugiura focused on learning the lay out and direction that Nakayama had for the JKA. He wanted to push the dreams and plans for the JKA that the chief instructor held and make them become a reality. He also had a great deal of time training under the master and learning the system and style that Nakayama viewed as being the JKA specific Karate system.

In 1963 Sugiura resigned this post to take a full time job teaching physical education at the Asai University. This is the reason that many give for him not automatically being elevated to the position of Chief instructor upon Nakayama Sensei's passing. The position he held was one of being the second in charge of operations under Nakayama and he had a tone of interactions with the chief instructor, however it was a brutally stressful position to be in and one that would cause a great personal pressure on anyone holding this post. From the few interviews I have read about Sugiura's position and how he worked within the position, most of the information suggests he was efficient, worked well with others and used his powers over the instructor corps only to organize and make others' lives easier.

While many people have stated that Sugiura Sensei was a great instructor, a very personable and effective manager and seen as the obvious heir to Nakayama Sensei, I have read from some Asai supporters that they felt Sugiura was a great "paper pusher, however he was not the right kind of person to lead an organization into the future. Most of them pointed out his lack of progressive thinking and his want to stick to the traditions and systems that Nakayama sensei had created. He was not overly ambitious to put his personal stamp on much of the Karate that was being taught and he was happy to maintain the Budo focused style that Nakayama Sensei had established. While this was seen as a weakness by those that area associated with and pushing for Asai to have been the chief, the reality is that this may have been one of the key reasons that he was picked. Sugiura Sensei was a traditionalist and respected the way that Nakayama was going, he was not as radical a selection as Asai Sensei and people knew he would continue to drive the JKA towards the same horizon that Nakayama Shihan was aiming for.

While Sugiura Sensei had resigned and become a full time university instructor he continued to train with Nakayama and was granted his 7th Dan in 1968. During this time Sugiura Sensei became very heavily involved in defining the JKA Karate system by creating textbooks with Nakayama and making videos to forward overseas. He became the man behind Nakayama Shihan and was seen by many as his second in command despite not having a lofty official post in the organization.

In 1976 Sugiura Sensei was an 8th Dan and full time member of the technical committee and head of the Asai University general education department. Some stories of his interactions with Asai Sensei show a great deal of friction as Asai was the Technical director and Sugiura a member of the committee that often had to real in the flamboyant and eccentric Asai telling him that he could not introduce different aspects of his "personal" Karate to the rank and file as it would confuse people. They did not agree with his ideas and his methods of teaching on occasion and this would lead to confrontations that were civil but often seen as the preamble for the split once Nakayama was no longer there to buffer the issues. In the end the selection of Sugiura Sensei may have been seen as a direct slight and message to Asai that his rebellious ways were being directly called out by the rank and file of the Shihankai.

By the time that the split occurred between the Nakahara side and the Asai side of the JKA Sugiura was retired from teaching at the Asai University and held a position as an instructor away from the Hombu, meaning he had his own little club and taught many great Karate athletes here. He was an active JKA instructor but not as visible as other greats of the time. However most of the senior students still treated him with great respect as they knew he was a master planner and a great asset to the organization.

Sugiura Sensei was teaching in his small club and honestly probably would have maintained his position teaching there if the JKA had not been thrown into chaos with the fighting between the now Chief instructor Asai Tetshuhiko and Nakahara. From what I gather being called upon to run the whole organization as the chief instructor was not in Sugiura Sensei's plans of semi-retirement from the chaos of running the organization. But when he was called up he took the honor to heart and set about securing the JKA.

At the time of the split a great number of big name JKA members had moved over to back Asai Sensei, however the majority of the students and juniors remained with the Nakahara group. An overwhelming number of the general staff remained loyal to the Nakahara side and created many voids for Asai's group. They lacked secretaries, general staff and a board that could help them form business plans. It was felt that Asai would win any court battles and the others would simply go back to work with him, however the only real major void for the Nakahara side was a legitimate chief instructor. Nakahara reviewed his prospects and reached out to Sugiura sensei, a more senior practitioner than Asai, and asked him to step in as the Nakahara backed successor to the Chief instructor position.

Sugiura hesitantly agreed to take up the mantel and return the JKA to the ways that Nakayama had been aiming the organization in, he would forge ahead in the same way that Nakayama was progressed and he would not introduce radical ideas counter to the JKA methodology. He was selected partially because he was a stalwart that would keep things calm and focus on the technical development only as much as he had been taught by his mentor, more importantly however he was selected for his management skills and his ability to organize and act as a politician in the time of chaos. His appointment offered a kind of calming force as he had the ability to command respect and the kind of attitude that others naturally would follow. He would agree to step into a storm of chaos and vitriol and do battle for his beliefs. Sugiura had a small stature and small frame compared to some of his counterparts, but he was very astute and read people and situations very well. He knew that this was going to be an ugly, drawn out battle that would see lots of back and forth, but he was ready to do battle and hold the path that Nakayama had selected. He would keep traditional Karate progressing at the appropriate pace and maintain the status quo that offered everyone comfort till they had passed these turbulent times.

In 1991 almost 4 years after the JKA Chief instructor Nakayama passed away Sugiura Sensei was appointed the chief instructor of the JKA and started working with the Chairman and the board to bring the JKA back in line with the old JKA ways that Nakayama Shihan had created. Sugiura Sensei's selection also cut out a great deal of minor infighting that was occurring as senior members, both in Japan and internationally, jockeyed to see if they could gain this position. Many senior members saw Sugiura Sensei as the only viable option to win a battle with Asia's Sensei's group as well as appeal for calm and create common vision with a new architect leader at the head.

I remember stories and instances where I saw senior instructors commenting on how "such and such" should have been picked and felt, at the time that they should have picked a more recognizable instructor. Having the gift of perspective and time however I can honestly say that Sugiura Sensei was not only the best choice, he was the only choice that the JKA had in this terrible time. The wave of stability came over the JKA and the Nakahara side forged ahead with the plans to take on the other sides claims to be the only JKA. A real sense of calm confidence could be felt as far away as our little Dojo in Canada. A sense of assurance and stability set in with Sugiura Senseis' appointment.

To counter the many changes that Asai Sensei had initiated in his 4 years of being the recognized chief instructor of the JKA, the newly formed Chief instructor and technical council came out with a set of five technical texts to clarify the Nakayama books and make sure that all the instructors were teaching Karate the same around the world. The books that were produced laid out a format for the system and were recognized by the JKA as "THE" Technical manual for all Karate training that would be stamped as JKA style Karate. These books quickly became seen as the Bibles of Karate Kata and became a rally point for JKA instructors to work on Kata from. The JKA was pushing to be the legitimate leaders in Shotokan Karate that they had felt they were before Nakayama passed away. They were trying to take back the name and ideals that made them JKA and they felt that Sugiura Sensei at the helm was going to push them past these issues with Asai and his breakaway group of "heretics".

The court battle that began with lower courts was long and drawn out, both sides still tensely training in the Honbu dojo and asserting that they had full ownership and rights to the JKA finances, name and assets. The battle involved a great number of court appearances and was very embarrassing for the JKA in general. This process put a halt to many of the growth initiatives that had been planned and highlighted the personalities involved in the spat. The Court battle did not put a stop to many of the tournaments but it added great stress to the seniors as each proceeding court date came and news of the arguments spread. In 1995 the Tokyo local court ruled that Nakahara group was the correct owners of the JKA name and had the rights to the name and possession or ownership of all JKA held assets. I remember hearing about the win in court and felt that this was a good thing for us as JKA students.

The fight could go away and the focus would go back to growth and development. We were told that the first big hurdle was over and my instructor got a clip from Japan that announced the win.

The Asai group then brought the case to the Tokyo higher court, which again ruled in favor of the Nakahara group after both sides pled their case before the court. Again the battle had been rough and the seniors all felt that the battle would be the last and the Asai group would not have the energy to push on. This could have been the sign that the Asai lead group had lost and should have moved on, but they then pushed even harder and brought the matter before the Japanese Supreme Court as an appeal stating that while the Nakahara group had been hand-picked by Nakayama Sensei to chair the business end of things that Asai Sensei was groomed to be his heir in the technical side, which was of course the more important side as it was the essence of why the group existed in the first place. The argument that without the Technical director the board would not be necessary was the tactical approach that Asai and his senior lead group took.

The battle went before the Supreme Court and in 1999 the Court officially rejected the appeal and stated that the Nakahara group officially had won the previous court cases and the decision would stand. This effectively ended the long court battle and gave the Nakahara run, Sugiura led JKA group the sole right to use the JKA name and the group moved on to continue building the organization the way that Nakayama had envisioned it. The headquarters and all of the assets were officially the Nakahara group's possession and a push to restart many of the abandoned endeavors began. However the court battle had cost the JKA many of its seniors as several in Europe and America had viewed the battles in the courts as embarrassing. However the end of the court battles also took a great deal of pressure off the JKA and allowed for expansion and growth again.

As for the united front that the Asai group had presented, this quickly fell apart when the court ruling was made. As it began to set in that they were not the owners of the JKA name, title or heirs to the legacy of Nakayama the seniors began to scramble to find an identity post court battles. Within a few years the senior membership of the group had fractured and while

Asai Sensei set up his Japan Karate Shotorenmei group to continue on his teachings and working on his version of the Shotokan style many others left him to form groups that would continue to teach the old ways and develop a more centralized system.

Some of the other main players, such as Yahara Mikio, left the Asai group to form their own systems and group. In the case of Yahara Sensei he formed the Karate-no-michi world federation and returned to a more traditional style of Karate based on his experiences and his ideas of Karate. Not a system that is purely JKA and not one that has a great deal of Asai's influence.

The KWF system is unique unto itself and probably would not have been allowed to grow and develop had they stayed JKA or stayed with Asai sensei. After watching hours of Youtube videos of Yahara I have gained a great deal of respect for his ideas and mastery of the human body. His focus on creating spring and explosiveness in training is inspirational. But you can see the divide between his system and JKA style Karate.

Other supporters of Asai's group also left him after the court battle left them without the JKA name or titles. Keigo Abe formed his own group, the very conservative and traditional JSKA. The JSKA sought to teach the original teachings of Nakayama Sensei as its standard and fundamentals as they attempted to remain "orthodox" and traditionally represent Abe's links and training lineage under Nakayama Sensei. Abe's group was supposed to be more "JKA than the JKA" and his standards were apparently very high. The irony of Abe being with Asai, a man bent on changing the very core syllabus, curriculum and feel of the JKA, is not lost on me. I have never met Abe but all the articles I have read suggest that this man would have been more of a perfect match for the Nakahara group and their dedication to Nakayama than Asai and his penchant for changing the JKA core values.

While Asai outranked him and was the choice of Nakayama at the time, it may not have been appropriate for him to be named the new Chief instructor, even if he would actually have been a better choice than Asai if traditionalism was the focus.

Abe rejected the overt changes that Asai had been making to the JKA fundamentals and refused to teach anything that Nakayama Sensei had not taught himself. Many people felt that his ultra conservative traditionalism and focus on keeping his group very small and controllable was the reason that he left the JKA's expansion based ideology. The JKA also may have rejected him as the chief instructor because he insisted that the teaching should be done on a smaller scale with less students, something categorically opposed to what the JKA was working towards at the time.

At the end of the day Asai Sensei was left with his vice Chair Kagawa Masao, who himself never fully changed his training or teaching to follow the more eccentric style that Asai Sensei had adopted. Kagawa was very loyal to his instructor however. Active as a competitor until the early 90's Kagawa enjoyed great success in both Kumite and Kata and was seen as a power house and kicking expert. His dedication to Asai Sensei led to his taking over Asai Senseis organization when Asai Sensei passed away.

The court battle ended with the Nakahara group claiming the position of Heir to Nakayama Shihans dream and the Asai group did not leave the lasting power that they once thought they would have after having backed the then chief instructor in Asai. In the end the JKA was seen as stronger for the efforts and commitment they put into the court case and battles that they had to go through to own the very identity they felt they should have already had. They pushed on to bring new Karate spirit to the JKA and establish a solid political, business and technical focus that brought them back to the greatness they once had.

While the JKA was busy avoiding implosion and battling each other, other groups like the World Karate Federation made headway and grew their influence, something that the JKA would find difficult to correct once the courts settled their internal quibbles.

In the Asai side did not win the court battles, but both sides left with a more defined idea of who they were. The Asai Side also left and splintered into the different groups as they are now, with different ideas, identities and ideologies that make them all strong and unique.

The Asai Branch of Shotokan

While the court battle was going on the Asai group was super close knit, they were strong and they taught a brutally traditional system of Karate, Asai holding close to the most detailed traditional system he could as he wanted to following Nakayamas path and then veer slightly when he could. The court ruling however allowed him to pull off his gloves and make changes to the training as he wanted to, he began showing his own ideas and creating an *"Asai Karate"* system that he had previously not demonstrated openly. He had researched Chinese styles and had implemented some

Kata changes previously but it was when he realized he was not going to be the next JKA chief instructor that the changes started coming fast and furious.

Abe Sensei and Yahara Sensei split to form their own separate groups shortly after the court battle saw them "no longer JKA". Abe formed his JSKA to keep super traditional and honor his instructor and Yahara formed his KWF to also go back to a more Budo style art that he could put his own personal stamp on. However the whole point of this blog is to look at what Asai did after finding himself on a splinter group side and no longer the leader of a JKA group.

When Asai Sensei lost the court battle he formed the JKS or Japan Karate Shotorenmei as well as the International Japan Karate-do Association or IJKA. The JKS was a Japanese based group that began to teach the altered system of Asai Sensei and allowed him to experiment and develop his system. Asai went about creating many new Kata and introduced them to the students. The result was a style very unique and different than JKA style Karate with roots in the Japanese art but with a great deal of personal changes that he implemented after studying White Crane Kung fu.

The JKS became the Japan arm of Asai's teaching and much of his mainstream changes began with this group. He began introducing different kata and movement drills to reflect changes he was making. His students who had trained with him in the JKA Matsuno faction mostly moved to this group when he lost in court. The changes in syllabus and curriculum soon put the JKS membership at odds with each other and members like Yahara, Abe and others left.

Asai Sensei developed his system and expanded it for six year, Unfortunately the Karate genius passed away in 2006 from liver cancer and again a master passed away with no real plan to have a successor to all of his hard work. Instead Asai Sensei left several leaders to split up his empire and create different groups with different focuses.

After Asai Sensei passed away the JKS organization was headed by Kagawa Sensei, a man whom had a great tournament record and was perhaps more JKA than he was in line with the New Asai Karate. The JKS began to change and move away from the change that the former founder had put in place and move back towards solid traditional JKA style Karate.

Along with the JKS the IJKA was being run by Asai as his European branch. The main instructor was Kato Sensei, who unlike Kagawa moved a great deal like Asai did and the changes became second nature. The IJKA is probably the closest to the changes that Asai wanted to put into effect of the two groups. Flowing, relaxed and more Chinese than the JKS version of the changes the differences between the two are striking when you see seniors practice side by side. However watching their Kata demonstrations and Kato showing the proper form, you can still see a great deal of Nakayama Sensei's Karate influence.

My impressions of the different movement skills of Kagawa, Kato and seniors from these groups, the focus of the groups was similar, to spread the teachings that they were introduced to by Asai Sensei. The JKS was based in Japan and had a great deal of hype about being "The Asai" Sensei group. However the IJKA was heavily represented in Europe, with a headquarters in the UK. The JKS has stretched out to some of the world, but the IJKA seems to have started in Europe after Asai passed away.

Other than the two group that were created dirctly by Asai Sensei only one other group follows the Asai Karate ideals to maintain the training that Asai Sensei had created. The ASAI group teaches 26 of Asai Sensei's additional Kata as well as a solid JKA based curriculum. The group was forged out of Yokota Sensei's trying to maintain the Asai Karate system .

After Asai Sensei passed away he, much like his mentor Nakayama Sensei, did not really leave one single person to continue in his quest. Asai Sensei and his Karate are perpetuated by qualified instructors like Yokota, Kagawa and Kato Sensei and their many followers, while I remain JKA I respect the fact that Asai Sensei had some different ideas that may very well be worth looking into and these men openly teach and train in the system that he generated and perpetuated.

Major splits in the JKA

I often find myself explaining how the JKA was originally one group, who had formed after the original students of Funakoshi split into the "Shotokai" and the "JKA" groups. I have to back pedal and state that the split was not complete or totally down the middle with both sides 100% fighting and not talking. The same is said for the JKA and its splits. I remember reading a quote from Asai Sensei who once said that the court battle the split him and his peers off from the JKA was not a complete battle that saw all the masters on each side not talking to each other or really fighting with each other. Asai famously stated that most of the instructors got along outside of politics, the infighting was done and they, for the most part, got along well with each other. Even early instructors who left like Kanazawa Sensei, who created his own system and left to pursue his own non-JKA style training would often go to camps and teach at seminars for JKA instructors/groups.

If you doubt this all you have to do is look to the ISKF summer camps and how masters from the JKA still go and teach at the camp. Even after Okizaki Sensei had said for years that Kanazawa was not JKA and he had different ideas that got him in trouble with the old guard of the JKA so he left. The JKA has gone through tones of changes, splits and has seen masters jump ship and start their own groups or move back to the JKA from groups that they had joined in a split. This blog is going to outline the bigger ones, the larger and more impactful splits to the JKA.

By 1999 the JKA had mostly returned to normal and while they won the Japan Supreme Court ruling they had already caught their wind and put their feet back under them, moved on and saw positive growth and the feeling, in Canada at least, was that when the Asai group lost the first court battle in 1995 that the fight was essentially over already. Most of us had moved on and were seeing the split as what it was, the Chief instructor had been ousted by the management and executive and the replacement Chief instructor was well respected, we all kind of just moved on.

I had a nice sit down with a member who was training with us from South America and we had been chatting about the difference in systems that we teach here in Manitoba compared to his home country and I had to point out that he was not from the JKA directly. His instructor was a very nice and skillful gent that is training in SKI Karate under Kanazawa, so it's not just that our systems are different, our styles are actually different. I was asked to describe the fracturing of the JKA world organization and try to explain the separations and splits. I have been asked to explain why this happened and what caused them…..and to be Frank; I don't often feel comfortable talking about the splits.
The truth is that the JKA has been home to me off and on for more than 35 years, and mostly on. I have had a great amount of respect for all the instructors I have trained with, even those have left the JKA, and while I know they are all human, a great deal of the splits seem to have been done for petty reasons or may have been out of frustrations with the JKA for its policies to protect its heritage. I will present, with respect the splits, but realize that I am bias as a JKA guy and yet I also see things could have been handled a bit better. But I will try.

Most of the splits are a result of sour grapes and to understand the situation I will be showing a bit of the "dirty laundry" that the different groups tend not to show when talking about why they left. Often it is one person feeling that they are entitled to certain things and then they get upset when they don't get what they want. Most of us see their histrionics as them just stamping their feet and picking up their ball and going home. Often I see the splitting people as grown men acting like children, but some of the fractures were just timing. The timing was perfect for a new group to be formed, it was time and a void had to be filled. Or a master passes away and then a new group is formed or in the case of Asai his two groups move apart from each other and a third or even fourth is formed when people take the name of the master after he passed away. The natural progression away from each other seemed to be...well natural.

I am very aware that there are people who are "Anti-Organization" or more specifically "Anti-JKA". They don't like organizations; they see them as big and cumbersome or counter to the focus of training. They are jaded and don't like the groups, they have personal issues and when you talk to them they are totally against the groups....Be it JKA or other. For those that seem bitter because they could not grow and flourish under groups and spit vitriol and venom at them whenever they talk about the masters, the JKA or other groups I have to say....whatever!

I was not personally involved in any of the splits that I am going to talk about and if you don't respect someone like Ueki Sensei, Kanazawa Sensei, Yahara Sensei, the late Asai Sensei or the rest of them and their contributions to Karate, well I have little time for small minded people who do not respect the people that helped form the art that they are actually training in. I only say this as I have had many online and in person conversations with people who show such a lack of respect for one or more of these masters that I could literally fill a book with them...but I won't! Let's leave it at no matter what side of a split you come down on, both sides did some things "Less than above board" and also had good reasons for doing what they did. No one is 100% clean or innocent in these things and jawing on about how one person was a "Such and such" or caused issues is digging up old issues, move on and train!

So, as gingerly as I can I will try to explain the larger splits, fractures and rebirths that have occurred over the years in the life cycle of the JKA and Shotokan as well as those that grew out of this group or affiliated groups. And I am simply going on the facts that I know from what I saw, what I was told or read (so some of it may not be "Facts" but more an interpretation of the events by my Sensei's and seniors or friends) and what I have read in interviews over the years. I pre apologize if I step on any toes, tell tales out of school or simply make you uncomfortable.

One factor to keep in mind, at the highest level of the splits, the chief instructors...all still getting along and would enjoy sitting together and chatting if put in a room. Why can't the zealous followers do this as well? Point in fact, one ISKF instructor once told me "heretic" Kanazawa would never be welcome at a ISKF camp or event by any students who trained under Okizaki Sensei. He went on how Kanazawa Sensei had different ideas that would never be okay to teach to his students, he felt that they were to different and he went on and on about how the JKA had given him the boot because of his ridiculous and heretical ideas. Fast forward about a decade and a half and who is teaching at the ISKF summer masters camp….Kanazawa! And who was posting selfies training with Kanazawa…said instructor…standing next to the man he branded a heretic to Karate.

Basically Okizaki Sensei and Kanazawa Sensei were not enemies nor did they dislike eachother, but the "us or them" mentality took over and the students began to speak out against an instructor simply because of the perception that Karate should be an" us or them" thing. Honestly the seniors tend to ignore this stuff, but I think they let the juniors behave and act this way to guarantee that they won't lose members. If you hate everyone but your own instructor…you pretty much have to stick around. Anyways I digress….again….

One of the first splits occurred before Kanazawa left, some may not feel that this split was very significant however as the instructor was a JKA Member, but had stronger roots in the Shotokai at the period when the Shotokai was gearing up for the first big split. Oshima Tsutomu had been a member of the Wasada Karate team and traveled to the US to continue his education in 1955. He began studying at UCLA and began teaching Karate at his University. He was the first person to known to teach Shotokan style of Karate in the US. Oshima Sensei had been a direct student of both Egami Sensei and Funakoshi Gichin Sensei he was by default a member of both the JKA and the Shotokai at that time and while both were somewhat interchangeable as far as membership he left for the states two years prior to Funakoshi passing away and as such two years before the big split. In 1959 he started the Southern California Karate Association and opened clubs all over the US's western states. The organization renamed itself the SKA or Shotokan Karate of America several years later. By this time Oshima had been promoted to 5th Dan under Funakoshi Gichin and was told to go teach in the states by Funakoshi himself. Oshima Sensei had great success and when Funakoshi Sensei passed away he floated between the JKA and the Shotokai for some time interacting with both groups.

While never a full member of the JKA or The Shotokai, Oshima Sensei maintained good relations with both sides and was very close to several JKA members. Oshima's organization was building and very popular. He had built up a solid base and many members were dedicated to him and his group. In 1960 Oshima Sensei invited a very talented JKA member to come train at his club. At that time some serious issues between Nakayama Sensei and Nishiyama Sensei had come up. Nishyama was looking to consolidate and crate a base for himself and a new group to support him and Nakayama Sensei was not happy with the power struggle.

At that time Oshima Sensei opened the door for Nishiyama to come to the states the JKA instructor jumped at the offer. He trained in Los Angeles at Oshima Sensei's Dojo for a few months and when Oshima Sensei felt comfortable he left the states for a short period of time to attend to some family matters back home. Oshima had given Nishyama the chance to earn some money, practice his English and experience the States, possibly creating a base for him to move to the states and teach at his own clubs. However Nishyama Sensei began to recruit Oshima's students themselves by telling them that his Karate was outdated. He started this as soon as Oshima left for Japan. He began to campaign for the members to keep him in the states and even established several clubs in the US aside from Oshima Sensei's' club, which began to suffer as Nishyama peeled off members and had them train at his own clubs and not pay through Oshimas Dojo. To be fair, Nishyama did open his own clubs and did not just recruit out of Oshima Sensei's clubs, however he did recruit the seniors and many of the seniors then joined the JKA through Nishyama. Also, Oshima was teaching old style Shotokan/Shotokai style Karate and had not been around to see the updates that the JKA had made, but honestly it was nearly the same and the changes that were made were minor...in fact he may have had a more robust system as he knew of the additions that the Shotokai was teaching at the time and the JKA had not and would not be approving for practice.

When Oshima Sensei returned from Japan in 1963 he took over his clubs again; however he found out quickly that Nishyama had created his own organization, the AAKF which later became the ITKF. He had taken a large number of Oshima Sensei's students and a lot of his seniors had transitioned over after being advanced by Nishyama in Oshimas absence. This created a double split as Oshima sensei would not work with the JKA again and Nishiyama formed the ITKF and basically left the JKA. And Ironically would introduce some ideas that the JKA did not back and he did not see any of the changes that Nakayama had put into effect. To this date the ITKF based groups have some very notably non-JKA style habits that I have seen training with members who were ITKF.

In 1977 Asano Shiro, a JKA instructor course trained member left the JKA and started the SKIF or Shotokan Karate do International federation. Shortly after his departure he reached out to Kanazawa Hirokazu, a senior and friend, and invited Kanazawa Sensei to come and run the organization as the technical leader of the group. Kanazawa sensei had already been at odds with several of the JKA higher ranked members for his interest in studying the origins of

Shotokan and also for his interest in Tai Chi as an alternative to Karate. Its ironic that this one item stuck out as a reason for JKA instructors not thinking that Kanazawa was JKA at heart....why? Well the Hoitsugan Dojo, Nakayama Senseis private Dojo, teaches Tai Chi several days a week and many of the JKA seniors participate in this very popular class.

However Kanazawa has proposed several practices that the JKA Leadership did not approve of other than Tai Chi and he had wanted to change the practices of the JKA in some areas as well as wanting to administer a small sub group of his own that would be under the JKA heading but would be used to research and develop his own system. Kanazawa's departure was seen as being a big split and rather harsh as his views on Karate had changed but he was still seen as a JKA Icon, being an early tournament champion and instructor program graduate. His ideas of merging Tai Chi practice with his Karate, specifically the idea of flow and other key concepts put him on the outs with the JKA higher ups, but he was still seen as the poster boy for early JKA success in tournaments.

The Senior members however felt that this evolution in his thinking was very disrespectful to the art and honestly they probably had some cultural racism towards China that may have affected their thinking. Kanazawa Sensei and Asano Sensei went on to form a large organization built a strong group in Europe but have never really had a large presence in North America or other parts of the world. They failed to grow to the level of the JKA had feared they would, but they continued to teach solid JKA style Shotokan even after the split. While Kanazawa and Asanos split from the JKA was not friendly or amicable in anyway, it is worth noting that Kanazawa Sensei himself at least, has kept contact with many of his peers and has taught at many summer camps over the years hosted by his old friends, seniors and junior alike.

With the success of the JKA instructor training program the JKA began to grow at an exponential rate. The marketing machine and genius of the group kicked in and the instructors who went through the program were marketed at the best. The training made them very good at teaching and others saw them as inspirational. The JKA also took its tournament participants that did well and promoted them as THE prototypes of Karate. This worked very well and as they grew and spread their influence and reach out to all countries across the globe they saw huge successes in Europe and North America, South America and Africa.

Nakayama Sensei adapted Funakoshi Sensei's approach of expansionism more over the years and the JKA began to expand and invite more Western members to the Honbu Dojo. The JKA grew and continued to expand its self with few drop offs and only small numbers of members leaving. Nakayama and the JKA undertook a world tour that took him across the globe to shore up allegiances in the smaller groups and show the world that the JKA was strong and could continue to develop and grow even further. This is the period that Nakayama Sensei came to Manitoba and gave Dingman Sensei the task of growing the JKA in Manitoba and across the Canadian Prairies to the west. It was a time of prosperity for all the JKA and a time of growth.

As primed as they were for even further growth the bubble was about to burst. Nakayama Sensei had ruled the JKA with his charisma and authority and very few big time names wanted to leave, Nishyama had moved to the states and while he was still associated with the JKA he pretty much did his own thing, but when Nakayama passed away in 1987 a string of splits and chasms began to grow and occur that would cause the JKA to lose a lot of ground that otherwise would not have been given. By not specifically naming a successor Nakayama himself caused a great number of these splits to occur. When he died a number of sub groups were formed naturally with lines of allegiances being drawn out by different members and depending on their influence the groups would grow and form opposition to the leadership in the JKA, some left and others folded in on themselves and stayed associated with the JKA or were removed all together.

With the issues at the Honbu creating the biggest split when Asai Sensei's leadership as the new chief instructor came into question and was opposed by the Nakahara side, many small fissures began to open and members split away. The split in the JKA created a great deal of turbulence in Europe and other overseas groups. The majority stayed loyal to the JKA but smaller groups began to form and move to be associated with the JKA but not full time members.

The first group to form was headed by long time and famed JKA Dojo enforcer **Kase Taiji** and his junior Shirai Hiroshi. While the organization was very popular in Europe, this new group steered clear of North America as Kase and Shirai were based out of Europe and had a big organization to deal with which did not leave much interest in expansion.

Kase Sensei had been the JKA enforcer, taking on any physical challenges to the JKA honor in the old days, he moved to France and taught at his Dojo while Shirai opened up his clubs in Italy. By all accounts the Kase and Shirai Karate groups in Europe were JKA through and through. Kase had been a student of Nakayama, Gichin and Gigo Funakoshi and Isao Obata, his training was unique in the JKA as he represented the old Funakoshi Karate and yet he transitioned with the JKA system. A graduate of Senshu University in Chiyoda Tokyo he graduated from this private university and moved into the JKA immediately to teach before traveling and finally ending up in France teaching with his Kohai in Italy. Another unique aspect of Kase practice was that he maintained a close tie with both factions of the JKA and Shotokai which did not make him very popular with some in the JKA.

Both men began to teach a uniquely Kase off shoot of Shotokan to the students in Europe and just prior to Kase's passing he formed the Kase-Ha Shotokan Ryu group that eventually changed to the Kase Ryu style after his passing. In 1989 both Kase and Shirai had founded the World Karate do Shotokan Academy (WKSA) to promote Kase's system of Karate. This group was not a complete divergence and split from the JKA but it created some sub groups that would end up leaving the JKA.

The Kase style is now known as the Fudokan style and has some very unique Kata that were added by one of Kase's students Vladimir Yorga and Ilija Yorga. The two men not only created the new Kata but upon Kase's passing they formed the Fudokan organization and split from the JKA completely.

After Kase Sensei passed in 2004 the mainstream group that he over saw fell to Shirai Sensei to lead and reverted to a model that made them more a mainstream JKA group. The Shirai group decided to join the ITKF and Shirai was awarded the 10th Dan. Shirai had been a student of Nishiyama and Nakayama Sensei as well as Kase and Sugiura Sensei after graduating from Komazawa University. The move to join the ITKF and leave the JKA was a natural one for Shirai. The story I was told is that it allotted him the transition from Kase to Nishiyama Sensei without really leaving the JKA sphere, but not totally entering it.

Next to leave the JKA was instructor graduate Okuda Taketo in Brazil. Okuda was a graduate of the instructor training program and was assigned to teach JKA Karate in Brazil. The country had shown an affinity for Karate as the Shotokai had a strong presence as did several Goju-ryu Karate groups. Okuda Set up his dojo in San Paulo Brazil and began teaching as the JKA representative to Brazil.

After several years teaching JKA style Karate Okuda left the JKA to focus on his own style of Karate he had named Butoku Kan style Karate. Okuda had graduated from Takushoku University and then moved on to the instructor training program of the JKA. He left the JKA as a 8th Dan in 1972 ,and being assigned the head instructor of the JKA Brazil he began training and exploring other eastern philosophies and changing his ideas of Karate, This lead to him leaving the JKA with his entire student body. While it was seen as a minor loss for the JKA as

Okuda did not have a large base that he left with, but it did set the president for smaller groups leaving to form their own systems.

Other groups split from the JKA and larger Shotokan Organizations over the years, some movement being very fluid. Some smaller groups were formed to accommodate individual's needs and ideas, and of course some of the newly formed groups imploded or merged back with bigger groups. The result was that the JKA had lost a great deal of talent, but the benefit to the international market was that smaller countries had more control over their future, on the down side often quality was lost and ranking advancement was often questionable.

Groups like the WSKF, led by Kasuya Hitoshi and Kamiyangi Tekaeki, were formed in response to wanting to maintain a loyalty to the art that Nakayama Sensei established without being part of the JKA and under their direct control. Many of the smaller groups had become comfortable not relying on the JKA for direction and while not happy with their host organizations, returning to the JKA was out of the question. The new groups formed and grew or withered and were lost. The natural flow of new organizations that cater to those not wanting to be part of the JKA or other larger groups continue today. However for the most part the JKA itself has not lost any big groups since the Asai led split was shut down by the courts….with one more recent exception.

Perhaps the largest split from the Nakahara run JKA group was the loss of the ISKF (International Shotokan karate federation) when they left in 2007. The ISKF was formed by Okizaki Teruyuki in 1977 when Okizaki and Yaguchi Yutaka formed the group to govern a JKA growth spurt in North America. The focus of the group was originally on developing a solid JKA base in the United States and Canada, but over the years Okizaki and his Seniors began to see themselves as growing away from the JKA. Okizaki had been a core member of the JKA in the old days and a senior student of Nakyama Sensei. In 1955 Okizaki was appointed the head of the instructor training program for the JKA and as part of an expansion program by the JKA he was sent to the states in 1961. He originally planned to stay for only 6 months, but opened his Dojo in Philadelhia later that year and settled in the states.

Over the years Okizaki Sensei was promoted to 8th Dan and was often back in Japan helping the JKA direct its business. Okizaki Sensei was the most senior black belt Member teaching abroad at this time and some suggested that his own organization was not enough for him; he was expecting to replace Sugiura when the Chief instructor retired, when that did not happen many say he felt hurt and abandoned by the JKA.

While I have trained with Okizaki several times I can only say that his personality on the floor is much different than his personality off the floor. I would not characterize him as anything other than business like and unfriendly to myself and others when not teaching, but when he was on the floor he was a charismatic leader and honestly one of the best technical practitioners I have ever trained with. His demeanor off the floor was one that suggested to me that "he was the boss" and the stories of him wanting to lead the JKA do not surprise me at all. If they were true then I would assume that his departure from the JKA came when he realized he was not going to be the leader of the group and the decision make changes to the rules for the organization was the breaking point for him.

The spit with the JKA came at a time when the JKA was seeking to shore up its membership and put in place very specific rules to make sure that the organization was strong and each area had only one local organization governing ONLY in the country they were registered in. It also hoped to ensure that no one high ranking Karate "personality" would form sub groups or associated organizations that would lead to undermine their efforts to grow, such as those that Kase and others had inadvertently created in the past. Essentially this meant that Okizaki and his seniors could ONLY run the organization in the states, they could not continue to lead the Canadian organization nor could they branch out into the Caribbean as they had or move south to Mexico as they had as well. They would see a large number of their membership become independent from them and JKA governed groups unto themselves.

Okizaki Sensei attended the JKA meeting and was not happy with the resulting vote to implement the changes. Along with his junior, Yaguchi Yutaka, Okizaki went home and had a meeting with his senior instructors in June of 2007. The group sent a letter of resignation to the JKA that month stating that the entire ISKF was opposed to the new rules and was resigning amass; however several of the seniors who Okizaki felt would join him split from the ISKF and formed the nucleolus of the new JKA group that would govern the united states branch of the JKA. Senior members who had held a great number of members left Okizaki. Koyama in Arizona, Takashina in Florida and Mikami in New Orleans remained with the JKA and build the JKA-America and leave the ISKF to stay with the JKA as the US representatives of the JKA. This rebuilding drew a great number of instructors from the ISKF at that time and the new focus of Okizaki and his ISKF was on global expansion, this put a great strain on other ISKF members in the states as they tried to grow the group back.

As the focus of the ISKF began to move to European and world expansion and it looked like the group was going to grow to rival the JKA internationally, The ISKF began to implement the same rules that saw them leave the JKA and rolled out several changes at their 2011 Masters Camp. Ironically, because they selected to move in the same direction as the JKA, Okizaki Sensei and his organization began to have issues with one of his seniors who had a very strong organization in the Caribbean and Canada. The new rules did not sit well with Frank Woon-a-tai, a senior who taught in Canada but had strong ties to the Caribbean nations. At this time the ISKF was looking at huge growth and wanted to show that they could do well without the JKA, but upon implementing the new rules it became an internal issue for the ISKF. Woon-A-Tai may also have felt he was next in line to head the organization when Okizaki eventually retired, but when the new rules came out Okiazki Sensei also publically stated his Nephew Hiro would be the next head of the ISKF. This lead to a great deal of drama at a camp an a very public dressing down of Woon-A-Tai at the masters camp, the group suffered its second big loss as Woon-A-Tai returned home from the embarrassing meeting camp and resigned along with a large group of Canadian , North Eastern US and Caribbean members from the ISKF.

While my history will show that I was a ISKF member many years ago when they were JKA I have to admit that we left long before this incident occurred and the only way I knew of the very public spat was the internet. Many of the letters and accounts of the chaos and in fighting made their way to the web and I had occasion to be forwarded many of the documents, letters and personal accounts of the camp and the events leading up to and following the camp. Its best to leave it as vague as I have in this writing, suffice it to say Mr. Woon-A-Tai reacted as any person who had dedicated his life to supporting the masters would have if they had treated them that way.

Within 2 weeks Woon-A-Tai sensei had established his International Karate Daigaku or IKD and was accepting membership from all over. He was promoted by the board of his new group and began to grow a large group that had its focal point in membership from the Canadian East coast, Ontario and the Caribbean nations. He had essentially stripped the North East from the ISKF and his new group was now challenging to be as force in these areas. While the IKD is never going to be as big as the JKA or even the ISKF the loss of the IKD has slowed the ISKF's growth and revealed some very uncomfortable political issues in this organization and how they treat senior members.

As you can see, internal troubles, bickering over licenses, rank and recognition are not an isolated occurrence when they happen. In fact the infighting is often the least responsible for groups splitting. It appears to me that rank, recognition and financials tend to be the most responsible for groups splitting. Ranking and recognition are all about power, some people forget that as Karate instructors they are PAID to do a job, they feel that recognition of a false power makes them untouchable and this leads to ego and issues with those under them. The finances or money from licensing rank is another big issue. If you pay someone to get rank, and you are not able to charge the students to rank them, the only people benefiting are those at the top, eventually the instructor will leave an organization if they see money flowing up past them and none of it sticking with them.

Case in point, Ray Dalke was very public in why he left Nishyama Sensei. He once said that he went to Nishyama about Kyu grading money and was told to not ask about this again. A short time later Dalke left to form his own organization and get paid what he felt he was worth. When masters expect students to teach for free or pay them huge sums to teach when the instructors are not making any money, or when masters lie to the instructors to get them to fall into line, it never lasts and does not end well for the organization.

Rank is another big issue for some, it goes hand in hand with perception of the level of respect one is getting and the recognition one is afforded. Some instructors say they don't care what their rank is, but then when they leave an organization it's often followed by a big Rank bump in the new organization they form or the one they join. The head guy gets one and then his students are bumped up a rank as well.

A prime example is Okizaki Sensei hitting the glass ceiling with the JKA of 9th Dan. He was not up for a rank advancement and honestly no one was looking at going past 9th Dan, but when Okizaki took his group out of the JKA and within a year he is sitting with a certificate that says he is a 10th Dan (the highest legit level ever awarded in Shotokan). All his students got bumps as well. And I don't want to seem like I am picking on Okizaki because he was far from the last one to do this. Woon-A-Tai was given his 9th Dan by his group (most of the votes coming from people like his wife and brother), Asai Sensei took his 10th Dan from his group, Kanazawa was given his 10th Dan by his group, Nishyama took his 10th Dan from the ITKF/ISKA, and many others have self-graded or given the orders to their squad of students to prepare fresh ink for certificates then grand them to the "master" and they too will get rank bumps. The only person I know of who has tested for and graduated into a rank, be it questionable if he would ever been allowed to fail, was Mikio Yahara who tested for his 8th Dan, but like I said, I saw the grading....was he worthy of a 8th Dan, maybe...but by all accounts and my observation...he would have passed a Yondan as quickly with that performance. In other words, performance of Karate is not often equal to rank...in any way.

I am not going to start a debate about the rankings of senior Karate people and if they warrant a bump or not. I obviously think that men like Okizaki Sensei, Kanazawa Sensei and Yahara Sensei are Icons of Karate and I actually have nothing against them being voted all 11th Dans for what they have done for Karate, heck if they want to be 32nd Dan masters of masters I could care less and think they may have an argument for advancement regardless. They have done so much for their own members and Karate it's not a debatable subject. But I tend to fall along the same thinking as Oshima Sensei, who has my deepest respect for staying at the last rank that Funakoshi Sensei gave him and not accepting rank advancements from his students. He proudly holds the rank of 5th Dan and won't accept any farther from anyone for any reason.

Some people just cannot get along and this can lead to splits as well. I still say that the original reasons I posed cause most of the splits, in cases like the Asai side vs Nakahara Side it was a clash of ideals and ideology and also a battle for control over a group that no one had inherited from the Master when he passed away. I can see both sides to these arguments and with a bit of research anyone can see both sides of a battle like that one. Most splits happen because one person gets to a point that they have invested so much time and energy into an organization and they start to feel like they have ownership of the group now, when they are challenged the fight is on. They feel they should be given more respect, more recognition or more control and or they should just be obeyed, the problem is when two sides feel the same way and neither gives any ground. And often it's just about money or control over their own destiny.

I hope that at this point in history most of the splitting and issues do not paint any one side darker with responsibility than the other side in the issues. Really I have the utmost respect for most Karate instructors and seniors that have contributed to Shotokan Karate, the JKA and the other groups formed after they left the JKA. Some of the splits occurred well before I began Karate and I had no dog in those fights. I wish that the splits had not occurred but to be honest....it has probably improved training today. The training has benefited by creating a special set of circumstances that allowed instructors to research, develop and grow their own styles and pass them on to us. They have grown and influenced systems and styles that would not have grown if the JKA had managed to not split up.

I tend to not think of it as Okizaki and his ISKF leaving the JKA…..but a chance for a specific focus of Karate to stay alive in its purest unchanged form, and grow new ideas. I see Yaharas leaving the JKA and then Asai sensei as the reason for the KWF's power system being developed, Kanazawa left and we see a smoother system that was created with his influence from Tai Chi, Asai Sensei created nearly 100 Kata and some very Chinese ideals in his system and Kase Sensei maintained a very strict system that grew with his moving away from the JKA. This has created many sub systems that all have their own benefits and positives, so splits have an upside.

The nice thing about all of this, even if I just used really inaccurate and broad generalities to get my point across, is that we live in a very modern electronic age when you can You-Tube any of these men or groups and get ideas for training that transcend one system or style but still stick to the traditional Shotokan roots. You see various alterations, interpretations and changes that can influence your own growth and you can do so without worry of any politics or stepping on toes. The splits created this opportunity for all of us training in Karate who take the research and development of their own personal style seriously.

For those feel I was overly harsh to any one group or person in this blog, I am sorry. To be honest I don't dislike any of these groups. I find value in almost all groups and individuals and honestly while I love being JKA I would be happy training in the KWF, ITKF, SKI or any other group that can help me learn, grow and help my students. I have trained with a great number of peole from the ISKF, ITKF, SKI, KWF and of course the JKA and all of them are valuable people in my memories and all have influenced my training. Masters like Tanaka, Okizaki, Yaguchi, Koyama, Takashina, Ueki, Imura and countless others have all been great influences on my training and my instructors training. So, how can I not respect all of them!

I honestly don't want to be in charge of anything but my own Dojo and would love to train with just about any one. I like training in groups that promote thinking and training over just giving out ranks, I would get along with almost anyone that has a solid point of view and ideals that can be backed up with solid practice and proof….Honestly I just want to be invited to play! This blog was just to show that there have been many splits, for many reasons. No one side has a monopoly on the truth or being "right", each side of each split has done things, said things or caused things that would not be seen as nice, respectful or ….in some cases….mature. The key is getting past that as a student and just training.

Suigura Sensei Retires…leaves a successor.

After the Nakahara lead JKA won the court battles against the Asai lead opposition it has pushed on and grown a great deal. They have navigated through some tough times in the beginning and moved the headquarters to a new location in Bunkyo-ku Iidabashi Omagani area of Tokyo and built an ultra-modern facility with two massive training areas, class rooms, change rooms and new offices for the headquarters. This new space is a massive upgrade compared to the old location; the upgrades tended to attract and assist new members who were looking to train at the historic JKA headquarters and ushered in a new type of younger membership who were looking for a more dynamic system and style now offered at the JKA.

The membership drastically changed but the JKA's spirit remained the same and was even reinforced by the new members and the seniors who were not in charge of the JKA classes now. This was only possible with the direction and management offered under Suigura Motokuni Sensei, the established and accepted Chief instructor who was brought in after Asai Sensei was toppled as the Chief instructor and the court battles began. Suigura Sensei was a stable force that would hold close to the Nakayama Traditions and avoid brining radical ideas into training. He was also a scholar who knew what was needed for the JKA to grow and shore up its interests internationally. He allowed the continued growth and popularity of the tournament style Karate to grow and develop.

Master Sugiura was born on October 4th, 1924 in Aichi prefecture. His Karate career had begun in his youth when he became a student of Shotokan Karate. At university he studied under Funakoshi Sensei and had trained a great deal with his son Yoshitaka (Gigo). He had been granted his 1st Dan at 20 years of age. After graduation from University in 1944, Suigura sensei had spent a year in the Tsuchiura Navy Flying Corps, but soon returned to Karate, now training under Nakayama while holding a job at a junior college in Tokyo. He earned his 3rd Dan around this time.

In 1955, Suigura Sensei gave up his job at the junior College and began working full time in the JKA's Guidance division. He was also Appointed director of the JKA and assigned to manage the instructors at the headquarters club. He taught at the JKA as well as managing some of the most famous of the JKA instructors. Suigura Sensei was also part of the team that established the rules for tournament matches and coached at as many as 5 different universities at the same time all around Tokyo. His reputation as a solid administrator and a Karate instructor were growing. His best students were always placing well at tournaments and many became instructors and coaches as well.

Suigura Sensei worked tirelessly to promote JKA Karate and in 1958, a year after the Japanese government granted the JKA official recognition, Suigura Sensei received his University license as a Physical Education instructor. Over the next 5 years he would teach part time as a physical education teacher and lecturer at Asia University and also taught at the JKA as well as managing the other instructors, he was granted his 6th Dan at this time.

Over the next decade he began producing materials to help promote the way of Karate around the globe. In 1961 he helped to edit the text book "Basics of Karate-do" which identified some common basic errors in Karate techniques. In 1963 Sugiura created a six volume English language film entitled "Karate seminar" which help teach basic Karate techniques. This film was very forward thinking and one of the first of its time. In the summer of 1963 Suigura Sensei resigned from the JKA as the Director for the instructors at the headquarters and took up a full-time teaching position teaching Physical Education.

While he had left the JKA Honbu his activities in Karate did not stop, in fact he took the free time he now enjoyed and expanded his influence and work with Karate. He served as president of the Koganei City Karate do Federation and he also joined the Japan Martial Arts Society as an active and influential member. Suigura sensei also created a partnership with Kodansha international Ltd and created a five volume set of Japanese and English videos on Kata only. Kodansha became the print partner of the JKA as well through the relationship that Sugiura Sensei began.

Sugiura Sensei's efforts were attracting a great deal of attention outside of Japan as well. He traveled to China and Taiwan for the Japan Frenship Karate-do Cup and formed friendships with masters all over Asia who were teaching JKA Karate and acted as the eyes and ears for Nakayama Sensei while traveling. In 1975 Suigura went to Los Angeles and Hawaii to attend the International Amateur Karate federation general meetings and to see the JKA Sponsored 7th IAKF Championships. He wrote about this in a monthly magazine he had a column in. Sugiura Sensei was often a fixture at these events and reported the happenings to the JKA as well as assisting at events and brining members to train and compete at events.

In 1976 Sugiura sensei, now an 8th Dan and member of the technical committee as well as a full time professor at Asai University, accompanied the university Alumni association on a historic visit to Indonesia and was then sent to observe how Karate was being taught at several

US universities. The next year saw Sugiura sensei complete his thesis "a system of Karate do" which discussed the true essence of Karate. He spend the next few years creating teaching materials for Karate as a physical education professional and in 1989 he drafted supplementary karate guidelines for these materials. His activities helped cement the JKA in the university and colleges in Japan and helped coaches and instructors identify talented members who went on to represent their colleges and universities at national level tournaments and Japan at international level competitions. In 1990 however Sugiura retired from his post at the Asia University and went into retirement hoping to continue helping the JKA grow and develop educational plans and policies that would develop solid instructors.

March of 1990 the retired University professor was approached by the JKA and asked to take on the position of Chief instructor. He was appointed as chief in March and began his new position by enacting many of the policy changes that he felt would solidify the traditional stance that the JKA had regarding training and competition. Two years later he received his 9th Dan by the JKA. Sugiura Sensei was focused on providing Karate with solid Kihon and he never taught fancy techniques. He felt that he should stick to the traditional basic Karate that Nakayama sensei had emphasized. This ensured that the focus was on providing flawless Kihon and execution of the proper Kihon when performing Kata and Kumite. He also put a great deal of emphasis on proper attitude and the connection of the body and mind in training as that, in his opinion, was the true soul of Karate.

Suigura Sensei had brought the JKA through the big court battle and organized and managed the huge organization as it moved the headquarters into a more modern facility; he had served as a stabilizer during a very turbulent time and done so with grace and often a very forceful but respectful final word on things. The JKA had focused a great deal of its efforts on expanding the Honbu and moving into a new facility and left the grass roots to the overseas instructors. Moving into the new age of the JKA the main organization seemed to allow a great deal of latitude and personal freedoms to the outlying countries and let their seniors run them as small fiefdoms. Before Suigura retired he saw this and started a series of rules changes that upset a great many seniors. Like the 70's splits with Asano/Kanazawa and Kase/Shirai, the turmoil of the great split with the ISKF was set. Okizaki Sensei in the US insisted that he was the next in line for the Chief spot and he also did not like the new rules that Suigura Sensei and the JKA had passed.

Just as the painful split with the Matsuno faction led by Asai Sensei had begun to heal, the ISKF, a traditionally Nakayama JKA Based group, splintered and left the fold. Many of the instructors loyal to Okizaki sensei had voted to the split siting over reach by the JKA. The JKA had been watching the goings on outside of Japan as they were focused on strengthening the JKA in Japan after the court battle had been won and noted that several instructors were now reaching beyond the boarders that the JKA had established for them and were forming international bodies, this was counter to the JKA plan.

The ISKF leaving was a hard time for the JKA; they had just gotten over the court battles and completed their reformation of the New JKA Honbu as well as growing local programs to help feed the JKA new and younger instructors. They found talented instructors and built the new club up around them. The JKA had established itself as the one and true holder of the JKA name and cemented the lineage that they had shown was legally theirs. The ISKF split hurt them in the Pan American areas but they quickly formulated a plan to reform JKA organizations in these areas and they provided great support as well as creating better controls for these organizations to ensure that they would not break rules that were set up to protect the JKAs interests. Suigura Sensei also oversaw the JKA's plans to rebuild itself worldwide and draw back names like Kawasoe Masao, a Japanese instructor based out of England who joined the ITKF under Nishyama, but who had maintained a lose affiliation with the JKA. Upon Nishyama passing away Kawasoe had decided to rejoin the JKA and bolster the JKA England group.

The JKA formed smaller national groups and put single groups in charge of local Karate. They licensed Dan grading instructors and offered to send out new and young instructors to teach. They promoted and grew tournaments and created a new feel for the JKA as the "keepers of the highest tradition". Suigura Sensei had seen the JKA through the worst of it and had done so with a focus on the future. He kept the JKA traditional but also worked to provide more modern training and insight. He kept his sights on a process of regrowth that was in line with Nakayama Sensei's dream of what the JKA could be and he built up the next generation of instructors while using the fame of several key instructors to build up the JKA and push it into a more successful place.

After years of hard work and toil as a master that never wanted the keys to the kingdom and shied away from the lime light letting others shine as representatives of the group, Suigura Sensei retired officially on April 15th 2010. Suigura sensei had always preferred to work from behind the scenes and never seemed comfortable front and center as the Chief instructor. It would seem he was much more effective dealing with the JKA from a managerial position and pushing others out to be the face of the organization. Members like Osaka, Tanaka and many others flourished as they traveled to spread the JKA spirit and forge territories for the organization while they were managed by the chief instructor from Japan. As a student I recognized his name mainly from my grading certificates and honestly I don't have any memories of seeing pictures of him till near the end of his tenure.

As he stepped down as technically the fourth chief instructor of the JKA he was replaced by Ueki Massaki. Ueki Sensei was selected because he was a solid traditionalist and had been a student of both Suigura and Nakyama Sensei. His karate is solidly basic, sound and fundamentally based and his dedication to the JKA had been unwavering as he assisted with the growth and formation of the new ideals that the JKA were developing to help them grow and maintain control of the technical soundness of the system they were teaching. Ueki Sensei also places a great deal of emphasis on being true to the traditions established by Nakayama and he was the best representative to replace Suigura Sensei upon his retirement regardless of what overseas instructors may have felt.

Moving into the future the JKA had shuffled the deck of instructors at the headquarters and had assigned two vice chief instructors with Tanaka Sensei and Osaka Sensei being recruited to reinforce Ueki Sensei in the future development. Tanaka Sensei represented the "Star power" that his tournament Karate history had brought him as well as a great deal of skill in representing Shotokan Karate in seminars around the world and Osaka Sensei was said to be the man with the best form and techniques in Karate by Nakayama. Both men were solid choices and brought different strength to help support Ueki Sensei and the JKA.

Both men also had solid support internationally and were in agreement that the JKA needed to stay traditional but also needed to evolve the way Nakayama had intended upon establishing the JKA. The New Shihankai (seniors' council) of the JKA was a true mixture of the old guard and newer seniors which showed that the JKA was looking towards the future and creating a solid organization based on traditions that had been put in place by Nakayama Sensei.

Sugiura Sensei and the new group received a great deal of support from Nakahara Nobuyuki, the "War time" chairman of the JKA board. Nakahara is a distinguished Japanese business man and financial leader who began his career in Karate in the mid 50's when he joined the Karate club at the prestigious Tokyo University, a premier university in Japan. After graduating from Tokyo University he attended Harvard and earned a master's degree in political economy and government. Subsequently he made his name in the Japanese oil industry, where he served in a number of important executive positions, including the president and chief operating officer of one of Japanese foremost oil companies. He also translated many books on oil and business and contributed articles to business magazines and lectured on business and finance at Japanese universities, including his alma mater Tokyo University.

Nakahara also was very close to many of the Japanese Prime Ministers and other Cabinet ministers and consulted with them on Oil issues and how to advance Japanese interests in the world economy. This helped Nakahara branch out and become a member of the policy board of the Bank of Japan. Nakahara also served as a Chairperson on a number of scholarship and social welfare foundations, including the famed American Studies Foundation, which provided financial assistance for Japanese scholars and institutions, engaged in US Studies. On top of all of this he worked tirelessly through his adult life to advance the interests of the JKA and Karate in general. He ultimately was given the rank of 9th Dan for his efforts on behalf of the JKA. He was appointed chairperson of the JKA in 1986 and went to work promoting the interests of the JKA with in the Japanese government and used his fame and influence to help the organization. Under his leadership the JKA finally succeeded in buying land and moving the Honbu into a multi-story facility that would assist in growing the organization and act as a focal point for the group. He was the longest running Chairperson in JKA history.

When Sugiura Sensei stepped down Nakahara remained as the Chairperson and allowed for a great deal of stability. However he was a "war time" kind of chairperson who had become very attached to the idea that he ran the JKA and the board was his to rule. The instructors at the Headquarters and the Shihankai were his to run, which was point of fact…not correct. As Ueki Sensei was appointed the JKA chief instructor and many changes were put in place the Chairman began to have issues with outside organizations like the JKF and even with the Honbu instructors began to dislike many of his ideas and his orders on how to run the headquarters. Some of his more disliked orders caused large waves in the JKA headquarters that again brought up the unrest of the past. This lead to a great deal of stress in the headquarters and change was again in the air.

Ueki Sensei a new Era

Ueki Masaaki Sensei was born in 1939 on March 24th in Tokyo. He began his Karate training at 16 in his high school under Sugiura Sensei at the Kimonenba Dojo (Now Koganei branch), with only one other student training alongside him. He had started training in Judo prior to his Karate training, but found he was too small and disliked the sport itself. He became very interested in Karate because of its focus on speed and mobility and it seemed to be made for his build. After high school he attended Asia University and continued training with Sugiura Sensei and refined his approach to Karate training.

Ueki Sensei graduated from Asai University in 1961 and was encouraged by his instructor to join the instructors training program at the JKA, which had only began 5 years prior and was still very much in the process of development. Ueki, in a French interview, recalled how harsh the classes were and how difficult training was and how the classes were very repetitive having the members of the program repeat basic techniques till they were exhausted. Thousands of punches and thousands of kicking repetitions done over and over to the count of a Sempai as the candidates soaked through their Gis in the hot Dojo under the watchful eye of the seniors and the instructors. They worked to forge solid Kihon and develop the spirit and understanding of hard work and near psychotic dedication that they needed to work towards graduation in the program.

Many years later I recall one of my Sempai joining the Instructor training program and writing home for more Gi's as his had been torn and worn so bad from the near homicidal Kumite matches that they had to engage in and the wear of the Kihon practice. His mother once told me that he had written her and told her about the amount of his own blood that soaking his Gi and how his instructors and seniors were agast that he did not have a fresh uniform to train in. All of his Gis were soaked, in tatters and colored crimson with the blood liberated from himself and his sparring partners. The training was not for the light hearted and even the most Lion-ish would contemplate constantly the idea of leaving, but out of fear of shame and embarrassment they pushed on and reached even new levels of technical and tactical proficiency.

Truthfully, I have trained under seven graduates in my time in Karate and save only one of them you could actually feel the proficiency they held in their Karate. Not to say that they all had amazing form or that they all looked the same, they don't....but they had a certain confidence in their techniques and a "reliability" in their teaching that showed. As I said only one was not up to this standard and he was not a full graduate. The rest of them seemed to be robotic in their technical ability, always doing the movements the same way with the same form and mechanical power. It is something to be inspired by.

Ueki Sensei's hard work led too many championship titles in Japan in both Kata and Kumite. In 1965, at the 8th All Japan Karate Championships he became the tournament grand champion by placing 1st in Kata and 2nd in Kumite. Ueki was also used in Nakayama Senseis "Best Karate" series as Nakayama took notice of Ueki and his skills. Nakayama wrote of Ueki "The hands and feet of Ueki Masaaki are worth watching, for they are very fast and truly sharp. It is not surprising that many opponents have been defeated".

Ueki Sensei settled into the JKA instructor corpse and became known as a very traditional and well liked instructor who brought the best out of people. He was made the managing director of the JKA in 1997 and helped support Suguira Sensei as the Chief instructor. His deep emphasis on very strong basics and stance was reflective of his learning from both Nakayama and Sugiura Sensei's and he developed a belief that in order to fully appreciate and totally benefit from Kata and Kumite training you need to pull them apart, practice the sequences and try to understand the nature of the techniques.

Despite his many tournament successes and rank advancement he remained humble and became very popular. He was seen as a favorite instructor at the JKA Honbu for many years and while he avoided the lime light his training and dedication to the JKA helped the group through the rough waters of the splitting and issues that they had, his stalwart dedication to the organization made him undeniably essential to the JKA growth and the success that the Honbu had. Ueki was one of the most senior instructors in the organization after time and assisted the Chief instructor teaching and running the instructor program. He eventually earned his 8th Dan and worked hard with the JKA to develop strategies for success and growth after groups left the organization and was part of the team of leaders who set out the new rules that would lead the JKA going forwards.

On May 29th of 2010, after Sugiura Sensei signaled that he would be stepping down as Chief instructor to go back into retirement Ueki Sensei was selected to be the next JKA Chief instructor. The record books for the JKA record him as being the third chief instructor, after the white wash of Asai Sensei's time as chief instructor was completed. At that time he was also given the rank of 9th Dan by the JKA to address his new position. Ueki Sensei began to make major changes, first of which was to address a well-established power struggle internally between the technical wing of the organization and the management end of the JKA that had set in and then to work to mend fences that this issue had created. After this he continued to push for the JKA to grow and build into the future.

The JKA had gotten to the point that many of the issues that were externally created were dealt with, it was time to turn inward and see what could be fixed, Ueki Sensei and the new Shihankai were set to look at the organization and see what needed to be fixed internally as well as a key relationship in the sport world of Karate, This was a priority for him to really make the JKA work effectivly and continue to be the holders of Nakayama Sensei's legacy. It seemed to me that it was a new day and that that the Chief instructors stamp on the organization would be to level the issues and deconstruct the problems, dealing with them in a methodical but sweeping fashion. In the end Ueki Sensei's dedication to the path his instructors had set forth made him the perfect candidate to move the JKA in to a new era.

Honestly, Ueki Sensei was known very well in Canada but my recollections of him were mainly from his being in the Best Karate books. He was not as big a name here as say Tanaka Sensei or Osaka Sensei. This was mainly because the masters who held sway over Canada, being mostly Okizaki and Yaguchi Sensei, did not really invite him out to attend camps as much. Also the US camps were often run by great masters like Koyama, Takashina and the odd visitor.

Years after we left the ISKF I had occasion to take a class from Ueki Sensei in Phoenix and was blown away by how basic it was, but how deep his understanding of the minutia of Kihon was. We did some partner drills and fun things but the highlight for me was when he stopped us and instructed on key fundamentals. I was struck by how detailed he was, his complete understanding of the movements, the way the joints had to turn and how the body reacted to a movement and affected the outcome of a basic move. He was teaching Soto Uke and was telling us how your back foot had to be placed, the way you had to drop your weight at a given second, the way that the core had to work and the power was from the hips, you can't do this or you had to pay attention to that. It was a masterful example of a man that truly knew his art and was an example of teaching ability. This was one more reason I feel he may have been the perfect candidate for the position.

End Notes

It has taken me months to put my blogs into written format that "resembles" a book .... somewhat, I apologize only if the stories seem a bit disjoined, but I don't apologize for my ideas or interpretations of the history that I am presenting. The blog itself was a meandering of thought and the often crooked and disjointed process of learning. I have rewritten several parts as I have grown and had a chance to review and think about several of my original stances and found them lacking. I promise you one thing only, I am continuing to learn and grow and my views on several of the current entries will change. The historical part of the book however is going to stay put!

The History of Karate has not always been rocky; however, it was often chaotic with points in time of smooth flowing growth and development. The stories we are told tend to be injected with more drama and histrionics than is needed. Mostly this is done to "Sell" the ideas that the instructors and organizations are trying to put over on us to fill the Dojo's however and the addition of the over the top chaos stories have very shaky ground when it comes to the truth. I can also say from my research that a great deal of the animosity that is presented is not held by the leaders of the different factions, groups and organizations. For instance, Asai Sensei told a story to an interview once that he was still good friends with many of the seniors in the JKA and when he passed away it was noted that when many high level masters and representatives attended his memorial service. When Master level instructors meet they are more often than not friendly to each other and often you can see the respect and friendship they share.

I can however say that without hesitation the followers of the different masters do not follow the same course and have friendly conversations. I have witnessed on line fights between 5th and 6th Dan practitioners of two different organizations, they were very heated and did not show good manners to be honest. I have been parts of conversations where instructors gossip, complain and put down their peers, locally and on international levels. It's very sad that some can't just recognize that politics has its place and personal views aside, most of us are not completely horrible people.

A few things I want to leave the readers with, that may help in your training, is first don't trust what you are told all the time...research and read...be open to opposing thoughts and focus on the Dojo Kun when training. And secondly the idea that Karate in the future is going to be defined by Karate of the past. We must strive to review research and truly understand the core values and fundamentals of the systems we are training in to allow us to absorb them and make them ours. You cannot just play at something like Karate, it's had historical significance and many people suffered and toiled to bring it to you.

It was based in a self-protection art that was used to protect royalty and now it often suffers as being used as a daycare activity used by parents to baby sit kids while they go shopping or worse to some degree, a sport that takes the Budo spirit out of the training and replaces it with medals and trophies. The spirit of the art is replaced with flashy moves and while the Budo systems focus on intrinsic development the sport aspect pushes a kind of eye catching movement system geared towards making judges and referees give points. My suggestion as a parent, students and an instructor is to find a traditional club if you are looking at the benefits of training and then stay the course avoiding instructors who are seeking fame through the athleticism of the student and pushing students to gain notoriety through their sport competition participation.

As students of the art we must show it more respect and provide its teachings as clearly and unabridged as we can, we should not interject personal interpretations when we don't know answers, do the foot work and go research till you truly understand the questions and the answers, then research more so you know the next question…and also be aware…there is always a next question if you are dedicated to your studies. The Karate you do today has been created by the Karate of the past.

Karate is one of the many arts that, when done properly, realizes that innovation in practice is not always a good thing. New Kata, new Kumite systems and new training cannot replace the authentic training that has been put in place by the founders. A local dojo has a sign (I used small d for dojo on purpose by the way) that says "the innovation of martial arts". A martial arts organization actually uses this as its name as well. Innovation to me means that the students are not learning authentic martial arts but a modern fabrication or a personalized reproduction of the original system. It lacks the *"Oshie"* or spirit that traditional arts have. It can look fancy, shiny and new, but upon honest examination it is lacking in the credible and legitimate spirit of training.

Also, as most can tell, my take on sport Karate is that it's counterproductive and a dangerous practice for those of us seeking Bujitsu focused Karate. I only have to point to the increase in injuries under the WKF rules. Oh, I know many say that the injury rate has gone down under the WKF rules, but this is a proven fabrication! The WKF put out a report that was researched by a European sport federation. The report stated that injuries fell 45% under the new Kumite rules, however a year later the European sport group that did the research said that the injury rate had actually climbed by nearly 60%! When they had presented the research to the WKF/JKF the president felt that the statistics would hurt their work to get into the Olympics and "Doctored" the results.

The English Karate group under the WKF was the first to question the statistics and then came out with their own report showing that the Kumite injuries had increased and contact was the main issue. The other aspects of sport Karate like Kata changes and the "need to make them more interesting and exciting" really turn me off of the whole thing. Also the habit of sport federations giving out rank also bothers me. The over reach and gross alteration of Karate are specifically the things that have soured me on sport Karate for some time now.

One other aspect of Karate that I hope people who are starting out take to heart and if you miss the whole history and stories I have written out here for you, something I truly hope that you take in and READ over and over is this….**"Hold tight to the moral guidelines that Karate offers while keeping true to a Kihon centric approach to Karate"**! These are words my instructor, Philip Dingman, infused in me and drove home many times. He said that the two most valuable things you should get from Karate are an understanding of what it is to be a good person and how it feels to work hard. Not what you can get out of Karate or what you can even feel like after training hard, but the feeling of training hard and the fact that you should be a good person. He also said that Karate often magnifies the poor behavior and morals of some. You can see a good person get better, and a bad person find ways to get worse.

Just from my observation of some of my instructors and peers I have seen a total lack of humanity and good character in some cases. I have seen peers of mine jailed for various crimes (and honestly I would throw the book at them again and again if given the chance) and I have seen seniors behave poorly, instructors abuse students and their perceived power over the students. I have seen some seniors become thieves when money came into the picture and I have seen the worst character flaws become the norm with some. Not to repeat myself to often but it's very much like my instructor has said "Karate does not necessarily make you a better person, it often amplifies and magnifies your personality, flaws and all".

I have also seen a great deal of peer bad behavior with some that Toss aside friendships for the new shiny thing and even jumped from organization to organization ignoring the family they had in their first organization. While I recognize that change is often necessary, the sheer lack of back bone that some have in regards to working with others is appalling. Some people should realize that "finding ways" to change organizations is not the morally correct way to approach change…..and no, I am not going to elaborate.

Karate also should not be used as a fancy adornment! You should not be pushing to do fancy kicks and add "flair" to your Karate. Adorning your skills with fancy and often useless, if not dangerous, fluff is not the point of Karate. Stick to a training regimen of Basic and fundamental karate and you will see your body grow and your skills increase. Also, keep in mind that modern additions to karate do not make it better, it just makes it different. Our time tested systems of Karate are meant to be used by anyone; the athlete, the leisure karate-ka, the child and the elderly. The systems that are traditional can be used by anyone. I have personally trained beside 79 year olds and 7 year olds, man, woman and child, able bodied and physically challenged. The systems are designed to be taught to anyone and so that everyone who trains can see success and reap the rewards and benefits of training!

The Future of Karate is now with the students, instructors and seniors of the Dojo today. We have to show respect to the founders and the systems and we need to learn, train and build our knowledge of the traditional base that forms our art. We need to veer away using Karate to advance our own agendas and just enjoy training in the art form, protect it from being corrupted by ideas that don't fit the traditional roots of the art. Our goal as instructors and students should be to train to understand and internalize the tenants and practices of Karate and build it in strength, to support our membership and bring them the most unadulterated training possible.

Use this book to see one side of each of the stories and opinions that are printed here, Use it as a source for one side of often a mixed and complex issue and then use it as a motivation to research and to continue growing. To grow as a student and make this fantastically magnificent art part of your life and part of you. And if it was not clear enough before, this book is often one sided, it offers my views based on research, personal experience and is written as my understanding of the facts, but it's as flawed as any other persons opinion is and even if I tried to be as accurate as I can be often the opinions are based on information found on the web or told to me and may not be as accurate as possible. I have tried to not take sides, I gave credit to those that I don't owe any allegiance to and I have pointed fingers at some I do, it's my attempt to call truth to power and at the same time show that I am were I want to be despite a tad bit of hero worship of senior Karate instructors that may have colored my view of events…and sometimes it very obvious to even me that my thoughts and those that I present are affected by these feelings. I make no secret of my open hero worship of men like Tanaka

Sensei and even Saeki Sensei, I find both men are exceptional instructors and should be seen as national treasures. All this while I have to reveal that my clubs have recently left Saeki Sensei and his CJKA for another JKA group in Canada because I feel that the new group is a much better fit for me.

Last I also don't hide my dedication to the JKA. I am an international affiliate who may never make it to the JKA HQ and at my age I probably will never meet people like Ueki Shihan again, but I am JKA through and through! I have been doing Karate for 38 or more years (depending on when you read this) and I am set in my ways, socially awkward and often far too honest, bull headed and sometimes accused of being abrasive. Please take that into account when reading this and realize my point of view may be such that you don't agree with me...but isn't that the great part about reading others opinions, you may not agree...but you are participating in a exercise of sharing.

Figure 1 King Sho Shin

Figure 2 Kumemura Village

Figure 3 Young Funakoshi Sensei Center

Figure 4 Funakoshi the Karate school teacher

Figure 5 Funakoshi far right, western clothing.

174

Figure 6 Early Class in Karate, Funakoshi Sensei center

Figure 7 Karate Master Anko Azato

Figure 8 Karate Master Anko Itosu

Figure 9 the first Shotokan Dojo

176

Figure 10 Funakoshi with members of the US Airforce exchange group.

Figure 11 Funakoshi Sensei Memorial

177

Figure 12 Karate early fighting

Figure 13 Masatoshi Nakayama Sensei

Figure 14 JKA instructors under Nakayama Sensei

Figure 15 Funakoshi Retired school teacher in Japan

Figure 16 Funakoshi Sensei at his sons funeral.

Figure 17 Obata helpf Funakoshi into a car

Figure 18 Yaguchi Sensei with Dingman Sensei

Figure 19 Nakahara Nobuyuki Chair JKA

Figure 20 more members of the Matsuno group

Figure 21 JKA under Sugiura and Nakahara

Figure 22 Asai and his JKS group

Figure 23 Sugiura Sensei

Figure 24 Sugiura Motokuni

Figure 25 Asai as cheif instructor at the Honbu

Figure 26 Suigura Sensei with Ueki Sensei

Figure 27 Ueki with other JKA masters

Figure 28 The Great Ueki Shihan!

After Thoughts

It has taken me months to edit the book and I have removed big chunks of information that was present in the blog posts. I would encourage you to check out my blog and review the notes I have left their to view the ideas that were taken out. However I want to update the reader on a few things that have happened as of late.

The JKA had been in a bit of a spat with the WKF, basically it was a pissing contest to see who would blink first. This game of chicken was more over power and influence and the idea that the WKF was becoming the significant Karate body worldwide. Something that the JKA balked at and a spat occurred. This spat centered around the use of the Emperor and Empresses cup. Essentially in Japan there is a trophy that is used by ALL SPORTS and its meant to be a sign that the official and traditional seat of power recognized the sporting event as a cultural event as well as brining a bit of prestige to the event.

The JKA got permission to use the Emperors cup for one of their national tournaments, however the WKF felt they had the right to approve this or at the least the right to use the cup over the JKA. Expected childish spats ensued between the WKF and Nahakara as the Chair of the JKA, and the JKA left or were kicked out of the WKF!
My feeling is that the WKF just tried to boot out the JKA. However, as Nakahara has proven in the past…he is in love with litigation. Eventually the courts ruled in favor of the JKA and they were allowed back into the WKF. This is of course a very simple and short add on story that was much more important and had even bigger ramifications inside the JKA.

At the same time as the court spat Nakahara was making waves inside the JKA. He was making life hard on the Dojo Honbu instructors by putting rules in place, fighting with outside organizations and ordering the JKA headquarters around. More so he cut Tanaka and Osaka from being the Vice Chief instructors. I have to admit here that there is a lot of info that is not said openly and there may be other reasons for the move, but as expected it tended to tick off the youth teaching at the Dojo as they were all training with Osaka and Tanaka Sensei's and very loyal to them.

Very shortly after all of this went down, the removal of the co-vice chairs, leaving the WKF and the issues created by Nakahara regarding the general teaching staff at the JKA...a letter was sent to the board requesting that Nakahara step down as the teaching staff at the Headquarters could not work under this. When Osaka left the board may others left as well or were removed, kick out of the JKA, One such person being Nemoto Sensei out of Chiba area. I was told that he was booted out by Nakahara and his area given to a junior.

In the end 12 of the Dojo seniors stood up to Nakahara and the board and drew a line in the sand. They had enough of the issues with the JKF, which many of them enjoyed participating in JKF tournaments and the expulsion of the JKA from the JKF had been taken hard. They complained about inconsistencies in dealing with European members and that the instructors who were on the board were never consulted about accepting memberships or removing members from the world federation.

Finally a letter was sent to the board and specifically Nakahara to voice their concerns:

"We, Headquarter Instructors cannot overlook these problems. To do nothing is to approve of these wrongdoings. We do not want to betray the members' trust.

We are instructors of not only techniques but also ethics of budoka, as a role model to other members in Japan and overseas. We are responsible for correcting the wrongdoings by the certain members of the management.

We hereby declare the foundation of Headquarter Instructor Association to correct the wrongdoing of the current management and change the current organization to allow for all members to take part in the future decision making process for a further development of JKA and karate-do.

It is clear that, despite the rhetoric of 'trust' and 'ethics', the group's emphasis is on amending the current JKA political structure, implementing a top-down form of change rather than one that necessarily incorporates the values of karate. It is likely that, unless the JKA changes the way it deals with internal problems, the group will continue to fracture, as it becomes more politicised; without a renewed mutual understanding, powerful individuals and powerful groups are more likely to splinter to set up their own rules, rather than play by someone else's."

After the group stood up and basically said "yah, no more" and emphasized that they were the teaching group, not the management group...and without the teaching group...no management group! Well it became very evident that change had to occur. Nakahara Stepped down and while the JKA was strengthened with the new chairman's position being filled by Kusahara Katsuhide, a highly educated man with a strong history in Budo, they also lost an effective wartime chairman who had done a lot for the JKA, but like Churchill suffered from his ego and a lack of war to fight.

The new chairman moved very quickly to correct many of the issues inside and outside the JKA. Kusahara mended fences with the JKF, he fortified the instructors at the JKA and gave them a say in a lot of political issues, Sent out a general letter to overseas instructors and made sure to mention the instructors at the Hombu and how important their work was. He however made a statement that reassured many of the traditionalist in that the JKA was going to continue development of "Ippon" style martial arts, meaning sport Karate was on the back burner…important…but not as much as traditional style training was. The letter illustrated the moves that the JKA were making, the instructors and seniors were in charge, the war was over!

Since this event the JKA has held a great number of training events, promotions and grading for overseas members and the JKA is now in the throes of a huge push to grow and to move the JKA into a position to build overseas and in Japan. They have a solid focus on numbers and not making power moves that help the board only. The focus is growth and taking advantage of traditional training again, and one other new event that will help out. The Olympics!

In the mix of all the turmoil that Nakahara had created the announcement that the WKF had finally convinced the IOC that Karate should be an Olympic event came out. The Olympics will welcome the WKF version of Karate into the Olympics in 2020 and with that a wave of new members will potentially grace the Dojos of Karate clubs around the world. However it will be WKF Karate and not JKA's Shobu Ippon focused Karate. It will be more sport than Budo!
While some are very sad that the advent of Karate into the Olympics is going to be pure sport, some, such as myself see it as an opportunity to grow their clubs, get people in the door and educate them about the difference. To me this is a win!

In the end, or as of now, the JKA is still strong…if not stronger for the changes, and the true and honest history of Shotokan Karate continues to be written. The many splits, changes and modifications continue on and the strong traditional JKA also continues on, perhaps in a much better place than in years past. The JKA represents my wing of the Shotokan world and honestly the more successful we all are the better. I have trained with SKIF people, ISKF was my home for years, I have worked with IKD people, WKIF people, KWF people and the Karate is similar, its Shotokan and its strong!

Read this book then go out and explore, read more blogs and chat sites, keep your filters on as there is a lot of BS and grudges being worked out but think about history, tradition and build your own ideas. That's all this book is, my building my ideas! I have had the good fortune of training with Dingman Sensei most of my childhood and into my adult hood (not saying I grew up…just older) and I have been privy to a great deal of "Secret" chats and events that others were never allowed to see. I have been told things by instructors that may never have been said in front of other students. I have been very lucky and wanted to share a bit with you. Most of the book is not controversial, and that's just the way it is. I don't get mad at people for things they did or said, it's all history and it's all how I got to be where I am today and how I am today. I have learned a lot about Karate and people and I encourage anyone reading this book to go out and study a bit, dig a bit and search out what you think is the truth as well.

And one last thought, The JKA and all Shotokan groups are made up of humans, flawed and fantastic! I have met many of them and no matter what group they belong to they have all shared with me, spoken to me and enriched my experience as a student, instructor and human. In the age of the internet I have had so many conversations, personal, Karate and just chatting with people from the JKA Japan, ASAI Karate, KWF, ITKF, ISKF, JSKA, and so many others that my research into the history, stories that I am told and little factoids that the general public do not get to see or hear about are always growing. This book was made up of blogs, research and stories or memories that I have collected over the years and I am sure I will have another one in me before I end my trek through the Karate world.

I want to thank the many people whom I have chatted with, reached out to and spoken with over the last two years of putting this book together, from the world of Karate and I want to again thank my Sensei Philip Dingman who was one of the greatest guides in Karate I could have ever hoped to have had. He was my second father for many years, my mentor and often my persecute when I was not working hard enough. I want to thank him for fostering my curiosity and my ideals in Karate and life. Without him I would be just another East K kid who had no focus and no interest, getting into trouble and wondering what was happening to all the time as it passed through my life. Well, at least he tried to keep me out of trouble………

To the future of Karate! Gambatte!

Figure 29 Author with Del Philips Sensei and Dingman Sensei

Printed in Great Britain
by Amazon